DISAGREEING AGREEABLY

This book facilitates civil discussion of controversial political issues. Unique to this book is a section that explains how to discuss politics without feeling angry or hostile toward people who hold different beliefs. In addition, the book provides concise and accessible debates of contemporary policy issues including gun control, immigration, the Electoral College, voting, and affirmative action. For each topic, readers are shown that opposing arguments are based on values and concerns that are widely shared by most people regardless of their political leanings. Perfect for students, professors, and citizens alike, this book promotes civility without shying away from controversy.

Glen Smith is a professor of political science at the University of North Georgia. Although he teaches a variety of courses in American politics, Glen has spent most of his career teaching Introduction to American Government to students from all backgrounds and educational interests. Glen's research focuses on the causes and consequences of political hostility, and he has written articles on this topic for political science journals including *American Politics Research, Political Research Quarterly*, and *Public Opinion Quarterly*. Summaries of his work have also been featured on political news websites such as *Psypost.org* and *Newsweek*.

"*Disagreeing Agreeably* will get students to think about political disagreement in new ways, get them interested in talking with others about politics, and encourage them to get better educated about the issues they care about."

—**Philip Neisser**, Dean of Business and Liberal Arts,
SUNY Canton, USA

"Glen Smith has written a highly readable text for students to better understand why polarization happens in the context of framing and civility. I highly recommend this engaging text that will help students make sense of major policy debates in American politics. This is an important book at an important time in our country."

—**Paul E. Lenze**, Jr., Northern Arizona University, USA

DISAGREEING AGREEABLY

Issue Debates with a Primer on Political Disagreement

Glen Smith

Routledge
Taylor & Francis Group

NEW YORK AND LONDON

First published 2020
by Routledge
52 Vanderbilt Avenue, New York, NY 10017

and by Routledge
2 Park Square, Milton Park, Abingdon, Oxon OX14 4RN

Routledge is an imprint of the Taylor & Francis Group, an informa business

© 2020 Taylor & Francis

The right of Glen Smith to be identified as author of this work has been asserted by him in accordance with sections 77 and 78 of the Copyright, Designs and Patents Act 1988.

British Library Cataloguing in Publication Data
A catalogue record for this book is available from the British Library

Library of Congress Cataloging-in-Publication Data
Names: Smith, Glen (Professor of political science), author.
Title: Disagreeing agreeably : issue debates with a primer on political disagreement / Glen Smith.
Description: New York : Routledge, [2019] | Includes bibliographical references. |
Identifiers: LCCN 2019008709 (print) | LCCN 2019019403 (ebook) | ISBN 9781000019988 (Adobe Reader) | ISBN 9781000020090 (Mobipocket Unencrypted) | ISBN 9781000020205 (ePub3) | ISBN 9780367228262 (hardback) | ISBN 9780367228279 (pbk.) | ISBN 9780429277054 (ebook)
Subjects: LCSH: Political culture--United States. | Communication in politics--United States. | Polarization (Social sciences)--Political aspects--United States.
Classification: LCC JK1726 (ebook) | LCC JK1726 .S644 2019 (print) | DDC 320.97301/4--dc23
LC record available at https://lccn.loc.gov/2019008709

ISBN: 978-0-367-22826-2 (hbk)
ISBN: 978-0-367-22827-9 (pbk)
ISBN: 978-0-429-27705-4 (ebk)

Typeset in Bembo
by Taylor & Francis Books

CONTENTS

Acknowledgments   *vii*

1 An Introduction to Political Hostility   1

PART I
A Primer on Political Disagreement   9

2 Where Opinions Come From   11

3 How We Think and Reason about Politics   21

4 Consider the Source: News Media and Political Hostility   32

5 How to Engage in Civil Discussions about Politics   43

PART II
Taxing and Spending   55

6 Should Medicare be Expanded to Cover All Americans?   57

7 Should College Tuition be Free for All Americans?   66

8 Should Congress Increase Funding for the Military?   75

PART III
Social Policy   83

 9 Should the Federal Government Legalize Marijuana?   85

10 Should Universities Encourage Affirmative Action Policies?   94

11 Should Illegal Immigrants be Granted Work Visas?   103

12 Should Students be Allowed to Carry Guns on College
    Campuses?   115

PART IV
Government Reforms   125

13 Should Congress Have Term Limits?   127

14 Should Supreme Court Justices Be Elected?   136

15 Should Voting be Mandatory in National Elections?   143

16 Should a National Popular Vote Replace the Electoral
    College?   151

Index   *159*

ACKNOWLEDGMENTS

Writing this book was a long and fulfilling process, which I never would have accomplished alone. There are so many people that I would like to thank. My wife Joy provided me the constant love and support I needed to write this book. Words cannot express how grateful I am that she inexplicably chose me. My son Jackson constantly inspires me to make the world a better place. My mother Helen spent all those days watching Jackson while I worked. My father Ray, and my sister Brooke, helped me think through some of the important questions in this book. Going further back in time, I would like to thank John Gaddy for recognizing the intellectual curiosity in me that I didn't know was there. I am also grateful to Phil Neisser, who inspired me to become a professor and taught me that political disagreement was something to be celebrated. This book was made possible by the Presidential Semester Scholar Award, which provided funding for my sabbatical. As such, I would like to thank the University of North Georgia for its continued support of my scholarly endeavors. Finally, I want to thank a few of my friends and colleagues that have provided me encouragement and emotional support over the last few years. Thank you Joe Huseby, Paul Lenze, John and Katie Nickerson, Jeff Rosky, Kathleen Woodward, and anyone else I may have accidentally left out.

1

AN INTRODUCTION TO POLITICAL HOSTILITY

Since the turn of the 21st century, there has been an alarming rise in anger and hostility in American politics. Political commentators in the news media, as well as prominent politicians, have expressed a great deal of concern that the members of the two political parties seem to increasingly dislike each other. A recent report by the Pew Research Center provides numerous examples illustrating a stunning increase in political hostility. For example, "More than half of Democrats (55%) say the Republican Party makes them 'afraid,' while 49% of Republicans say the same about the Democratic Party" (Pew Research Center 2016). The most widespread complaint about the other party is that they are closed-minded. In 2016, 70 percent of Democrats said they believed Republicans were more closed-minded than most Americans, while a majority (52%) of Republicans said the same about Democrats (Pew Research Center 2016). There is additional research showing that partisans feel increasing animosity toward people in the opposing party (Iyengar, Sood, and Lelkes 2012; Iyengar and Westwood 2015).

The increasing political hostility between opposing partisans has important consequences for how we get along with other people. Political differences can result in the loss of valuable friendships and even estrangement from family members. For example, one survey found that roughly a quarter (26%) of those using social media have "hidden, blocked, defriended or stopped following someone" because of a political disagreement (Pew Research Center 2014). For some, political differences have even strained relationships with family members and romantic partners (Pesce 2016; McCarthy 2016; Holmes 2017). During the 2016 presidential campaign, a Pew Research Center survey found that 41 percent of couples—that supported opposing candidates—said they had argued about politics (Holmes 2017). Perhaps to avoid future conflict, partisans are ruling out members of the opposing Party as potential romantic partners (Huber and

Malhotra. 2017). Additionally, parents are increasingly likely to say that they would be uncomfortable with their child marrying someone in the opposing political party (Iyengar, Sood, and Lelkes 2012). In short, the inability to rationally and productively deal with political disagreements can have important consequences for people's personal relationships.

Political animosity also extends to political leaders in opposing parties. According to Gallup, the election year gap in presidential approval between Republicans and Democrats is wider than at any point since approval has been recorded (Jones 2014). For example, Barack Obama's approval rating among Republicans in 2012 was 10 percent, compared to 86 percent approval among Democrats. This partisan divide is similar to his predecessor George W. Bush, who recorded a 13 percent approval rating among Democrats in 2004, which dropped to 6 percent during his last year in office. By comparison, Democrat Bill Clinton had a 23 percent approval rating among Republicans during his reelection bid in 1996, and Republican Ronald Reagan had a 29 percent approval rating among Democrats in 1984. During his first year in office, Donald Trump had 83 percent approval among Republicans, but only *8 percent* among Democrats (Jones 2018). As much as we may dislike members of the opposing party, we dislike their elected representatives even more.

Although there are numerous explanations for this increasing political intolerance, most scholars point to a lack of exposure to opposing political viewpoints (Mutz 2002; Badger and Chokshi 2017). For a number of reasons, people are less likely to hear opinions that they disagree with, and when they do, they often come in the form of caricatures. Americans increasingly live around people that share their political worldview, where large cities are populated with liberals, while rural areas are dominated by conservatives. Even when people do associate with ideologically diverse groups, they tend to avoid discussing political topics because they are afraid of emotional conflicts (Mutz 2002; Pew Research Center 2014). Furthermore, diversification of the American news media has allowed Americans to get news from ideologically-consistent sources, while sheltering themselves from opposing arguments (Stroud 2011). For all of these reasons, many Americans rarely come into contact with facts and arguments that oppose their beliefs.

The best way to reduce political anger and hostility is for people to learn the arguments and values underlying opposing opinions. One way that learning opposing arguments lowers political hostility is by challenging the stereotypes we have about members of opposing political groups. Much of the animosity we feel toward opposing political groups results from negative stereotypes about why they hold their opinions. Research in social psychology suggests that people believe that members of social out-groups act in more stereotypical ways than members of in-groups (Judd et al. 1991). For example, when it comes to assistance for the needy, liberals tend to see conservatives as heartless, while conservatives see liberals as bleeding hearts (Farwell and Weiner 2000). Likewise, partisans often believe that members of the opposition are ideologically extreme (Brady and Sniderman 1985;

Sherman et al. 2003; Ahler 2014). These negative stereotypes can lead people to see their political opponents as more "evil" than they actually are (Sabatier et al. 1987). Hostility also stems from how people explain *why* other people disagree with them. Without an awareness of opposing arguments, people tend to attribute disagreement to negative causes, such as ideological bias, ignorance, self-interest, lying, or some ulterior motivation (Kennedy and Pronin 2008). For example, Reeder and colleagues (2005) found that people were more likely to attribute negative motives to George W. Bush's decision to invade Iraq when they disagreed with his decision. Moreover, people are less willing to negotiate or seek compromise when they believe the opposition is somehow biased in their thinking (Kennedy and Pronin 2008). To some extent, animosity toward opposing groups results from misperceptions of their policy positions and motivations.

Learning opposing arguments reduces political hostility by helping us understand the *actual* reasons that people hold different beliefs and opinions. The more we learn why people disagree with us, the less likely we are to attribute disagreement to negative motivations or stereotypes about members of opposing groups. In other words, learning the actual arguments of opposing partisans helps us realize that their opinions are based on reasonable perspectives. According to the contact hypothesis, increased exposure to other groups can reduce prejudice by challenging negative stereotypes (Allport 1954). Learning about other cultures and viewpoints can increase tolerance by focusing attention on shared values and similarities across different social groups (Pettigrew and Tropp 2006; Kennedy and Pronin 2008). Furthermore, Ahler (2014) found that people were more likely to hold moderate opinions on policy issues after they learned that aggregate opinions were not as polarized as they thought. In short, learning the actual opinions and arguments of the opposition can help us be more tolerant of, and less angry toward, people who disagree with our political views.

The overall purpose of this book is to reduce political hostility by helping you understand the real sources of political disagreements. This book is composed of four parts, with Part I being very different than the following three. In the first part of the book, I make a case for political tolerance by arguing that all of our opinions are potentially "biased" by our backgrounds, personalities, cognitive biases, news sources, and discussion partners. In Chapter 2, I argue that many of our opinions are a product of the environments we were born into and the personalities we inherited. Too often people look at political issues as having one correct answer or solution, but that is rarely the case in politics. Instead, whether a policy is good or bad depends on an individual's values, beliefs, and position in society. The purpose of Chapter 2 is to help you understand that the best policy often depends on one's perspective. To that end, Chapter 2 discusses the sources of political disagreement, including personality, personal experiences and framing. Instead of disliking someone for holding different opinions, it is more logical to attribute disagreement to differences of perspective that naturally result from being different people and living different lives. From this perspective, disagreement is not something to be avoided, but instead something to be embraced because it provides an opportunity to learn the perspectives of other people.

In Chapter 3, I explain why we often do not think about politics objectively. Instead, we are all potentially biased by our preferences and perspectives on the world. Through a process called motivated reasoning, people process new information in a way that allows them to hold opinions that promote their goals (Kunda 1990; Taber and Lodge 2006). Since there is no way to know for certain that your opinions are *not* biased, it makes sense to hold beliefs with less certainty, and to seek to broaden our perspectives by understanding the opinions of others. The chapter begins with an overview of motivated reasoning and its consequences for American politics, and continues with a discussion of some ways you can guard yourself against motivated reasoning.

The purpose of Chapter 4 is to explain how the news media have the potential to help people learn opposing arguments, but only if they choose to challenge their opinions. On the one hand, partisan media allow people to isolate themselves in echo chambers where they rarely hear opposing arguments (Sunstein 2001; Cook 2010; Stroud 2011). These partisan media echo chambers can increase political hostility by furthering misunderstandings about why people disagree (Levendusky 2013; Smith and Searles 2014). On the other hand, people can get news from a variety of liberal, conservative, and mainstream news outlets, which can simulate productive political discussion (Smith 2017). Whether the media increase or decrease political hostility depends on what particular sources people choose. In Chapter 4, I discuss the role of the news media in promoting political discussion, why partisans think the media are politically biased, and how both partisan and mainstream media affect political hostility.

The first part of the book concludes with Chapter 5, which helps facilitate more productive dialogue about political and social problems. For a variety of reasons, people often have trouble engaging in civil discussion of controversial issues. While some are no doubt afraid of getting angry, many avoid discussions because they do not want to upset those who hold opposing views (Mutz 2002). The purpose of Chapter 5 is to address some of the common factors leading to uncivil discussions, and to provide tips to facilitate civil, informed, and productive discussion of contentious issues. Hopefully, this chapter will allow you to talk about politics without angering others or getting angry yourself.

In the remainder of the book, each chapter discusses the main arguments surrounding a political issue. The topics for these chapters were carefully selected because they provide specific examples of larger controversies in American politics. In each chapter, I present a brief historical background of the issue and then explain how each side is linked to competing values that most Americans share. The key point is that each individual holds numerous values that are relevant to political issues, but those values often conflict when put into practice. Unfortunately, we often think of issues in terms of one set of values and considerations, without considering other potentially relevant values that might apply to the same issue. Once we come to understand how our own conflicting values are tied to the same issue, we may become more accepting of other people who hold different opinions. The purpose of the issue chapters is to expose readers to the rationales behind opposing perspectives, which hopefully reduces animosity toward those that disagree.

For Part II of the book, the chapters focus specifically on issues of taxing and spending. Chapter 6 presents a debate over the merits of expanding the Medicare program to cover all Americans. I chose this topic because it is an example of the larger debate over health care, which is wide-ranging and complex, as it involves a variety of issues including: taxes, personal debt, hospitals, treatment options, prescription drugs, mental health, reproduction, contraception, and end-of-life decisions. At its most basic level, the key questions in the health care debate are whether health care is a right, and whether health care is better run by the government or the for-profit insurance industry. Chapter 7 debates whether college tuition should be free for all Americans. The debate over free college involves competing values that most people hold, such as equality of opportunity, personal responsibility, and a desire to reduce government inefficiencies. Chapter 8 also addresses questions of government waste, but looks at the military instead of higher education or health care. Specifically, Chapter 8 debates whether we should increase spending for the military, which involves competing perspectives on foreign policy and government spending.

Part III of the book focuses on social policies that deal with questions of personal freedom, federalism, racial equality and constitutional rights. Chapter 9 addresses a very prominent issue in current politics: the legalization of marijuana for recreational purposes. The debate over legalizing marijuana is an excellent example of the larger debates over personal freedoms and the arguments concerning state versus federal power. The topics of civil rights and racial injustice are discussed in Chapter 10, which debates the merits of race-based affirmative action in college admissions. Chapter 11 presents opposing arguments surrounding a guest worker program for illegal immigrants. The immigration debate is a perennial issue in American politics, but it is often difficult to discuss because of its racial undertones. To conclude Part III, Chapter 12 presents a debate over campus carry laws, which allow people to carry concealed weapons on college campuses. The debate over campus carry is an excellent example of the larger debate over gun control because it involves many of the same arguments over public safety, personal protection, and preventing mass shootings.

The topics discussed in Part IV deal with hypothetical reforms to government, with some having a more realistic chance of occurring than others. Regardless, the proposed reforms involve long-standing questions over the proper role of citizens in a representative democracy, and how to make government institutions more effective and responsive to the people. Specifically, Chapter 13 presents the debate over congressional term limits, in which the key question is how much faith we have in other voters to make good decisions. Although Chapter 14 debates judicial elections for the U.S. Supreme Court in particular, which admittedly will probably never happen, the larger debate is over the tradeoffs between political accountability and judicial independence. Popular elections give people what they want, but voters often elect the most popular candidate rather than the most qualified person for the job. Chapter 15 debates the merits of mandatory voting in national elections. Although compulsory voting would certainly increase the incentive to vote, and reduce inequities in representation, some question whether democracy is strengthened by people voting when they have little information and are uninterested in the political system. To conclude the book, Chapter 16 debates whether the President of the United States should be elected by the people or the Electoral College. The main question in the Electoral College debate is whether the United States is one country or a collection of states. Of course, as with all of the policies discussed in this book, there are practical considerations at play that are also important to consider.

The issue debate chapters are designed to give a brief introduction to the debate. As such, they do not represent every point of view, possible argument, or piece of evidence. In order to keep the chapters (somewhat) interesting and concise, I had to make difficult decisions about what to include and what arguments and evidence to jettison. If you are interested in any of the issues, each chapter includes a section listing sources for further inquiry. My hope is that those sources will provide the interested reader a more complete examination of the topics.

References

Ahler, Douglas J. 2014. "Self-Fulfilling Misperceptions of Public Polarization." *Journal of Politics* 76(3): 607–620.
Allport, Gordon W. 1954. *The Nature of Prejudice*. Reading, MA: Addison-Wesley.
Badger, Emily, and Niraj Chokshi. 2017, June 15. "How we Became Bitter Political Enemies." *The New York Times*. Retrieved from https://www.nytimes.com/2017/06/15/upshot/how-we-became-bitter-political-enemies.html
Brady, Henry E., and Paul M. Sniderman. 1985. "Attitude Attribution: A Group Basis for Political Reasoning." *American Political Science Review* 79(4): 1061–1078.
Cook, Charlie. 2010, April 21. "Home of the Whopper." *National Journal*. Retrieved from: http://www.nationaljournal.com/njonline/po_20100420_2450.php
Farwell, Lisa, and Bernard Weiner. 2000. "Bleeding Hearts and the Heartless: Popular Perceptions of Liberal and Conservative Ideologies." *Personality and Social Psychology Bulletin* 26(7): 845–852.
Holmes, Lindsay. 2017, November 8. The 2016 Election is Still Straining Relationships. *The Huffington Post*. Retrieved from https://www.huffingtonpost.com/entry/election-relation ships-strain_us_5a00bd89e4b0c9653001a6a8
Huber, Gregory A., and Neil Malhotra. 2017. "Political Homophily in Social Relationships: Evidence from Online Dating Behavior." *The Journal of Politics* 79(1): 269–283.
Iyengar, Shanto, and Sean J. Westwood. 2015. "Fear and Loathing across Party Lines: New Evidence on Group Polarization." *American Journal of Political Science* 59(3): 690–707.
Iyengar, Shanto, Gaurav Sood, and Yphtach Lelkes. 2012. "Affect, Not Ideology: A Social Identity Perspective on Polarization." *Public Opinion Quarterly* 76(3): 405–431.
Jones, Jeffrey M. 2014. "Obama's Fifth Year Job Approval Ratings among Most Polarized." Gallup. Retrieved from http://www.gallup.com/poll/167006/obama-fifth-yea r-job-approval-ratings-among-polarized.aspx
Jones, Jeffrey. 2018, January 22. "Trump's First-Year Job Approval Worst by 10 points." Gallup. Retrieved from http://news.gallup.com/poll/226154/trump-first-year-job-app

rovalworstpoints.aspx?g_source=link_NEWSV9&g_medium=tile_5&g_campaign=item_201617&g_content=Trump%27s%2520FirstYear%2520Job%2520Approval%2520Worst%2520by%252010%2520Points

Judd, Charles M., Carey S. Ryan, and Bernadette Park. 1991. "Accuracy in the Judgment of In-Group and Out-Group Variability." *Journal of Personality and Social Psychology* 61(3): 366–379.

Kennedy, Kathleen A., and Emily Pronin. 2008. "When Disagreement Gets Ugly: Perceptions of Bias and the Escalation of Conflict." *Personality and Social Psychology Bulletin* 34(6): 833–848.

Kunda, Ziva. 1990. "The Case for Motivated Reasoning." *Psychological Bulletin* 108(3): 480–498.

Levendusky, Matthew. 2013. "Why Do Partisan Media Polarize Viewers?" *American Journal of Political Science* 57(3): 611–623.

McCarthy, Kelly. 2016, October 13. "Let's Not Talk Politics: Why the 2016 Election is Dividing Family and Friends." ABC News. Retrieved from http://abcnews.go.com/Lifestyle/talk-politics-2016-election-causing-family-friends-divide/story?id=42769919 ;

Mutz, Diana. 2002. "Cross-cutting Social Networks: Testing Democratic Theory in Practice." *American Political Science Review* 96(1): 111–126.

Pesce, Nicole. 2016, November 5. "The Presidential Election is Dividing Spouses, Families and Friends." *New York Daily News.* Retrieved from http://www.nydailynews.com/life-style/presidential-election-dividing-spouses-families-friends-article-1.2858614

Pettigrew, Thomas F., and Linda R. Tropp. 2006. "A Meta-Analytic Test of Intergroup Contact Theory." *Journal of Personality and Social Psychology* 90(5): 751–783.

Pew Research Center. 2014, June 12. "Political Polarization in the American Public." Retrieved from http://www.people-press.org/2014/06/12/political-polarization-in-the-american-public/

Pew Research Center. 2016, June 22. "Partisanship and Political Animosity in 2016." Retrieved from http://www.people-press.org/2016/06/22/partisanship-and-political-animosity-in-2016/

Reeder, Glenn D., John B. Pryor, Michael J. A. Wohl, and Michael L. Griswell. 2005. "On Attributing Negative Motives to Others Who Disagree With Our Opinions." *Personality and Social Psychology Bulletin* 31(11): 1498–1510.

Sabatier, Paul, Susan Hunter, and Susan McLaughlin. 1987. "The Devil Shift: Perceptions and Misperceptions of Opponents." *The Western Political Quarterly* 40(3): 449–476.

Sherman, David K., Leif D. Nelson, and Lee D. Ross. 2003. "Naïve Realism and Affirmative Action: Adversaries are More Similar than They Think." *Basic and Applied Social Psychology* 25(4): 275–289.

Smith, Glen. 2017. "Sympathy for the Devil: How Broadcast News Reduces Negativity Toward Political Leaders." *American Politics Research* 45(1): 63–84.

Smith, Glen, and Kathleen Searles. 2014. "Who Let the (Attack) Dogs Out? New Evidence for Partisan Media Effects." *Public Opinion Quarterly* 78(1): 71–99.

Stroud, Natalie. 2011. *Niche News: The Politics of News Choice.* New York, NY: Oxford University Press.

Sunstein, Cass R. 2001, June 1. "The Daily We: Is the Internet Really a Blessing for Democracy?" *Boston Review.* Retrieved from: http://bostonreview.net/cass-sunstein-internet-democracy-daily-we

Taber, Charles S., and Milton Lodge. 2006. "Motivated Skepticism in the Evaluation of Political Beliefs." *American Journal of Political Science* 50(3): 755–769.

PART I

A Primer on Political Disagreement

2

WHERE OPINIONS COME FROM

Far too often people view political disagreement as an obstacle to overcome, a problem that must be solved, or a disease that needs a cure. This perspective assumes that every question has a right answer, and disagreement occurs because one of the two parties is somehow mistaken. It is tempting for us to blame others for not seeing the correctness of our beliefs. We often assume that our opinions are based on a rational look at all of the available evidence, and if people disagree it must be because they are irrational or uninformed. Social psychologists call this belief "naïve realism" and it stems from a common problem in human perceptions; we can only see the world from our own perspective (Robinson et al. 1995; Ross and Ward 1996; Pronin et al. 2004). The naïve realist believes that they view the world in a more or less objective manner. Their political opinions are simply a result of an unbiased processing of information they have obtained from objective reality. As such, it is easy to figure out the one correct solution to every problem.

When the naïve realist encounters someone who holds a contrary opinion, they confront a problem. If my opinions come from objective reality, and someone holds a contradictory opinion, one of us *must* be wrong. Since I know how much *I know*, and usually do not know how much others know, my first assumption is that others disagree because they lack information. My assumption is that if everyone knew what I knew they would hold my beliefs. If someone holds a contrary opinion, it is probably because they are less informed on the topic. If I learn that they know a lot about this particular topic, our disagreement cannot be explained away by their ignorance. In this scenario, I may assume that their view of the world is biased by their ideology, party affiliation, self-interest, or some ulterior motive. An underlying assumption of naïve realism, and one that I challenge throughout this book, is that there is *one correct* way to look at the world, and hence one correct opinion or solution to a problem.

An alternative perspective is that whether a policy is good or bad often depends on one's perspective, which is shaped by their life experiences and place in society. When it comes right down to it, all thoughts can only come from a mixture of three sources: genetics, experiences and randomness. Each one likely contributes to variation in our opinions, but to a greater or lesser extent depending on the individual and the opinion in question. As a result, human beings will be unable to completely agree on everything, because we are all looking at the world from different perspectives. The same policy that benefits one person is likely to harm other people. Society will never achieve perfect agreement on every issue as long as people are different. Disagreement is a natural outcome of people having different personalities, leading different lives, and thinking about political issues in different ways. In other words, we disagree about politics because we are different people, and the only way to eliminate disagreement is if all of us were the same. What a boring world that would be!

To be clear, I do not argue that all beliefs and opinions are equally correct! Some beliefs are factually wrong, some arguments are illogical, and some opinions are morally bankrupt. It is perfectly fine to believe your viewpoint is correct. What I argue in this chapter, and throughout this book, is that we should resist the urge to *dislike* others *simply* because they hold different political opinions. People are born with different personalities, have different experiences during their lives, and as a result they think about political issues in very different ways. Since many of the reasons that we hold different opinions are largely out of our control, it makes little sense to feel anger toward people who happen to hold different perspectives. The purpose of this chapter is to explain the basis for our political disagreements, which will hopefully help alleviate some of the hostility that may arise during political discussions.

Genetics, Personality, and Political Attitudes

In many ways, human beings are born to disagree about politics. The fact that we are born with different mental and physical characteristics predisposes us to eventually disagree about political issues. In fact, recent research suggests that people are *born* with cognitive processes that, all things being equal, make them more likely to hold liberal or conservative opinions during their lifetimes. In their seminal study, Alford, Funk, and Hibbing (2005) examined the role of genetic predispositions in political opinions. The researchers set out to determine how much of our political differences could be attributed to experiences, and how much were inherited. To that end, they compared the similarities between fraternal and identical twins. This is a clever approach because it allows the researchers to, more or less, control for the upbringing of the twins. Both types of twins are born at the same time, to the same parents, and raised in the same environment. The only difference is that identical twins share the same genetic makeup. If all political opinions come from experiences, fraternal twins would be just as similar in their political opinion as identical twins. Conversely, if identical twins are more similar in their political opinions, it likely resulted from their greater share of genetic material.

The results of the research showed that roughly *half* of the variation in political attitudes could be attributed to genetic inheritance rather than social upbringing. Indeed, identical twins were more similar in their eventual ideology and issue attitudes than fraternal twins. Meanwhile, party identification had no relationship with genetics, and instead was based on one's upbringing. Likewise, what religion one chose is based more on upbringing, while how strongly one practiced religion was more determined by genetics. Both religion and party identification are largely social constructions that change over time, while ideology and religiosity are related to one's personality, which is more strongly related to genetic predispositions.

It is important to make the distinction between being predisposed to hold an opinion and being predetermined. Having conservative parents does not *predetermine* someone to become a conservative, as of course there are people who grow up with different political attitudes from their parents. Instead, genetics predisposes people to eventually hold political attitudes similar to their parents, when all things are equal. Our genetics interact with our environments in important ways to produce our eventual political opinions (Settle et al. 2010). Likewise, having alcoholic parents does not guarantee that you will become an alcoholic, though children do inherit personality traits that predispose them to eventually abuse alcohol. For example, if someone inherits higher anxiety from their parents, they are more likely to use alcohol to reduce their anxiety. There are many children with anxiety that never abuse alcohol, but the probability that they will is greater than someone who is born with lower anxiety.

Traits also predispose people to interpret their experiences in ways that, all things being equal, will result in them holding similar attitudes to their parents. For example, Oxley and colleagues (2008) found that conservatives are more likely to react negatively to fear inducing stimuli, which helps explain why they support conservative policy positions—such as military spending and capital punishment—that will protect them from perceived threats. In other words, if someone is born with more sensitivity to fear, they are predisposed (all things being equal) to grow up to hold certain policy attitudes as a result of their genetics. Furthermore, Gerber and colleagues (2010) found that personality traits can predict political opinions. In short, the very fact that people have different personalities causes them to disagree about politics.

If political disagreement results from birth characteristics, of which we have little control, it makes little sense to dislike someone because they hold opposing perspectives. Instead, it is more rational to accept that our minds are different, and we are predisposed to view the world in different ways. There is evidence that people are less likely to hold animosity when they attribute social differences to a birth condition. For example, the best predictor of support for gay marriage is the belief that people were born gay, and thus had no choice in their sexual orientation (Haider-Markel and Joslyn 2008). As more people believe homosexuality is a condition of birth, and hence out of an individual's control, they are more willing to allow them to have equal rights. My point here is not to argue about the origin of sexual orientation, but instead to point out the role of *causal attributions* in hostility toward different social groups. Perhaps if we come to believe that political disagreements are a natural consequence of birth characteristics, we may feel less anger toward the people who hold opposing opinions.

Past Experiences

Another reason that we disagree about politics is because we live different lives. Political opinions are shaped by our upbringing, experiences, friends, information sources, positions in life, and even pure randomness. If someone grows up in a poor area and knows more people receiving welfare, they may be more likely to understand the problems that poor people face than someone who grows up in a rich neighborhood and believes welfare recipients lack personal responsibility. Personal experiences shape our understanding of the situation, which will inevitably affect our political opinions.

Past experiences can have large and lasting effects on political opinions because they create differences in our knowledge and interpretations. For example, research suggests that personal contact with homosexuals increased support for gay marriage (Barth et al. 2009). One of the main reasons that Americans have become more supportive of gay marriage since the turn of the 21st century is because more people realized that they had friends and family that were homosexuals. As it became more socially acceptable to be openly gay, thanks in no small part to popular culture and the entertainment industry (Slater et al. 2006), closeted homosexuals started revealing their sexual orientations to friends and family. When people learned that they had loved ones that were homosexuals, they became more supportive of gay marriage because they wanted their loved ones to have that right (Lewis 2011). Former Vice President Dick Cheney famously supported legalizing gay marriage—possibly because his daughter was a lesbian—even though his President George W. Bush campaigned strongly against legalizing gay marriage in the 2004 presidential campaign. As for Rob Portman, a Republican U.S. Senator from Ohio, he changed his position to support gay marriage after finding out that his son was a homosexual (Peter 2013). Both of these instances provide high profile examples of politicians whose personal experiences affected their policy opinions, even at potentially high costs to their careers considering that they both were Republicans and accountable to socially conservative voters who were very much opposed to gay marriage.

Experiences affect our opinions beyond the people we know. Public support for marijuana legalization is strongly related to personal use of the drug. According to the Pew Research Center report in 2015, roughly half (49%) of Americans had used marijuana at some point in their lives. Among previous users, 65 percent believed marijuana should be legal, while only 34 percent of non-users supported legalization (Pew Research Center 2015). Perhaps the best explanation for the link between use and support is the knowledge of the actual effects of marijuana rather than supposed effects that one might hear in public school curricula or anti-drug advertisements. Again, this is not to say that the anti-legalization side is wrong, but instead that experiences bring with them knowledge that influences opinions. The point is that disagreement is based largely on knowing different people, living different lives, and having different experiences.

There is also a cyclical aspect to the effect of experiences on opinions, as our experiences shape our worldview and personality. These differences in personality and worldview affect how we see and interpret future experiences and the ways we structure our information environment. For example, if a person is prescribed pain medication after an injury and becomes addicted, it will affect how they view the issue of opioid addiction even after they no longer use the drug. Suffering through drug addiction may make them more sympathetic to those addicted to all types of drugs, not just prescription pain medication. Likewise, the family one is born into will affect how they interpret the speeches and actions of political candidates, their preferred news sources, and with whom they associate. For example, someone born into a Republican family is more likely to give Republican candidates the benefit of the doubt, listen to conservative talk radio, and avoid talking politics with Democrats. Conversely, someone born into a Democratic home is likely to favor Democratic policies, watch MSNBC, and associate mostly with other liberals. Given these structural differences in their information environments and how they interpret the world, is it any wonder that they would have trouble seeing the other's point of view when discussing politics in a college classroom?

Framing and Value Salience

Disagreements can also result from differences in how people think about political and social issues. Even if people have the same information and values, they may still disagree because they do not see all values and considerations as relevant to every issue. Framing occurs when the way an issue is discussed emphasizes particular values and deemphasizes other potentially relevant considerations. Opinions on political issues are often a reflection of the information that comes to mind at the moment we are asked a question or make a decision (Zaller 1992). Rarely do we think of all of the values and information that are relevant to an issue. When political elites or the news media frame political issues by focusing on certain values, it makes it more likely that we will consider those values when choosing our policy opinion. Thus, we often disagree because we are thinking of different values surrounding the same issue.

There is abundant research showing that how an issue is framed can shift public opinion by making different considerations appear relevant at the time. For example, Nelson, Clawson and Oxley (1997) conducted an experiment that tested the effects of media framing on public support for civil liberties. In the experiment, participants were exposed to one of two versions of a news story about a potential Ku Klux Klan rally in their town. While one story framed the issue as a civil liberties question, the other story focused on the potential threat to public safety posed by a rally that could spark violence. Watching the public safety frame made participants less supportive of allowing the KKK to hold a public rally. In other words, simply reframing the question around public safety made American citizens more willing to deny other citizens a constitutional right to assemble.

What makes frames so effective at changing opinions is that most people have conflicting values and considerations at any one time. Frames make some values and considerations appear more relevant to the issue at hand (Nelson, Clawson and Oxley 1997; Druckman 2004). If the topic is public education funding, whether one frames the issue as a question of government spending or promoting equal opportunity, will go a long way to determining whether people support increasing funding to public schools. Most people support promoting educational opportunity for children, but those same people want to limit government spending and reduce taxes. Those supporting increased funding focus on the opportunity it will create for children, and probably assume that those opposing more funding do not care about educating children. In reality, those opposing increased school funding probably support equal educational opportunity, but believe that institutional reforms could improve educational outcomes without increasing taxes. Each side likely assumes that the other side does not share their values, while they likely are not thinking of them or do not consider them as relevant to this particular issue.

Where do frames come from? Although frames come from a variety of sources, the most common sources are political elites, such as elected officials, think tanks, government officials, and media commentators (Entman 1993 and 2004). When elites in a political party consistently frame an issue a certain way, members of the party in the general public will usually adopt that frame when thinking about the issue. Druckman (2001) found that frames were much more persuasive when they came from a trusted source. Thus, Republicans adopt the frames from the Republican Party, while Democrats adopt frames espoused by leaders of the Democratic Party. Leaders of each party have an incentive to consistently frame political issues in ways that persuade voters to their side. People will be more likely to vote for Republicans, and support Republican policies, if they are able to effectively frame the issues. Consequently, political elites talk past each other by framing issues in different ways, with ordinary citizens usually adopting the frames of their party.

Partisans come to disagree because they are connecting different values and considerations to the issue, even if they share the same underlying values. For example, most people believe that individuals have a right to privacy, but also believe the government should have the tools to stop criminals. Those values conflict when the question is whether government should be able to access library records, e-mails, phone calls, and records of gun purchases. Although people want both privacy and safety, they will often only focus on the values framed by their side and argue that the opposition's concern is either not relevant to this issue or is not a big deal. Next time you are discussing politics, try considering the values that others are linking to the issue and whether you hold them to some degree. If so, your disagreement may simply be a matter of intensity of support for the value, or the fact that you have not considered other relevant considerations. In fact, Americans share many of the same values, but we usually focus only on the values that support our preferred policy positions.

In sum, disagreement results from people being different, living different lives, and thinking about issues in different ways. When people are born different and have different experiences, they are bound to hold different opinions. Even if people hold the same underlying values and goals, they could still disagree because they frame the issue differently. That is, people think about political issues differently because they mentally connect different values and considerations to the same issue. Thus, there are many different factors that cause us to disagree about political issues. This does not mean that nobody is right, or that no policies, arguments, or facts are better than any other. Instead, the point is that we should be more understanding if people don't happen to share our political views. They hold different opinions because they have not lived your life, and *you* have not shared *their* experiences. In short, it makes little sense to dislike someone because they just happened to live a different life.

Review Questions

1.   What is naïve realism and why does it increase political hostility?
2.   How do genetics predispose people to hold different political attitudes?
3.   In what ways do personal experiences cause political disagreements?
4.   What is framing, and why do people accept some frames and not others?

Discussion Questions

1.   Has a political disagreement ever caused you to end a friendship or to limit contact with a family member?
2.   How much do you believe your genetics predisposed you to hold your current political beliefs?
3.   Do you dislike people who hold different opinions? If so, did reading this chapter alleviate any of that hostility?
4.   Can you think of any ways to increase people's understanding of how other people see the world?

Sources for Further Inquiry

Books

Hatemi, Peter K., and Rose McDermott, eds. (2011). *Man is by nature a political animal: Evolution, biology, and politics.* Chicago: IL: University of Chicago Press.

Hibbing, John R., Kevin B. Smith, and John R. Alford. (2013). *Predisposed: Liberals, conservatives, and the biology of political differences.* New York, NY: Routledge Press.

Houghton, D. P. (2014). *Political psychology: situations, individuals, and cases.* New York, NY: Routledge.

Lakoff, George. (2010). *Moral politics: How liberals and conservatives think.* Chicago, IL: University of Chicago Press.

Schaffner, B. F., & Sellers, P. J. (Eds.). (2009). *Winning with words: the origins and impact of political framing.* New York, NY: Routledge Press.

Westen, Drew. (2007). *The Political Brain: The Role of Emotion in Deciding the Fate of a Nation.* New York, NY: Perseus Books.

Journal and Newspaper Articles

Alford, John R., Peter K. Hatemi, John R. Hibbing, Nicholas G. Martin, and Lindon J. Eaves. 2011. "The politics of mate choice". *The Journal of Politics*, 73(2):362–379.

Bartels, Larry. (2013, November 12). "Your Genes Influence Your Political Views. So What?" *Monkey Cage Blog.* Retrieved from https://www.washingtonpost.com/news/monkey-cage/wp/2013/11/12/your-genes-influence-your-political-views-so-what/?utm_term=.fa81a0501fd0

Byrd, Carson W., and Matthew W. Hughey. (2015, September 28). "Born That Way? 'Scientific' Racism is Creeping Back into Our Thinking," *Monkey Cage Blog.* Retrieved from https://www.washingtonpost.com/news/monkey-cage/wp/2015/09/28/born-that-way-scientific-racism-is-creeping-back-into-our-thinking-heres-what-to-watch-out-for/?utm_term=.d75afdaf973f

Carney, D. R., Jost, J. T., Gosling, S. D., & Potter, J. 2008. "The secret lives of liberals and conservatives: Personality profiles, interaction styles, and the things they leave behind." *Political Psychology*, 29(6), 807–840.

Dinas, Elias. 2014. "Why does the apple fall far from the tree? How early political socialization prompts parent-child dissimilarity". *British Journal of Political Science*, 44(4): 827-852.

Grossmann, Matt, and David A. Hopkins. 2015. "Ideological Republicans and group interest Democrats: The asymmetry of American party politics". *Perspectives on Politics*, 13(1):119-139.

Hibbing, John (2013, November 27). "Why Biology Belongs in the Study of Politics," *Monkey Cage Blog.* Retrieved from https://www.washingtonpost.com/news/monkey-cage/wp/2013/11/27/why-biology-belongs-in-the-study-of-politics/?utm_term=.1c4b8db5c61c

Jensen, Carsten, and Michael Bang Petersen. 2017. "The deservingness heuristic and the politics of health care". *American Journal of Political Science*, 61(1):68-83.

Smith, Kevin B., Christopher W. Larimer, Levente Littvay, and John R. Hibbing. 2007. "Evolutionary theory and political leadership: Why certain people do not trust decision makers". *The Journal of Politics*, 69(2):285–299.

Swanson, Ana. (2016, May 13). "The Disturbing Thing that Happens When You Tell People They Have Different DNA," *The Wonkblog*. Retrieved from https://www.washing tonpost.com/news/wonk/wp/2016/05/13/the-disturbing-thing-that-happens-when-you-tell-people-they-have-different-dna/?utm_term=.949be7fe1220

References

Barth, Jay, L. Marvin Overby, and Scott H. Huffmon. 2009. "Community context, personal contact, and support for an anti—gay rights referendum". *Political Research Quarterly*, 62(2):355–365.

Druckman, James N. 2004. "Political preference formation: Competition, deliberation, and the (ir) relevance of framing effects". *American Political Science Review*, 98(4):671–686.

Entman, Robert M. 1993. "Framing: Toward clarification of a fractured paradigm". *Journal of Communication*, 43(4):51-58.

Entman, Robert M. (2004). *Projections of power: Framing news, public opinion, and US foreign policy*. University of Chicago Press.

Gerber, A. S., Huber, G. A., Doherty, D., Dowling, C. M., & Ha, S. E. (2010). Personality and political attitudes: Relationships across issue domains and political contexts. *American Political Science Review*, 104(1), 111–133.

Haider-Markel, Donald P., and Mark R. Joslyn. 2008. "Beliefs About the Origins of Homosexuality and Support For Gay Rights: An Empirical Test of Attribution Theory". *Public Opinion Quarterly*, 72(2):291–310.

Lewis, Gregory B. 2011. "The friends and family plan: Contact with gays and support for gay rights". *Policy Studies Journal*, 39(2):217–238.

Peter, Jeremy W. (2013, March 16). G.O.P. Senator says he has a gay son, and backs gay marriage. *New York Times*. Retrieved from http://www.nytimes.com/2013/03/16/us/politics/ohios-portman-says-he-supports-gay-marriage.html.

Pew Research Center. (2015, April 14). In Debate over legalizing marijuana, disagreement over drug's dangers. *Pew Research Center*. Retrieved from http://www.people-press.org/2015/04/14/in-debate-over-legalizing-marijuana-disagreement-over-drugs-dangers/#about-half-say-they-have-tried-marijuana

Pronin, E., Lin, D. Y., & Ross, L. 2002. The bias blind spot: Perceptions of bias in self versus others. Personality and Social Psychology Bulletin, 28:369–381.

Pronin, Emily, Thomas Gilovich, and Lee Ross. 2004. "Objectivity in the eye of the beholder: divergent perceptions of bias in self versus others". *Psychological Review*, 111 (3):781.

Robinson, R. J., Keltner, D., Ward, A., & Ross, L. 1995. "Actual versus assumed differences in construal: "Naive realism" in intergroup perception and conflict." *Journal of Personality and Social Psychology*, 68:404–417.

Ross, L., & Ward, A. (1996). Naive realism in everyday life: Implications for social conflict and misunderstanding. In T. Brown, E. S. Reed, & E. Turiel (Eds.), Values and knowledge. The Jean Piaget Symposium Series (pp. 103–135). Hillsdale, NJ: Erlbaum.

Ross, Lee, and Richard E. Nisbett. (2011). *The person and the situation: Perspectives of social psychology*. Pinter & Martin Publishers.

Settle, J. E., Dawes, C. T., Christakis, N. A., & Fowler, J. H. 2010. "Friendships moderate an association between a dopamine gene variant and political ideology." *The Journal of Politics*, 72(4):1189–1198.

Skipworth, Sue Ann, Andrew Garner, and Bryan J. Dettrey. 2010. "Limitations of the contact hypothesis: Heterogeneity in the contact effect on attitudes toward gay rights". *Politics & Policy*, 38(5): 887–906.

Slater, Michael D., Donna Rouner, and Marilee Long. 2006. "Television dramas and support for controversial public policies: Effects and mechanisms". *Journal of Communication*, 56(2):235–252.

3

HOW WE THINK AND REASON ABOUT POLITICS

In the previous chapter, I explained how our perceptions of the world are affected by our personalities, previous experiences, and position in society. Political disagreement is a natural outcome of people being different, and living different lives. After reading the previous chapter, you might still dislike political opponents because they have the *opportunity* to change their minds, but fail to adopt the correct opinion. On the one hand, just because people are born with a predisposition to hold a stupid opinion, it does not relieve them of the responsibility for changing it based on new information. Likewise, being predisposed toward alcoholism does not relieve someone of their responsibility to get treatment. On the other hand, we all suffer from cognitive biases that make it very unlikely that we will change our minds. A mountain of research shows that people engage in motivated information processing on a largely unconscious basis, and even do so when they are *made aware* of their cognitive biases. Furthermore, politically informed people are more likely than the uninformed to engage in motivated reasoning, which means that educating people will not solve this problem. If we all suffer from biased thinking from time to time, we should cut people some slack if they don't immediately change their minds when presented with opposing evidence.

The purpose of this chapter is to explain how all of us are subject to cognitive biases that lead us to believe that our preferred opinion is the objectively best policy option. Even if we were fortunate enough to support the correct policy, there is no way to know that our opinions and beliefs are not the result of cognitive biases. Since we are not aware of our own biases, it is best to hold opinions and factual beliefs with humility rather than certainty. Intellectual humility will make political discussion more productive and rewarding because you will accept the possibility that you may be wrong. In this chapter, I explain the main components of motivated reasoning including: confirmation bias, biased interpretation, and selective memory. I also explain why we tend to see bias in the opinions and beliefs of others, but usually fail to notice any biases in our beliefs. To conclude the chapter, I discuss how we can be more objective in our thinking, but because we can never be sure we are free of bias, we should strive for intellectual humility.

Motivated Reasoning

One of the most important problems in politics is that people process information in a way that supports what they desire to believe. A process called motivated reasoning occurs when people see the world in a way that supports their desired opinion. There are three parts to motivated reasoning: confirmation bias, biased interpretation, and selective memory. Altogether, they result in people resisting persuasion even when faced with evidence contrary to their opinions. Consequently, disagreement tends to persist even if everyone encounters the same information.

The first step in motivated reasoning is confirmation bias, which occurs when people seek out and notice information that confirms their views, while avoiding and ignoring contrary information. When people search for information on an issue, they tend to seek out sources that they expect will confirm their preferred opinion. Those opposing gun control will go to the National Rifle Association website to learn about gun control legislation. Likewise, people get news from sources that they deem trustworthy, but they tend to trust sources that confirm their views. Think about it, if you see the world through a liberal point of view, a news source that presents pictures from a liberal perspective will appear to be a better reflection of reality than a non-partisan news source. Conservatives trust conservative news sources, while liberals trust liberal outlets.

The recent proliferation of partisan news sources makes it easier for people to get news from sources that reinforce their political opinions. There is plenty of research showing that partisan media such as Fox News, MSNBC, and Conservative talk radio increase negativity among the American public (see Chapter 4). The more Republicans watch Fox News, or Democrats watch MSNBC, the more negative they feel toward members of the opposing party. Additionally, research suggests that partisan media are much more likely to increase negative feelings toward the opposition than to make partisans like their own candidate (Smith and Searles 2014). While it is true that partisan media do not command large audiences, those that do pay attention are much more politically active than ordinary Americans, which increases their power in the American political system (Abramowitz 2012; Levendusky 2013). In fact, Dilliplane (2011) found that partisan media even increase political activity among their audiences, further enhancing their political power. In short, confirmation bias is facilitated by partisan media outlets that increase negativity among the most politically active members of each party.

Even if people are exposed to the same information, they are likely to *interpret* the world in ways that support what they already believe. In a process called biased interpretation, people focus on aspects of information and events that make it seem like it supports, rather than conflicts with, their previous opinions. For example, partisans tend to believe that negative ads from their candidates are fair, while attack ads from opposing candidates are out of bounds and inappropriate, even when the candidates level the *exact same* attack (Stevens et al. 2012). In other words, partisans interpret the content of ads in ways that benefit politicians in their party. Moreover, Claassen and Ensley (2016) found that motivated reasoning made partisans more accepting of dirty electoral tricks among their own party, but saw the same tricks as outrageous when perpetrated by political opponents.

Biased interpretation can also have important consequences for people's pocketbooks if they make financial decisions based on their biased interpretations of the economy. Bartels (2002) found that people's factual beliefs about the economy were biased by their partisanship. Specifically, Democrats were more likely to incorrectly believe that the unemployment rate and inflation had gotten worse during the Reagan administration. More recent research confirms that fears of the opposing political party gaining power make partisans less likely to make major purchases (Krupenkin, Rothschild, and Hill 2018). If partisans act on these biased interpretations of the economy, it could have lasting consequences for their financial situations. For example, if Republicans pulled their money out of the stock market at the beginning of Barack Obama's presidency—because they believed he would surely wreck the economy—they would have lost a lot of money during the next eight years. This is not to say that Obama caused the economic turnaround, but merely to point out the dangers of basing one's financial decisions on biased interpretations of the economy rather than objective economic indicators.

Another consequence of biased interpretation is that people have trouble understanding how others could disagree with them. After all, you saw the same thing I did, so I assume you interpreted it the same way. It is very difficult to imagine that someone could see the same event, but interpret it differently. Consider a football game, where it seems every pass interference call draws boos from half the crowd and cheers from the other half. Perhaps they are lying to themselves, or maybe they saw the event differently, in a way that benefits their team. In a classic example of motivated reasoning, Hastorf and Cantril (1954) interviewed fans of Dartmouth and Princeton about a college football game. Perhaps not surprisingly, supporters of each team had very different accounts of what took place during the game, even though they watched the *exact same event*. Their perceptions of objective reality were biased by their preferences.

Subsequent research found similar biases in interpretations of negotiations and protests. Specifically, after viewing a negotiation, partisans tend to believe their party to be friendlier than the other party. In another interesting study, Kahan and colleagues (2012) conducted an experiment where all participants watched video of the exact same protest, but some were told the protest was against abortion, while others were told it was against the military's "don't ask, don't tell" policy that restricts gays from serving openly. Despite watching the exact same events, viewers disagreed over objective facts such as "whether the protestors obstructed and threatened pedestrians." The problem is that we tend to believe that there is only one way to look at reality, but in fact, we often interpret objective reality differently depending on our preferences, previous experiences, and mental constructs. Our first instinct is to assume that the other person is biased in their interpretation of the event, but we could just as easily be biased in our interpretation.

The final step of the motivated reasoning process is selective memory, where people are more likely to remember information from long-term memory that supports their desired opinion (Taber, Cann, and Kucsova 2009; Sanitioso, Kunda, and Fong 1990). In other words, people are more likely to remember reasons why they are right than reasons why they are wrong. Meffert and colleagues (2006) found that partisans were more likely to remember negative information about opposing party candidates than their preferred candidate in an election environment. When we evaluate the correctness of our opinions, our brains do not conduct an objective search for information. Instead, we seek memories that confirm what we want to believe. Is it any wonder that we frequently talk ourselves into objectively bad decisions?

The process of selective memory has an additional consequence of making people more certain of their original position. After all, if you are more likely to remember all of the reasons why you are right, and few of the reasons why you are wrong, you are likely to grow more confident in your opinions. In other words, the more people hear information opposing their opinions, the more certain they are that they are right (Lord, Ross and Lepper 1979; Taber and Lodge 2006). Rather than increasing intellectual humility, our natural processes make us more certain that we are seeing the world objectively. It also makes it difficult to understand how other people could possibly disagree with us given all of the objective facts that we just remembered that prove the rightness of our viewpoint. For someone to disagree with us, they must either be ignorant, biased or perhaps they have some ulterior motivation. If this is how people interpret political disagreements, perhaps it should not be surprising that political discussion often results in animosity and hostility.

Perhaps the most dangerous aspect of motivated reasoning is that it occurs largely outside of conscious awareness. People usually have no idea that they are engaging in motivated reasoning (Kunda 1990; Taber and Lodge 2016). Indeed, motivated social cognition is nearly automatic in the human mind when people encounter new information (Taber and Lodge 2006; Taber and Lodge 2016). In other words, motivated reasoning occurs so quickly that our conscious mind is incapable of knowing that it happened. As a result, there is no way to know for sure that our thinking was *not biased* by our motivations. Retroactively checking for biases does not solve the problem, because the way we check for biases is itself biased by our motivations to be correct! The key point is this: even if our opinions and beliefs reflected objective reality, we would have no way to know that with absolute certainty.

One might assume that motivated reasoning only occurs among the ignorant, but in fact it is the politically informed who are *more* likely to engage in motivated reasoning than the uninformed (Lodge and Taber 2005). For example, Braman and Nelson (2007) found that formal legal training did little to reduce motivated reasoning on legal rulings. More informed people have more ability to dispute counter-attitudinal information and arguments, and to create more elaborate rationalizations to support their opinion or belief in the face of contradictory evidence. This has at least two implications. First, educating the population will not solve the problem. The more information people have, the more they will remain obstinate in their preferred opinion. Second, those with political power are more likely to engage in motivated reasoning than ordinary people. Political elites have more information than the average American, but that means they are better able to defend their positions, and better able to find opinion-confirming information. Motivated reasoning will not be cured with more education unless it is accompanied by changes to how we approach learning and reasoning.

Bias Blind Spot

Another problem is that we are much more likely to notice bias in other people's opinions than to recognize our own biases. This phenomenon is referred to as the "bias blind spot" because we can clearly see bias in the opinions of others, but are blind to any biases in our opinions or beliefs (Pronin et al. 2002). The bias blind spot occurs because we engage in an "introspection illusion" where we believe that we have accurately assessed the sources of our own opinions and beliefs, and in doing so eliminated any potential biases. Since we do not have access to the introspection of others, we rely on observable evidence of bias in their opinions. For example, if we have a personal connection to a person, issue or an event, we see it as enhancing our knowledge, but we see others' personal experiences as biasing their opinions (Ehrlinger et al. 2005). This is why sports fans can simultaneously point out bias in the other team's fans, but not in their own observations.

The bias blind spot makes us more likely to feel hostility toward other people who hold opposing perspectives. Importantly, this perception of bias in others escalates conflicts because we tend to explain disagreement by attributing it to the bias in other people's perceptions rather than reasonable difference of opinion (Kennedy and Pronin 2008). When the opposition persists in holding incorrect beliefs or opinions, even after we graciously point out their wrongheaded thinking, it further frustrates us because they are just being hard-headed. Additionally, we tend to believe that we are being more fair and rational than the other side during any arguments or conflicts (Frantz 2006). As a result, we attribute disagreement to others not thinking clearly, rationally, and objectively.

The bias blind spot also makes people less likely to support negotiation and compromise with opposing political groups. In an interesting experiment, Kennedy and Pronin (2008) made some participants more likely to notice bias in political opponents. When people believed that negotiating partners were biased in their beliefs, they were less willing to cooperate in negotiation to resolve conflicts. The thinking goes "if the only reason we disagree is because you are biased, there is no reason to cooperate and negotiate to resolve our disputes." Instead, I will try to explain why your opinions are wrong. This refusal to negotiate is often glorified by saying we are "standing by our convictions." But if both sides think the opposition is biased, neither side will be willing to negotiate or compromise. In a political system such as the United States, where compromise is required to pass legislation, opposition to negotiation and compromise frequently ends in gridlock and inaction.

Increasing people's awareness of the bias blind spot does nothing to prevent it from occurring (Pronin et al. 2002). Again, people engage in the illusion of introspection and conclude that they are not biased. The bias blind spot is also not a symptom of low intelligence or naive and lazy thinking. Research suggests that smart people are *more likely* to suffer from the bias blind spot (West et al. 2012). Rather than trying to prevent the bias blind spot from occurring, or fruitlessly trying to assess our own biases, the best approach is to acknowledge that our opinions and beliefs might be biased. Despite the persistence of the bias blind spot, people often get offended by the mere suggestion that their opinions are biased, as if it is some defect to have opinions that stray from objective reality. As this chapter illustrates, we are all susceptible to cognitive biases and even if we were objective, we would have no way of knowing it for sure. Once we recognize that our political opinions and beliefs are biased, we may feel less animosity toward people who happen to hold conflicting views. After all, their opinions may be biased by their preferences, but it is highly likely that we are also biased in our perceptions of the world.

Possible Solutions to Motivated Reasoning

Although I paint a pretty grim picture, there are ways we can reduce the likelihood that we will engage in motivated reasoning. One way to reduce motivated reasoning is to increase one's self-esteem in other areas of their personal image, besides partisanship or ideology. Cohen and colleagues (2007) found that people were less likely to engage in motivated reasoning when they simply listed things that they liked about themselves. In a political context, Binning and colleagues (2010) found that self-affirmation made Democrats and Republicans more positive toward leaders in the opposing party. This self-affirmation exercise connected people's self-esteem to non-political sources—rather than political sources such as ideology and party identification—which made them more willing to be wrong when confronted with opposing information.

Another way to reduce motivated reasoning is to provide ourselves incentives for achieving accurate beliefs and predictions. Prior and colleagues (2015) found that providing people monetary incentives for answering factual questions made them less likely to give an answer that fit their preferred belief. Unfortunately, people rarely have *sufficient incentives* to avoid motivated reasoning. In some interesting experiments, participants were asked to wager on the outcome of sporting events in which their teams were playing (Babad 1987; Babad et al. 1992). Not surprisingly, fans were more likely to bet on teams they liked. At halftime, participants were given the opportunity to change their bets to the winning team, but many fans persisted in supporting their preferred team even when they were losing. These findings are also applicable to predictions of electoral outcomes. Even when we have monetary incentives to change our view, we often still engage in motivated reasoning.

Ultimately, the best way to combat motivated reasoning is to *accept that we could be wrong*. Once we recognize the possibility that we might be wrong, we can become more open to new information, and less hostile toward people who hold conflicting views. Hopefully, understanding our biases will help us hold our beliefs and opinions with more *intellectual humility* and less intellectual arrogance. Leary and colleagues (2017) define intellectual humility as "recognizing that a particular personal belief may be fallible, accompanied by an appropriate attentiveness to limitations in the evidentiary basis of that belief and to one's own limitations in obtaining and evaluating relevant information" (p. 793). In other words, intellectual humility is a recognition that we do not have complete information, and that our thinking may be biased in some way. When people hold opinions with humility, they accept that they could be wrong, and are open to changing their minds.

Importantly, recent research suggests that intellectual humility can make people less likely to engage in certain aspects of motivated reasoning. For one, intellectual humility makes people better able to evaluate the strength of arguments in an objective manner. Motivated reasoning causes people to classify arguments that support their opinions as stronger than opposing arguments (Taber and Lodge 2006). In contrast, intellectual humility allows people to remember and evaluate arguments in a more evenhanded manner (Leary et al. 2017). Furthermore, the more intellectually humble someone is, the less likely they are to attach their self-esteem to their opinions and beliefs (Krumrei-Mancuso and Rouse 2016). As a result, intellectual humility makes people less defensive when they encounter reasons why they might be wrong. Intellectual humility also has a variety of other benefits such as making people more: intellectually curious, tolerant of ambiguity, open to learning diverse perspectives, and willing to change their mind (Deffler, Leary and Hoyle 2016; Leary et al. 2017).

Most important of all for my purposes, intellectual humility decreases negativity toward people who express opposing opinions (Leary et al. 2017). When people accept that their own opinions could be wrong, they are less likely to hold negative feelings toward people that disagree. It makes no sense to dislike someone for holding opposing perspectives if you acknowledge that they might be right. Conversely, when we are absolutely certain that we are right, we often feel anger toward people who (we believe) are too stupid and hard-headed to understand that they are wrong. If you hold your opinions with humility rather than arrogance, you will find it much easier to engage in discussions with people who hold different perspectives. In short, intellectual humility is a valuable characteristic that can help facilitate productive discussions, while decreasing hostility toward people who disagree.

Review Questions

1. What are the three parts of motivated reasoning and why are they dangerous?
2. What are some ways people can overcome motivated reasoning and why are they effective?
3. What is the bias blind spot and how does it increase political animosity?
4. What types of people are more likely to engage in motivated reasoning?
5. What is intellectual humility and how does it facilitate productive political discussions?

Discussion Questions

1. How does motivated reasoning affect interpretations of science?
2. How does the electoral process in the United States encourage motivated reasoning among elected officials?
3. What steps can you take to be more critical of opinion confirming information?
4. How does motivated reasoning weaken accountability in a representative democracy?
5. After reading this chapter, would you classify Americans as more gullible or hard-headed?
6. On what types of issues are politicians better able to move public opinion?
7. What can schools do to make students less susceptible to motivated reasoning and the bias blind spot?

Sources for Further Inquiry

Books

Arceneaux, Kevin, and Ryan J. Vander Wielen. 2017. *Taming Intuition: How Reflection Minimizes Partisan Reasoning and Promotes Democratic Accountability.* New York, NY: Cambridge University Press
Church, Ian, and Peter Samuelson. 2016. *Intellectual Humility: An Introduction to the Philosophy and Science.* London: Bloomsbury Publishing.

Green, Donald, Bradley Palmquist and Eric Schickler. 2002. *Partisan Hearts and Minds.* New Haven, CT: Yale University Press.

Lavine, Howard G., Christopher D. Johnston, and Marco R. Steenbergen. 2012. *The Ambivalent Partisan: How Critical Loyalty Promotes Democracy.* New York, NY: Oxford University Press.

Lenz, Gabriel S. 2013. *Follow the Leader?: How Voters Respond to Politicians' Policies and Performance.* Chicago, IL: University of Chicago Press.

Lodge, Milton, and Charles S. Taber. 2013. *The Rationalizing Voter.* New York, NY: Cambridge University Press.

Weeden, Jason, and Robert Kurzban. 2014. *The Hidden Agenda of the Political Mind: How Self-interest Shapes our Opinions and Why we Won't Admit it.* Princeton, NJ: Princeton University Press.

Journal and Newspaper Articles

Baekgaard, Martin, Julian Christensen, Casper Mondrup Dahlmann, Asbjørn Mathiasen, and Niels Bjørn Grund Petersen. (Forthcoming). "The Role of Evidence in Politics: Motivated Reasoning and Persuasion among Politicians." *British Journal of Political Science.* Retrieved from: https://www.cambridge.org/core/journals/british-journal-of-poli tical-science/article/role-of-evidence-in-politics-motivated-reasoning-and-persuasion-among-politicians/6813A080C058E1BB4920661FF60BED6F

Bisgaard, Martin. 2015. "Bias will Find a Way: Economic Perceptions, Attributions of Blame, and Partisan Motivated Reasoning During Crisis." *Journal of Politics* 77(3): 849–860.

DeMarree, Kenneth G., Cory J. Clark, S. Christian Wheeler, Pablo Briñol, and Richard E. Petty. 2017. "On the Pursuit of Desired Attitudes: Wanting a Different Attitude Affects Information Processing and Behavior." *Journal of Experimental Social Psychology* 70: 129–142.

Edelson, Jack, Alexander Alduncin, Christopher Krewson, James A. Sieja, and Joseph E. Uscinski. 2017. "The Effect of Conspiratorial Thinking and Motivated Reasoning on Belief in Election Fraud." *Political Research Quarterly* 70(4): 933–946.

Flynn, D. J., Brendan Nyhan, and Jason Reifler. 2017. "The Nature and Origins of Misperceptions: Understanding False and Unsupported Beliefs about Politics." *Political Psychology* 38(S1): 127–150.

Gascó, Margarita, Pablo Briñol, David Santos, Richard E. Petty, and Javier Horcajo. 2018. "Where Did This Thought Come From? A Self-Validation Analysis of the Perceived Origin of Thoughts." *Personality and Social Psychology Bulletin.* Retrieved from: http://journals.sagepub.com/doi/10.1177/0146167218775696

Geher, Glenn. 2016, Dec. 13. "The Social Psychology of a Nation Divided." *Psychology Today.* Retrieved from: https://www.psychologytoday.com/blog/darwins-subterranea n-world/201612/the-social-psychology-nation-divided

Goren, Paul. 2005. "Party Identification and Core Political Values." *American Journal of Political Science* 49(4): 881–896.

Grimes, David R. 2014, Feb. 5. "Denying Climate Change Isn't Scepticism – It's Motivated Reasoning." *The Guardian.* Retrieved from: https://www.theguardian.com/sci ence/2014/feb/05/denying-climate-change-scepticism-motivated-reasoning

Kahan, Dan. 2011, May 4. "What is Motivated Reasoning and How Does it Work?" *Science and Religion Today.* Retrieved from: http://www.scienceandreligiontoday.com/2011/05/04/what-is-motivated-reasoning-and-how-does-it-work/

Mooney, Chris. 2011, May. "The Science of Why We Don't Believe Science." *Mother Jones*. Retrieved from: http://www.motherjones.com/politics/2011/03/denial-scien ce-chris-mooney

Taber, Charles S., and Milton Lodge. 2006. "Motivated Skepticism in the Evaluation of Political Beliefs." *American Journal of Political Science* 50(3): 755–769.

References

Abramowitz, Alan. 2012. *The Polarized Public: Why Our Government is So Dysfunctional.* New York, NY: Pearson Longman.

Babad, Elisha. 1987. "Wishful Thinking and Objectivity among Sports Fans." *Social Behaviour* 2(4): 231–240.

Babad, Elisha, Michael Hills, and Michael O'Driscoll. 1992. "Factors Influencing Wishful Thinking and Predictions of Election Outcomes." *Basic and Applied Social Psychology* 13(4): 461–476.

Bartels, Larry M. 2002. "Beyond the Running Tally: Partisan Bias in Political Perceptions." *Political Behavior* 24(2): 117–150.

Binning, Kevin R., David K. Sherman, Geoffrey L. Cohen, and Kirsten Heitland. 2010. "Seeing the Other Side: Reducing Political Partisanship via Self-Affirmation in the 2008 Presidential Election." *Analyses of Social Issues and Public Policy* 10(1): 276–292.

Braman, Eileen, and Thomas E. Nelson. 2007. "Mechanism of Motivated Reasoning? Analogical Perception in Discrimination Disputes." *American Journal of Political Science* 51 (4): 940–956.

Claassen, Ryan L., and Michael J. Ensley. 2016. "Motivated Reasoning and Yard-Sign-Stealing Partisans: Mine is a Likeable Rogue, Yours is a Degenerate Criminal." *Political Behavior* 38(2): 317–335.

Cohen, Geoffrey L., David K. Sherman, Anthony Bastardi, Lillian Hsu, Michelle McGoey, and Lee Ross. 2007. "Bridging the Partisan Divide: Self-affirmation Reduces Ideological Closed-mindedness and Inflexibility in Negotiation." *Journal of Personality and Social Psychology* 93(3): 415–430.

Deffler, Samantha A., Mark R. Leary, and Rick H. Hoyle. 2016. "Knowing what you Know: Intellectual Humility and Judgments of Recognition Memory." *Personality and Individual Differences* 96: 255–259.

Dilliplane, Susanna. 2011. "All the News You Want to Hear: The Impact of Partisan News Exposure on Political Participation." *Public Opinion Quarterly* 75(2): 278–316.

Ehrlinger, Joyce, Thomas Gilovich, and Lee Ross. 2005. "Peering into the Bias Blind Spot: People's Assessments of Bias in Themselves and Others." *Personality and Social Psychology Bulletin* 31(5): 680–692.

Frantz, Cynthia M. 2006. "I AM Being Fair: The Bias Blind Spot as a Stumbling Block to Seeing Both Sides." *Basic and Applied Social Psychology* 28(2): 157–167.

Hastorf, Albert H., and Hadley Cantril. 1954. "They Saw a Game: A Case Study." *The Journal of Abnormal and Social Psychology* 49(1): 129–134.

Kahan, Dan M., David A. Hoffman, Donald Braman, Danieli Evans, and Jeffrey J. Rachlinski. 2012. "'They Saw a Protest': Cognitive Illiberalism and the Speech-Conduct Distinction." *Stanford Law Review* 64: 851.

Kennedy, K. A., and E. Pronin. 2008. "When Disagreement Gets Ugly: Perceptions of Bias and the Escalation of Conflict." *Personality and Social Psychology Bulletin* 34(6): 833–848.

Krumrei-Mancuso, Elizabeth J., and Steven V. Rouse. 2016. "The Development and Validation of the Comprehensive Intellectual Humility Scale." *Journal of Personality Assessment* 98(2): 209–221.

Krupenkin, Masha, David Rothschild, and Shawndra Hill. 2018, August 27. "Partisanship's A Helluva Drug – And It's Reshaping the Economy." Politico. Retrieved from: https://www.politico.com/magazine/story/2018/08/27/trump-economy-partisan-influence-consumer-confidence-219602

Kunda, Ziva. 1990. "The Case for Motivated Reasoning." *Psychological Bulletin* 108(3): 480–498.

Leary, Mark R., Kate J. Diebels, Erin K. Davisson, Katrina P. Jongman-Sereno, Jennifer C. Isherwood, Kaitlin T. Raimi, Samantha A. Deffler, and Rick H. Hoyle. 2017. "Cognitive and Interpersonal Features of Intellectual Humility." *Personality and Social Psychology Bulletin* 43(6): 793–813.

Levendusky, Matthew S. 2013. *How Partisan Media Polarize America*. Chicago, IL: University of Chicago Press.

Lodge, Milton, and Charles S. Taber. 2005. "The Automaticity of Affect for Political Leaders, Groups, and Issues: An Experimental Test of the Hot Cognition Hypothesis." *Political Psychology* 26(3): 455–482.

Lord, Charles G., Lee Ross, and Mark R. Lepper. 1979. "Biased Assimilation and Attitude Polarization: The Effects of Prior Theories on Subsequently Considered Evidence." *Journal of Personality and Social Psychology* 37(11): 2098–2109.

Meffert, Michael F., Sungeun Chung, Amber J. Joiner, Leah Waks, and Jennifer Garst. 2006. "The Effects of Negativity and Motivated Information Processing During a Political Campaign." *Journal of Communication* 56(1): 27–51.

Prior, Markus, Gaurav Sood, and Kabir Khanna. 2015. "The Impact of Accuracy Incentives on Partisan Bias in Reports of Economic Perceptions." *Quarterly Journal of Political Science* 10: 489–518.

Pronin, Emily, Daniel Y. Lin, and Lee Ross. 2002. "The Bias Blind Spot: Perceptions of Bias in Self versus Others." *Personality and Social Psychology Bulletin* 28(3): 369–381.

Sanitioso, Rasyid, Ziva Kunda, and Geoffrey T. Fong. 1990. "Motivated Recruitment of Autobiographical Memories." *Journal of Personality and Social Psychology* 59(2): 229–241.

Smith, Glen, and Kathleen Searles. 2014. "Who Let the (Attack) Dogs Out? New Evidence for Partisan Media Effects." *Public Opinion Quarterly* 78(1): 71–99.

Stevens, Daniel, John Sullivan, Barbara Allen, and Dean Alger. 2012. "What's Good for the Goose is Bad for the Gander: Negative Political Advertising, Partisanship, and Turnout." *The Journal of Politics* 70(2): 527–541.

Taber, Charles S., and Milton Lodge. 2006. "Motivated Skepticism in the Evaluation of Political Beliefs." *American Journal of Political Science* 50(3): 755–769.

Taber, Charles S., and Milton Lodge. 2016. "The Illusion of Choice in Democratic Politics: The Unconscious Impact of Motivated Political Reasoning." *Political Psychology* 37(1): 61–85

Taber, Charles S., Damon Cann, and Simona Kucsova. 2009. "The Motivated Processing of Political Arguments." *Political Behavior* 31(2): 137–155.

West, Richard F., Russell J. Meserve, and Keith E. Stanovich. 2012. "Cognitive Sophistication Does Not Attenuate the Bias Blind Spot." *Journal of Personality and Social Psychology* 103(3): 506–519.

4

CONSIDER THE SOURCE: NEWS MEDIA AND POLITICAL HOSTILITY

The news media play a vital role in promoting a healthy democracy. Providing political information to the public allows voters to hold elected officials accountable. A free press is also essential for a vigorous and robust marketplace of ideas, where people are exposed to diverse perspectives surrounding political issues and events. People rely on the news media for information about the world that exists outside of their direct experiences. Perceptions of crime, the economy, wars, international conflicts, environmental pollution, and social unrest, are shaped largely by the news media. In fact, these *sociotropic* evaluations have more influence on our opinions than our personal circumstances (Mutz 1998). For example, perceptions of the national economy are a better predictor of voting behavior than people's personal economic situation—also called their *pocketbook* considerations. Where we get our news plays a large role in determining what issues we think are important (Iyengar and Kinder 1987), how we evaluate political candidates (Miller and Krosnick 2000), and how we think about political issues (Nelson, Clawson and Oxley 1997). In short, the news media help shape the way people understand the world.

For most of the 20th century, Americans received a similar portrait of the world from the mass media, regardless of the specific sources that they used. Many people lived in markets with only a single local newspaper, and television news was dominated by the big three broadcast television networks. West (2001) calls this period (1920s–1970s) the *objective era* of the news media, because news content was similar across the most popular outlets, and reporters presented fairly balanced coverage of public affairs (D'Allessio and Allen 2000). During this period, Americans found the news media credible and trustworthy (West 2001). One reason Americans trusted the media was because they received *similar* news from a *variety* of different sources. When there are only a few news sources, each source has a financial incentive to capture the entire market, which motivated news sources to be objective and balanced in order to avoid alienating liberals or conservatives. When people saw similar pictures of the world coming from all three nightly news programs, and their local newspaper, they had less reason to question whether it was true.

Technological changes resulted in an expansion of news sources on cable television and the internet. In this more competitive marketplace, some news sources found it profitable to cover politics from a distinctly partisan and ideological perspective. In the modern media marketplace, conservatives can watch *Fox News*, listen to the *Rush Limbaugh Show*, and read the *Drudge Report*, while liberals can watch *MSNBC*, and read the *Daily Kos*. These partisan news outlets are appealing to people who want to be told that they are right and the other side is wrong. Partisan media allow conservatives and liberals to get news that matches the way they see the world. As a result, many people are able to isolate themselves in like-minded echo chambers where they only get news that reinforces their previous beliefs.

The purpose of this chapter is to explain how the news media can *simulate political discussion* and provide vicarious contact with dissimilar political groups. In other words, the news media can help you learn diverse perspectives and challenge stereotypes about people who hold those perspectives. While the diversity of news media outlets provides you the opportunity to broaden your horizons, it also allows you to isolate yourself into like-minded media echo chambers that repeat your beliefs back to you. As I will show, if you only get news from like-minded partisan media, you are more likely to believe that only their facts are credible, and the opposing side is uninformed, immoral, corrupt, and evil. On the other hand, getting news from *liberal and conservative* outlets will expose you to the strongest arguments on both sides of prominent political issues. Meanwhile, paying some attention to mainstream media is likely to reduce political hostility by helping you learn the actual reasons that people disagree with you. In short, whether the news media increase or decrease political hostility depends on what news sources people use. In this chapter, I explain why some people rely exclusively on partisan media, how doing so increases hostility between opposing groups, and how mainstream media can reduce polarization.

The Appeal of Partisan Media

Why do some people choose to get news from like-minded partisan media outlets? The main benefit of like-minded media is that it allows people to avoid cognitive dissonance (Festinger 1957). Human beings desire to hold opinions that are—or at least appear to be—logically consistent with each other. When people encounter information that contradicts their opinions and beliefs, it causes an internal inconsistency between their previous opinions and this new information. The internal inconsistency causes people to feel psychological stress until the inconsistency is resolved, after which people feel relief. For example, Westin and colleagues (2006) monitored the brain activity of Democrats and Republicans while they read inconsistent statements from their preferred presidential candidate prior to the 2004 election. When partisans read the inconsistent statements, they experienced emotional discomfort, which turned to pleasure after they *rationalized* away the inconsistency. In other words, hearing negative information about their preferred candidate caused them stress, but their brain rewarded them with pleasure after they engaged in motivated reasoning (see Chapter 3).

One way to prevent cognitive dissonance is to avoid situations that are likely to result in exposure to information that conflicts with one's beliefs. When people encounter such counter-attitudinal information, they typically dispute the information, which requires mental effort on their part. Avoiding opposing information altogether means that people do not have to exert mental energy defending their opinions. In an interesting study, Frimer, Skitka, and Motyl (2017) found that the aversion to cognitive dissonance was so strong that people gave up the opportunity to *win money* just to avoid hearing arguments that opposed their opinions. The main reasons people gave for avoiding opposing arguments were that it would require too much effort and cause frustration (Frimer, Skitka, and Motyl 2017). In short, people have emotional and psychological incentives to avoid exposure to opposing arguments.

Getting news from like-minded media allows partisans to minimize the chances they will suffer cognitive dissonance. When partisans get news from mainstream or opposing sources, they typically have to exert mental energy to dispute arguments and facts that contradict their opinions. People do not necessarily make the *conscious* decision to avoid opposing information, but instead they simply find it more pleasing, and less mentally taxing, to get news from sources that reinforce what they believe.

Partisan media can also help *alleviate* dissonance that results from facts or events that contradict one's desired beliefs. If the economy is going poorly while a Democrat is president, Democrats can go to a liberal blog to learn why it is not really the president's fault. Likewise, if there is a scandal involving a Republican politician, *Fox News* can explain why it is not a big deal, and not at all hypocritical to continue voting for the Republican. For example, the day after Osama Bin Laden was killed, many Republicans probably faced cognitive dissonance. While they were glad Bin Laden was brought to justice, many of them probably did not want to give any credit to Barack Obama for ordering the raid. Conservative radio host Rush Limbaugh rushed to his listeners' aide by explaining that *any* president would have made the same decisions, so Obama deserves no credit whatsoever. In doing so, Limbaugh allowed his Republican listeners to be happy that Bin Laden was dead, but not have to feel any positive feelings about President Obama. Partisan media is attractive to partisans because it helps them both *avoid and resolve* the psychological stress that results from cognitive dissonance.

To be sure, avoiding cognitive dissonance is not the only reason people prefer to get news from partisan media outlets. Some people get news from partisan media because they believe mainstream media outlets are politically biased against their party or ideology. People are less likely to get news from sources they perceive as politically biased or lacking credibility (Tsfati and Cappella 2003). Instead, they more consistently rely on news sources that, in their opinion, are objective and trustworthy (Stroud 2011; Smith and Searles 2014). Perceptions of media bias are also important because they affect how people process information from the news. All things being equal, people are more likely to believe information when it comes from a credible source (Hass 1981; Druckman 2001; Levendusky 2013). If someone perceives bias in a news source, they are less likely to believe what they report. Of course, it is perfectly logical to ignore or avoid information sources that you believe are biased. Perceptions of media bias would be useful as long as they were accurate. Unfortunately, people are not very good at identifying political bias in the media (Dalton, Beck and Huckfeldt 1998; Ladd 2010; Smith 2010).

Perceptions of media bias come from three main sources: the hostile media effect, opinion content, and elite attacks on the media. The most common reason people perceive media bias is because media coverage deviates from their view of the world. In a psychological process called the *hostile media effect*, partisans tend to believe that media coverage of political issues is biased against their side (Vallone, Ross, and Lepper 1985; Giner-Sorolla and Chaiken 1994). The hostile media effect results from a process called selective categorization, where partisans are more likely to classify arguments and information as opposing their side of an issue (Schmitt, Gunther and Liebhart 2004). When news sources present balanced or neutral coverage, partisans classify more arguments against their side. As a result, Democrats and Republicans watching the same balanced news coverage can each think that it favors the other party (Vallone et al. 1985). Partisan news sources present strong arguments on one side, and criticize the (usually weak) arguments on the other side. Viewers are likely to view this coverage as more objective because it better aligns with the way they see the world.

A second source of perceptions of media bias is opinion content such as opinionated news programs on cable television, or opinion columns and editorials in newspapers. The purpose of opinion content is to present an argument on some political topic. In contrast to straight news, opinion content is not supposed to be unbiased, or present balanced arguments on each side. Quite the contrary, opinion columns are intended to express opinions on one side of the debate, while the other side is free to express their opinions in their own column. It is precisely because opinion content is unabashedly one-sided that it carries greater weight than straight news in people's perceptions of media bias (Dalton, Beck and Huckfeldt 1998). People are not very good at judging media bias in straight news because it presents balanced perspectives. Instead, they use opinion content as a proxy for the slant of news articles, and then judge the entire source as biased (Turner 2007). If you believe a news source is biased, perhaps you should ask whether you are judging the source based on its opinion content, rather than any bias in the actual news.

Another reason people perceive bias in the media is because politicians accuse the media of bias. Politicians commonly attack the news media for various reasons, but research consistently shows that those attacks lower overall media credibility (Watts et al. 1999; Ladd 2011). Furthermore, when politicians accuse the media of political bias, it increases perceptions of bias independent of any *actual bias* in the news source (Watts et al. 1999; Smith 2010). For example, I conducted an experiment where participants read the *same* newspaper article, but some people read a political candidate accuse the newspaper of a liberal bias, while others read an accusation of conservative bias (Smith 2010). Despite reading the exact same article, elite attacks were enough to convince people that the article was biased against the attacking politician. Additionally, accusations of bias were just as effective when they were read *after* the article, meaning it did not affect how people processed the news. In other words, politicians can convince people that a news source is biased even when there is no bias. It is important to note that elite attacks are most effective on members of the attacker's political party, but tend to be ignored by members of the opposing party (Smith 2010).

Despite the problems with our perceptions of media bias, they still affect where we get our news and whether we believe it. When people believe a source is politically biased, especially if it is biased against them, they are more likely to avoid that news source altogether (Stroud 2011; Tsfati and Cappella 2003). The widespread belief among Republicans that the media have a liberal bias is one reason why they have gravitated to conservative media outlets (Jamieson and Cappella 2008). While liberals also pay attention to like-minded media, such as *MSNBC*, they are more likely than conservatives to get news from mainstream sources from time to time (Mitchell et al. 2014). Nonetheless, both Democrats and Republicans are increasingly likely to get news from partisan media outlets rather than mainstream news (Stroud 2008 and 2011). Furthermore, surveys suggest that people find their like-minded news sources believable, which allows for increased persuasion (Smith and Searles 2014). In short, perceptions of media bias have important effects on where we get our news, and whether we believe it.

The point of all of this is to show you that people do not have very good reasons for isolating themselves into like-minded media echo chambers. Some people avoid mainstream and opposing outlets because they want to avoid cognitive dissonance. While it may be more comfortable to avoid hearing opposing arguments, it is a poor strategy if your goal is to make the best decisions possible. Avoiding opposing arguments only makes sense if you are absolutely certain that you are correct, but I hope most people are not that intellectually arrogant.

Some people rely exclusively on partisan media because they believe mainstream news is politically biased, which is certainly a plausible reason to avoid a news source. The problem is that your perceptions of media bias may be inaccurate, but nonetheless cause you to isolate yourself in a media echo chamber. This is not to say that media bias does not exist, but rather that when it does, we are unlikely to judge it in an objective manner. Instead, perceptions of bias stem from our personal biases, evaluations of intentionally biased opinion content, and blind faith in like-minded politicians to be honest about biases in the media. Could mainstream media be biased against your side? Of course it could! Unfortunately, our own biases make it difficult, if not impossible, to evaluate bias in the news media. If your perceptions of media bias are potentially inaccurate, it makes more sense to get news from ideologically diverse media outlets. Just in case you still want to live in a media echo chamber, the next section explains how doing so is likely to make you more angry and hostile toward people who hold different political opinions.

Partisan Selective Exposure and Hostility

When people get their news exclusively from like-minded partisan media, it has important effects on how they feel toward opposing political groups and their elected leaders. Before getting to the effects of partisan media, it is important to understand how their financial incentives shape the content of the news. Partisan media have a financial incentive to make you fearful and angry toward opposing partisans, and especially their political leaders. Previous research suggests that both fear and anger cause people to seek out information (Brader 2005; Ryan 2012), especially from like-minded partisan news media (Song 2017). Partisan media can increase their profits by telling you that the other side is stupid, immoral, corrupt, and evil (Jamieson and Cappella 2008). If you are content and happy, you may seek out other entertainment options, but if you are fearful and angry, you will spend more time watching, listening to, or reading partisan media outlets. Conservative talk radio hosts argue that Democrats are godless, lazy bums, who want to destroy everything America stands for, while liberal media personalities argue that Republicans are misogynistic, racist, homophobes. I wish I were exaggerating these portrayals, but I am sorry to say they are quite common on partisan media outlets (Jamieson and Cappella 2008; Hannity 2010). The narrative on both liberal and conservative media is consistent; we are fighting on the side of righteousness against the evil opposition.

All of this negative coverage of the opposing party has a predictable effect on viewers. The more people rely on partisan media for their news, the more likely they are to hold negative attitudes toward members of the opposing party (Morris and Francia 2010; Smith and Searles 2013). On the one hand, some of this correlation is people self-selecting into the partisan media audience. If you hate the opposing party, you are more likely to seek out partisan media that tells you they are evil. On the other hand, there is abundant evidence that partisan media actually *cause* people to dislike members of the opposing party (Jamieson and Cappella 2008; Feldman 2011; Levendusky 2013; Smith and Searles 2014). Some researchers have used controlled experiments to show that even small amounts of exposure to partisan media make people more negative toward opposing partisans (Feldman 2011; Levendusky 2013; Mutz 2015). Other researchers have used innovative techniques to show that partisan media increases negativity in the real world over time (Stroud 2011; Morris and Francia 2010; Smith and Searles 2014; Smith 2016). In my previous work, I showed that increased partisan media coverage of opposing party candidates made viewers of Fox News and MSNBC more negative and distrustful toward opposing party leaders (Smith and Searles 2013 and 2014; Smith 2016). Specifically, the more coverage partisan media devoted to opposing party candidates, the more negative viewers were toward that candidate the following day and week. Altogether, there is consistent evidence that partisan media make viewers more hostile toward opposing partisans.

Although it may seem that way, I do not argue that partisan media are all bad, or do not serve any good in society. For example, partisan media make people more likely to participate in the political system (Dilliplane 2011), which is a good thing! What I argue instead is that relying *exclusively* on like-minded partisan media is a bad idea. Partisan media can simulate productive political discussion, but only if people use an ideologically diverse mix of news media. The opinionated shows on partisan media provide strong arguments supporting their side of the policy debate. As already discussed, the problem with partisan media is that they usually present poor arguments supporting opposing perspectives. Relying exclusively on liberal or conservative news outlets is likely to lead people to believe that their side has strong arguments, while the other side has poor arguments and nefarious motivations. Getting news from both liberal and conservative news outlets will provide you with strong arguments supporting liberal and conservative opinions, and in doing so simulate productive political discussion. Partisan media allow you to access opposing perspectives, as long as you are willing to listen to the other side from time to time.

How Mainstream Media Reduce Partisan Hostility

In contrast to partisan media, mainstream news outlets expose people to strong arguments on both sides of public policy questions. Helping people learn diverse perspectives works to challenge negative stereotypes about the characteristics, opinions, and motivations of political opponents. Mainstream news is one of the few places where Americans get consistent exposure to diverse perspectives about political affairs (Mutz and Martin 2001). Exposure to diverse arguments helps partisans understand the rationales behind the opinions of opposing political groups. Although partisans are unlikely to change their voting decisions or policy preferences, understanding that opposing viewpoints are based on rational arguments can challenge stereotypes and reduce antipathy toward the opposition (Mutz 2002). Moreover, hearing opposing arguments on mainstream news might help partisans attribute disagreement to rational differences of opinion rather than some defect in members of opposing groups.

There is empirical evidence that exposure to mainstream media can decrease hostility toward opposing partisans. In some of my recent work, I showed that broadcast news programs made viewers more positive toward the opposition party (Smith 2017). Specifically, the more broadcast news programs someone watched, the more likely they were to have positive attitudes toward candidates in the opposing party. These effects were most pronounced among partisans with the strongest attachments to their political party. Meanwhile, there was no consistent relationship between exposure to broadcast news and feelings toward one's own party nominee, meaning mainstream news does not simply increase positive feelings across the board. People already knew the arguments of their party's candidate, but learning the actual arguments of the opposing candidate made strong partisans less negative toward the opposition party's nominee. Furthermore, I show that increased coverage of the candidate on broadcast news was followed by increased positive feelings among the opposing party one week later. In other words, mainstream news can help people learn the arguments of the opposition, which can challenge stereotypes of opposing groups, and result in less political hostility.

Review Questions

1. Why did the news media have higher credibility during the "objective" era?
2. What is cognitive dissonance and how does it push people to get news from partisan media?
3. What are the three main reasons that people perceive political bias in the news media?
4. How do partisan media increase political hostility?
5. How do mainstream news sources decrease negative feelings toward opposing partisans?

Discussion Questions

1. Are partisan media good or bad for democracy?
2. Where do you get most of your news and why?
3. How do you judge the credibility of individual news outlets?
4. What are some ways to avoid fake news outlets on social media?
5. Should the news media give people the information they want, or what they need to know?

Sources for Further Inquiry

Books

Arceneaux, Kevin, and Martin Johnson. 2013. *Changing Minds or Changing Channels?: Partisan News in an Age of Choice.* Chicago, IL: University of Chicago Press.
Baum, Matthew A. 2005. *Soft News Goes to War: Public Opinion and American Foreign Policy in the New Media Age.* Princeton, NJ: Princeton University Press.
Cappella, Joseph N., and Kathleen Hall Jamieson. 1997. *Spiral of Cynicism: The Press and the Public Good.* New York, NY: Oxford University Press.

Ladd, Jonathan M. 2011. *Why Americans Hate the Media and How it Matters*. Princeton, NJ: Princeton University Press.
Mutz, Diana C. 2015. *In-your-face Politics: The Consequences of Uncivil Media*. Princeton, NJ: Princeton University Press.
Uscinski, Joseph E. 2014. *The People's News: Media, Politics, and the Demands of Capitalism*. New York, NY: New York University Press.

Books

Arceneaux, Kevin, Martin Johnson, René Lindstädt, and Ryan J. Wielen. 2016. "The Influence of News Media on Political Elites: Investigating Strategic Responsiveness in Congress." *American Journal of Political Science* 60(1): 5–29.
Borchers, Callum. 2016, April 24. "The 'Nasty Effect,' and Why Donald Trump Supporters Mistrust the Media." The Wonkblog. Retrieved from https://www.washingtonpost.com/news/the-fix/wp/2016/04/24/the-nasty-effect-and-why-donald-trump-supporters-mistrust-the-media/?utm_term=.4480327d6b0e.
Druckman, James N., Matthew S. Levendusky, and Audrey McLain. 2018. "No Need to Watch: How the Effects of Partisan Media Can Spread via Interpersonal Discussions." *American Journal of Political Science* 62(1): 99–112.
Jamison, Mark. 2017, April 12. "The Great Media Divide: News Business on the Left and right Perpetuate out Political Divide. " U.S. News and World Report. Retrieved from https://www.usnews.com/opinion/economic-intelligence/articles/2017-04-12/how-left-and-right-media-models-perpetuate-partisan-politics
Levendusky, Matthew. 2014, February 3. "Are Fox and MSNBC Polarizing America?" Monkey Cage Blog. Retrieved from https://www.washingtonpost.com/news/monkey-cage/wp/2014/02/03/are-fox-and-msnbc-polarizing-america/?utm_term=.fea04e44de00
Smith, Glen. 2016, November 2. "Is it Too Late for Partisan TV News to Swing the Election?" *Newsweek*. Retrieved from http://www.newsweek.com/it-too-late-partisan-tv-news-swing-election-515731
Sweeny, Kate, Darya Melnyk, Wendi Miller, and James A. Shepperd. 2010. "Information Avoidance: Who, What, When, and Why." *Review of General Psychology* 14(4): 340–353.
Wemple, Erik. 2017, January 27. "Dear Mainstream Media: Why So Liberal?" *The Washington Post*. Retrieved from https://www.washingtonpost.com/blogs/erikwemple/wp/2017/01/27/dear-mainstream-media-why-so-liberal/?utm_term=.602085e3a31a

References

Aday, Sean. 2010. "Chasing the Bad News: An Analysis of 2005 Iraq and Afghanistan War Coverage on NBC and Fox News Channel." *Journal of Communication* 60(1): 144–164.
Bennett, Lance W. 1996. *News: The Politics of Illusion*. New York, NY: Longman.
D'Allessio, Dave, and Mike Allen. 2000. "Media Bias in Presidential Elections: A Meta-Analysis." *Journal of Communication* 50(4): 133–156.
Dalton, Russell J., Paul A. Beck, and Robert Huckfeldt. 1998. "Partisan Cues and the Media: Information Flows in the 1992 Presidential Election." *American Political Science Review* 92(1): 111–126.
Dilliplane, Susanna. 2011. "All the News You Want to Hear: The Impact of Partisan News Exposure on Political Participation." *Public Opinion Quarterly* 75(2): 278–316.

Druckman, James N. 2001. "On the Limits of Framing Effects: Who Can Frame?" *Journal of Politics* 63(4): 1041–1066.

Feldman, Lauren. 2011. "The Opinion Factor: The Effects of Opinionated News on Information Processing and Attitude Change." *Political Communication* 28(2): 163–181.

Festinger, Leon. 1957. *A Theory of Cognitive Dissonance*. Stanford, CA: Stanford University Press.

Frimer, Jeremy A., Linda J. Skitka, and Matt Motyl. 2017. "Liberals and Conservatives Are Similarly Motivated to Avoid Exposure to One Another's Opinions." *Journal of Experimental Social Psychology* 72(1): 1–12.

Giner-Sorolla, Roger and Shelly Chaiken. 1994. "The Causes of Hostile Media Judgments." *Journal of Experimental Social Psychology* 30(2): 165–180.

Hannity, Sean. 2010, August 27. "Hannity: The 'true agenda' behind global warming is to punish the U.S. and redistribute wealth." Retrieved from http://www.hannity.com/show/2010/08/27

Hass, Glen R. 1981. "Effects of Source Characteristics on Cognitive Responses and Persuasion." In *Cognitive Responses to Persuasion*, eds. Richard E. Petty, Thomas M. Ostrom, and Timothy C. Brock. Hillsdale, NJ: Lawrence Erlbaum Associates Inc.

Iyengar, Shanto, and Kinder, Donald R. (1987). *News that Matters: Television and American Opinion*. Chicago, IL: University of Chicago Press.

Jamieson, Kathleen Hall and Joseph N. Cappella. (2008). *Echo Chamber: Rush Limbaugh and the Conservative Media Establishment*. New York, NY: Oxford University Press.

Ladd, Jonathan M. 2010. "The Neglected Power of Elite Opinion Leadership to Produce Antipathy toward the News Media: Evidence from a Survey Experiment." *Political Behavior* 32(1): 29–50.

Levendusky, M. 2013. *How Partisan Media Polarize America*. Chicago, IL: University of Chicago Press.

Miller, Joanne M., and Jon A. Krosnick. 2000. "News Media Impact on the Ingredients of Presidential Evaluations: Politically Knowledgeable Citizens are Guided by a Trusted Source." *American Journal of Political Science* 44(2): 301–315.

Mitchell, Amy, Jeffrey Gottfried, Jocelyn Kiley, and Katerina Eva Matsa. 2014, October 21. "Political Polarization & Media Habits." The Pew Research Center. Retrieved from http://www.journalism.org/2014/10/21/political-polarization-media-habits/pj_2014-10-21_media-polarization-02/

Morris, Jonathan S., and Peter L. Francia. 2010. "Cable News, Public Opinion, and the 2004 Party Conventions." *Political Research Quarterly* 63(4): 834–849.

Mutz, Diana. 1998. *Impersonal Influence: How Perceptions of Mass Collectives Affect Political Attitudes*. New York, NY: Cambridge University Press.

Mutz, Diana C. 2002. "The Consequences of Cross-Cutting Networks for Political Participation." *American Journal of Political Science* 46(4): 838–855.

Mutz, Diana C., and Paul S. Martin. 2001. "Facilitating Communication across Lines of Political Difference: The Role of the Mass Media." *American Political Science Review* 95(1): 97–114.

Nelson, Thomas E., Clawson, Richard A., and Oxley, Zoe. 1997. "Media Framing of a Civil Liberties Conflict and Its Effect on Tolerance." *American Political Science Review* 91(3): 567–584.

Ryan, Timothy J. 2012. "What Makes us Click? Demonstrating Incentives for Angry Discourse with Digital-age Field Experiments." *The Journal of Politics* 74(4): 1138–1152.

Schmitt, Kathleen M., Albert C. Gunther and Janice L. Liebhart. 2004. "Why Partisans See Mass Media as Biased." *Communication Research* 31(6): 623–641.

Smith, Glen R. 2010. "Politicians and the News Media: How Elite Attacks Influence Perceptions of Media Bias." *International Journal of Press/Politics* 15(3): 319–343.

Smith, Glen. 2016. "The Timing of Partisan Media Effects during a Presidential Election." *Political Research Quarterly* 69(4): 655–666.

Smith, Glen. 2017. "Sympathy for the Devil: How Broadcast News Reduces Negativity Toward Political Leaders." *American Politics Research* 45(1): 63–84.

Smith, Glen, and Kathleen Searles. 2013. "Fair and Balanced News or a Difference of Opinion? Why Opinion Shows Matter for Media Effects." *Political Research Quarterly* 66(3): 671–684.

Smith, Glen, and Kathleen Searles. 2014. "Who Let the (Attack) Dogs Out? New Evidence for Partisan Media Effects." *Public Opinion Quarterly* 78(1): 71–99.

Song, Hyunjin. 2017. "Why Do People (Sometimes) Become Selective about News? The Role of Emotions and Partisan Differences in Selective Approach and Avoidance." *Mass Communication and Society* 20(1): 47–67.

Stroud, Natalie. 2008. "Media Use and Political Predispositions: Revisiting the Concept of Selective Exposure." *Political Behavior* 30(3): 341–356.

Stroud, Natalie. 2011. *Niche News: The Politics of News Choice.* New York, NY: Oxford University Press.

Tsfati, Yariv, and Joseph N. Cappella. 2003. "Do People Watch What they Do Not Trust?" *Communication Research* 30(5): 504–529.

Turner, Joel. 2007. "The Messenger Overwhelming the Message: Ideological Cues and Perceptions of Bias in Television News." *Political Behavior* 29(4): 441–464.

Vallone, Robert P., Lee Ross, and Mark R. Lepper. 1985. "The Hostile Media Phenomenon: Biased Perception and Perceptions of Media Bias in Coverage of the Beirut Massacre." *Journal of Personality and Social Psychology* 49(3): 577–585.

Watts, Mark D., David Domke, Dhavan V. Shah and David P. Fan. 1999. "Elite Cues and Media Bias in Presidential Campaigns: Explaining Public Perceptions of a Media Bias." *Communication Research* 26(2): 144–175.

West, Darrell M. (2001). *The Rise and Fall of the Media Establishment.* Boston, MA: St. Martin's Press.

Westin, Drew, Pavel S. Blagov, Keith Harenski, Clint Kilts, and Stephan Hamann. 2006. "Neural Bases of Motivated Reasoning: An fMRI Study of Emotional Constraints on Partisan Political Judgment in the 2004 U.S. Presidential Election." *Journal of Cognitive Neuroscience* 18(11): 1947–1958.

5

HOW TO ENGAGE IN CIVIL
DISCUSSIONS ABOUT POLITICS

Political philosophers have long recognized the virtues of political discussion for both individuals and society. In ancient Greece, Socrates was put on trial for engaging his fellow citizens in critical discourse. In *On Liberty*, John Stuart Mill argued that free and open discussion produced more rational and better informed opinions. The protections of free speech and a free press in the first amendment established James Madison's marketplace of ideas, where all opinions are expressed and truth will eventually win out over misperceptions and illogical arguments. More recently, Guttman and Thompson (1998) argue that political discussion has a variety of benefits including better quality opinions and increased tolerance of opposing groups.

More recent studies have provided compelling evidence that people benefit from political discussions. Talking about politics increases factual information and results in better quality opinions (Scheufele 2000). There is also evidence that political discussion makes people more likely to participate in the political system (Wyatt, Katz, and Kim 2000). Furthermore, talking with people who hold opposing opinions makes people better able to provide reasons for their own opinions and to understand the reasons behind opposing perspectives (Price, Cappella, and Nir 2002). Most relevant to this book, learning the reasons justifying opposing perspectives increases tolerance toward people who hold opposing opinions (Mutz 2002).

Although political discussion can be beneficial, the benefits depend a great deal on *how* people engage in political discourse. The effects of political discourse depend on *who* we discuss politics with and *how* we engage in the discussion. Political discussion is most beneficial when diverse perspectives are presented in a civil manner. Unfortunately, people are more likely to talk about politics in ideologically *homogeneous* discussion groups where most of the group members have similar political views (Huckfeldt and Sprague 1987; Huckfeldt, Johnson, and Sprague 2004). For example, homogeneous discussion groups would be Democrats only talking with other Democrats, or conservatives who mostly talk about politics with other conservatives. While discussing politics in these homogeneous discussion groups can increase participation, it can also increase hostility toward political opponents (Mutz 2006). Homogeneous group members are not exposed to the reasonable arguments behind opposing perspectives, so they fail to understand why people disagree with their opinions.

Political discussion tends to be more enlightening when it includes people who hold dissimilar political viewpoints. Discussing politics in these *heterogeneous* groups—that include Democrats and Republicans, liberals and conservatives—tends to increase tolerance because it helps people understand that political opponents have fairly reasonable arguments supporting their perspectives (Mutz 2006). Heterogeneous discussion groups also challenge stereotypes about opposing political groups. People often believe that opposing political groups are more extreme than they really are, but talking with members of opposing groups challenges those extreme stereotypes.

One downside to heterogeneous political discussion is that it increases ambivalence, which occurs when people have competing considerations about political issues or candidates (Mutz 2002; Huckfeldt, Mendez, and Osborn 2004). When people are ambivalent, they are less likely to participate in politics. In other words, homogeneous groups increase participation by reducing ambivalence, while heterogeneous discussion groups have the opposite effect. McClurg (2006) argues that heterogeneous discussion groups are less likely to decrease participation when they include political experts who can provide clearer arguments to group members, helping them understand which opinion they hold. Including politically informed people in heterogeneous discussion groups helps people understand politics better, which reduces ambivalence, while not also reducing participation. Unfortunately, people are more likely to avoid talking about politics in heterogeneous discussion groups because they are afraid of offending their discussion partners (Mutz 2006). In short, people are least likely to talk about politics when it would benefit them the most, and instead save political discussion for times when everyone already agrees with each other.

It is also important that political discussion be conducted in a *civil* manner. Research shows that most people are turned off by uncivil discussion about politics (Brooks and Geer 2007). Indeed, uncivil discussion results in more negative feelings, which causes people to be more closed-minded and to perceive greater disagreement with the opposing side (Hwang, Kim, and Kim 2016). In contrast, civil discussion is more likely to result in increased understanding of opposing arguments, respect and tolerance for the opposition, and increased trust in government (Mutz 2015). In other words, you are only likely to benefit from political discussion when it is civil, while uncivil discussion is probably a waste of your time and entirely unproductive.

The purpose of this chapter is to provide guidelines for readers to engage in civil and productive discussion of political issues. Based on my experiences leading political discussions in the classroom, I provide the following tips that should facilitate discussion of controversial issues, while minimizing the anger and hostilities that often accompany such debates. It should be pointed out that this list does not include obvious standards of appropriate behavior during discussions, such as not interrupting others, or engaging in childish name-calling. Instead, what follows is a list of ways to make ordinary political discussions more productive and less emotionally toxic.

Tip #1: Don't Take it Personally

My most important piece of advice is to disconnect your personal identity from your opinions and beliefs. In my experience, the main reason that disagreement causes anger is because people take their political opinions and beliefs personally. That is, they see their opinions as a part of their identity or self-concept. As such, any arguments against their opinions or beliefs are seen as a personal attack on who they are as a human being. Unfortunately, pride often gets in the way of a productive political discussion; it causes anger and defensiveness when people challenge our opinions. When people encounter political arguments that challenge their values and beliefs, they often feel cognitive dissonance, resulting in a negative emotional state (see Chapter 4). Steele and Liu (1983) found that cognitive dissonance is primarily caused by threats to one's self-concept, which causes people to feel lower self-esteem. People believe that if their opinion is incorrect, they must not be intelligent or informed, thus lowering their self-esteem. If exposure to opposing arguments threatens our self-esteem, it should come as no surprise that we dislike and avoid people who challenge our opinions.

It should be pointed out that it is illogical to have lower self-esteem when you "lose" a political argument. Imagine for a second that you hold an uninformed opinion or incorrect belief; as unthinkable as that might be, try it anyway! If someone helps you correct your belief or hold a more informed opinion, you are now smarter than you were before. In fact, it makes more sense to feel higher self-esteem after losing an argument, because you actually won the argument. The problem is that some people are so afraid of looking stupid that they would rather continue to hold an incorrect belief, but that approach to learning is the highest form of stupidity.

Another approach to solve this self-esteem problem is simply not to base your sense of self-worth on characteristics that are likely to change. People cannot judge their worth based on one characteristic or shortcoming because there are many different criteria of evaluation and no agreed upon standard of judgment. What one person views as a positive trait, another might view as a negative. While one person might view intelligence as the most important characteristic, another might view physical strength, material wealth, or even reputation. For example, if you lose an argument, and subsequently adopt a different opinion, you simultaneously hold the characteristics unintelligent and open-minded. Which characteristic is more desirable depends on who you ask. Some may see you as open-minded, while others see you as stupid. How one sees you is more about them than anything you did. Regardless, you should not live your life stressing about how everyone else, and usually complete strangers, will regard you. After all, if someone were to stop being your friend because you lost a political argument, were they really a worthwhile friend to begin with?

Tip #2: Don't Be a Partisan

One of the reasons people take issues personally is because they see politics as a competitive competition. In politics, people form emotional attachments to their political parties and ideologies. Green, Palmquist, and Schickler (2002) argue that most people identify with political parties the way a sports fan identifies with their favorite team. Similar to being a sports fan, people form long-lasting emotional attachments to their political party early in life. These emotional attachments affect the ways people perceive the world (see Chapter 3), and judge elected officials. Furthermore, Miller and Conover (2015) find that for many partisans, winning is the primary goal, regardless of whether that victory produces desired policies. Partisans are also willing to support their party engaging in dirty tricks and voter disenfranchisement as long as it helps their "team" win the election (Claassen and Ensley 2016). A simple explanation for this is that people feel higher self-esteem when their political party wins, because it affirms the correctness of their views. When someone speaks ill of their party on the other hand, it threatens their self-esteem. Moreover, partisans feel higher self-esteem when they denigrate members of the opposing group. That is, partisans feel better about themselves when they say or hear negative things about the opposing party.

Of course, it makes little sense to tie your self-esteem to your party affiliation. By the way, it is also silly and irrational to base your self-esteem on the success of a sports team, but that is an argument for another time. There is no reason that partisans should feel pride when their party wins an election, nor should they feel low self-esteem when their party loses. You are not a Republican or a Democrat! You are a human being who happens to vote for candidates who affiliate with a political party organization.

The problem with strong partisan attachments is that it can dominate your motivations for engaging in political discussion. Personally, during my years as a professor, I have found nothing more irritating than a partisan who absolutely must defend their party at every opportunity. For example, if I bring up Bill Clinton's impeachment and the Monica Lewinsky affair as an example of media coverage of sex scandals, a Democrat might chime in to say that Republicans have cheated on their wives too, or that George W. Bush is a war criminal. For these people, politics is a war between the two political parties, and political discussions in the classroom or at the kitchen table, are the battles that they absolutely must win. Political discussion becomes a means to score political points for your team rather than an attempt to find the right answer or to learn opposing perspectives. Unfortunately, too often these partisans can hijack a productive discussion by making sure their political party is seen in the best possible light.

If you ever have the urge to defend your political party or preferred elected officials, stop and think about your motivations. Ask yourself what you could possibly have to gain. How many people in that class will actually be persuaded to change their ideology, issue position, party, or voting decision based on what you are about to say? The answer is, very few! People rarely change their minds, and when they do, it does not happen because a fellow student hurls campaign rhetoric at them. In other words, stop being so cravenly partisan that you miss the larger point of the discussion. Let's say I am wrong, and you do change the minds of every person in the classroom with your brilliant arguments. Even in that highly unlikely scenario, you are only talking about a handful of people. Even persuading the entire class will not change the outcome of an election or get your preferred candidate elected. More realistically, you will appear so blinded by partisanship that you cannot engage in productive discussions.

Tip #3: Avoid Ad Hominem Arguments

Another important piece of advice is to avoid personal attacks on others. Perhaps this is obvious, but I have found that people often do not realize that they have attacked someone personally. As a general rule, it is best to attack arguments, opinions, and beliefs, and to ignore the characteristics of people who hold an argument. Remember, the quality of an argument has *nothing* to do with the person making the argument, unless they are basing it on their own credibility. For example, if the dumbest person alive believed that the earth was round, does it mean that the earth must be flat? Of course not, but that often seems like a compelling argument to make when one's back is against the wall and you are defending "your" opinions and beliefs.

When we criticize an argument by attacking the person making an argument, it is called an *ad hominem* attack. For example, imagine I argued that states should increase funding for higher education because it will improve the economy, but you respond that "of course you would say that, you're a college professor who would stand to benefit from funding increases." It may well be the case that I benefit from more higher education funding, but that has absolutely nothing to do with the strength of my argument. Is it not possible that I would benefit from more funding, *and* it would improve the economy? Argue the arguments and not the arguer.

Tip #4: Assume People Are Smart

A useful trick in political discussions, and all discussions for that matter, is to assume that other people have something of value to say. During political discussions, it is generally a good idea to assume that those you are talking with are intelligent people who hold informed and well-reasoned opinions. When we assume that other people are smart, we are more likely to listen to what they have to say, rather than simply waiting for our turn to talk. What you want to avoid is assuming that people are uninformed simply because they expressed an opposing point of view. As we saw in the previous chapters, just because some one disagrees with you does not mean they are stupid or biased. Maybe they have information that you are not aware of, or a different perspective that you have never thought of before. Maybe they can help clarify your opinions or change your mind altogether. You will never know unless you actually listen to and consider what they have to say. If you enter into a discussion assuming that you know everything, then political discourse is a waste of your time.

During discussions in my classes, I probably have every reason to assume that I know more about politics than my students. Well, at least I hope that I know more than them. Yet I assume that they have information, experiences, perspectives, and insights into political topics that I have not considered. Approaching discussion in this way makes me eager to hear their comments, and I end up learning more from them than they probably learn from me. Give people the benefit of the doubt and you may be surprised by how much they can teach you.

Tip #5: Accept that You Could Be Wrong

On a related note to the point above, it is usually best to hold your opinions and factual beliefs with humility. Too often people are certain that their way of interpreting the world is the "correct" way of looking at things, without acknowledging that others could have reasonable differences of perspective (see Chapter 2). One of the most troublesome obstacles to productive disagreement is overconfidence in the absolute correctness of our political opinions and beliefs. Some people even suffer from the Dunning-Kruger effect, which is a cognitive bias in people's perceptions of their own expertise. When it comes to political discussions, the Dunning-Kruger effect causes people to overestimate the amount they understand about a topic because they are not aware of how much they do not know. Consequently, those with low levels of information often believe that they know all there is to know about a topic, resulting in overconfidence and unwillingness to learn opposing perspectives.

Furthermore, overconfidence in the correctness of one's opinions can make people angry at those who express opposing arguments. If I believe that I know all there is to know about a topic, and you disagree with me, it must be because you lack information or intelligence. Opinion certainty also makes people more likely to engage in a competitive style of argument, in which discussion is seen as a sport rather than an exchange of ideas (Rios, DeMarree, and Statzer 2014). Treating political discussion as a competitive exercise results in a largely unproductive process that will usually end in hurt feelings, hostility, and frayed relationships.

Tip #6: Don't use an Individual Case to 'Disprove' a General Principle

This is one of the most frequent problems with political discussions among students in introductory courses. When discussing theories and evidence about general correlational or causal relationships in society, a student will present an individual case that defies the general relationship. Keep in mind that the social sciences do not deal in certainty, so no theory or principle will be 100 percent correct in every situation and for every person. You may know someone who has smoked cigarettes for most of their life and never developed lung cancer, but that does not disprove the argument that smoking causes lung cancer. In the political arena, just because you may know a black Democrat who voted for a Republican candidate, does not mean that blacks and Democrats do not usually vote for Democrats for political office. Understand that anecdotal evidence may be useful for theory building, but it occasionally runs counter to the general trend.

Tip #7: Establish Your Goals

What do you want to get out of political discussion? If you're like me, your goal is to understand the perspectives of other people. From a selfish standpoint, you will get more out of a debate by listening and learning from others than you will by simply waiting for you turn to speak. After all, you already know your opinion and why you hold it, so it does not benefit you to tell everyone else why you are right. Instead, you have much more to learn about the world, and other people, by trying to understand their perspectives. Please don't get me wrong, by all means talk! Pose clarifying questions or a counter-factuals to learn the nuances of opposing perspectives. State your opinion, while keeping an open mind. Make the goal of every discussion to understand opposing perspectives and work toward a practical solution.

If your goal is to persuade other people, you are likely to be disappointed. That being said, I am not arguing that is *wrong* to attempt to persuade people to your side. Indeed, much of the national political discourse is about trying to persuade people. The problem with attempts at face to face persuasion is that we often resent people when they fail to adopt our perspectives. More often than not, you will become angry with people who do not see your point of view, which is a very unhealthy way to live your life. Trying to persuade others is not wrong, but you need to accept that people are free to hold whatever position they choose.

More than anything, do not blame others when they fail to see the correctness of your views. A healthier response is to accept that some people are not going to be persuaded no matter how good your arguments are or how many facts you throw at them. As I explained in Chapter 2, people think about politics differently, while Chapter 3 shows that we are often motivated not to change our minds. Another response is to take responsibility for your inability to persuade others. Rather than blaming others for their stupidity, you should acknowledge that maybe your arguments simply were not persuasive in this particular instance. After all, if people were not persuaded, than your arguments (by definition) were unpersuasive. That does not mean that your arguments would not be persuasive in other contexts or when talking with other people. Placing the blame on yourself will likely motivate you to develop better arguments, seek more facts, or simply accept that people are different and respond to different types of arguments. All of these reactions are healthier, and will promote better interpersonal relationships, than getting angry at everyone who fails to recognize the brilliance of your political views.

Tip #8: Try Listening

All of the preceding discussion brings me to my last piece of advice, which is to actually *listen* to what other people have to say. In any discussion, not just political discussions, listening is an underrated skill. Too often people are so eager to explain their point that they fail to really consider what other people are saying. When other people are talking, try to understand their reasoning and perspective. After all, you cannot truly understand your own opinion without learning the arguments that oppose your side. In *On Liberty*, Mill (1869, p. 67) put it well when he argued that:

> He who knows only his own side of the case knows little of that. His reasons may be good, and no one may have been able to refute them. But if he is equally unable to refute the reasons on the opposite side, if he does not so much as know what they are, he has no ground for preferring either opinion.

Believing that you are right does not justify ignoring the arguments of other people, yet that is often why we have unproductive political discussions. You have far more to gain from learning the arguments of others than by asserting the arguments that you already know. Of course, I am not telling you not to express your views, because if everyone simply listened, there would be no discussion! Instead, when you are not talking, it is important that you actually listen to other people and try to understand their arguments. Doing so will allow you to better respond to what they said, and will make them feel like you actually respect their point of view, which will create a more civil and productive environment to exchange ideas.

Review Questions

1. What are the main reasons that people avoid discussing politics with friends and family?
2. What are the benefits of talking about politics with people who hold diverse opinions?
3. Why are uncivil discussions unproductive?
4. Why does political discussion make some people angry?
5. Why is it important to think clearly about your goals for political discussion?
6. Why is it important to listen carefully to opposing arguments?

Discussion Questions

1. What are some ways to make political discussion on the internet more civil?
2. Does the anonymity of online discussion boards benefit or harm political discussions?
3. Are there any political issues that you can't talk about without getting angry?
4. Do you believe political discussions are a waste of time?
5. What are your goals for political discussion?
6. How often do you hear opposing arguments from friends, family, or social media?

Sources for Further Inquiry

Books

Kling, Arnold. 2017. *The Three Languages of Politics: Talking across the Political Divides.* Washington D.C.: Cato Institute.
Klofstad, Casey. 2010. *Civic Talk: Peers, Politics, and the Future of Democracy.* Philadelphia, PA: Temple University Press.
Lakoff, George. 2014. *The All New Don't Think of an Elephant!: Know your Values and Frame the Debate.* White River Junction, VT: Chelsea Green Publishing.
Neisser, Phil, and Jacob Z. Hess. 2012. *You're Not as Crazy as I Thought (but You're Still Wrong): Conversations between a Die-hard Liberal and a Devoted Conservative.* Dulles, VA: Potomac Books, Inc.
Shea, Daniel M., and Morris P. Fiorina. 2012. *Can We Talk? The Rise of Rude, Nasty Stubborn Politics.* New York, NY: Pearson Higher Ed.

Journal and Newspaper Articles

Chan, Michael. 2018. "Reluctance to Talk about Politics in Face-to-face and Facebook Settings: Examining the Impact of Fear of Isolation, Willingness to Self-censor, and Peer Network Characteristics." *Mass Communication and Society* 21(1): 1–23.
Conover, Pamela Johnston, Donald D. Searing, and Ivor M. Crewe. 2002. "The Deliberative Potential of Political Discussion." *British Journal of Political Science* 32(1): 21–62.

Eveland, William. 2004. "The Effect of Political Discussion in Producing Informed Citizens: The Roles of Information, Motivation, and Elaboration." *Political Communication* 21(2): 177–193.

Gutting, Gary, and Jerry Gaus. 2015, June 11. "The Virtues of Political Disagreement." *New York Times*. Retrieved from https://opinionator.blogs.nytimes.com/2015/06/11/the-virtues-of-politicaldisagreement/?mtrref=www.google.com&gwh=CB2444B4FE5ECDBA05FD8F68684ADB56&gwt=pay&assetType=opinion

Hirsch, Alexander. 2016, August 8. "Why Political Disagreements over How the World Works May Be Easier to Solve than those over Goals." LSE USAPP Blog. Retrieved from http://blogs.lse.ac.uk/usappblog/2016/08/08/why-political-disagreements-over-how-the-world-works-may-be-easier-to-solve-than-those-over-goals/

Huckfeldt, Robert, and Jeanette Morehouse Mendez. 2008. "Moths, Flames, and Political Engagement: Managing Disagreement within Communication Networks." *The Journal of Politics* 70(1): 83–96.

Miller, Patrick R., Piotr S. Bobkowski, Daniel Maliniak, and Ronald B. Rapoport. 2015. "Talking Politics on Facebook: Network Centrality and Political Discussion Practices in Social Media." *Political Research Quarterly* 68(2): 377–391.

Morey, Alyssa C., William P. Eveland Jr, and Myiah J. Hutchens. 2012. "The 'Who' Matters: Types of Interpersonal Relationships and Avoidance of Political Disagreement." *Political Communication* 29(1): 86–103.

Pattie, Charles J., and Ron J. Johnston. 2008. "It's Good to Talk: Talk, Disagreement and Tolerance." *British Journal of Political Science* 38(4): 677–698.

Testa, Paul F., Matthew V. Hibbing, and Melinda Ritchie. 2014. "Orientations toward Conflict and the Conditional Effects of Political Disagreement." *The Journal of Politics* 76(3): 770–785.

Wells, Chris, Katherine J. Cramer, Michael W. Wagner, German Alvarez, Lewis A. Friedland, Dhavan V. Shah, Leticia Bode, Stephanie Edgerly, Itay Gabay, and Charles Franklin. 2017. "When We Stop Talking Politics: The Maintenance and Closing of Conversation in Contentious Times." *Journal of Communication* 67(1): 131–157.

Wojcieszak, Magdalena E., and Diana C. Mutz. 2009. "Online Groups and Political Discourse: Do Online Discussion Spaces Facilitate Exposure to Political Disagreement?" *Journal of Communication* 59(1): 40–56.

References

Brooks, Deborah Jordan, and John G. Geer. 2007. "Beyond Negativity: The Effects of Incivility on the Electorate." *American Journal of Political Science* 51(1): 1–16.

Claassen, Ryan L., and Michael J. Ensley. 2016. "Motivated Reasoning and Yard-sign-stealing Partisans: Mine is a Likable Rogue, yours is a Degenerate Criminal." *Political Behavior* 38(2): 317–335.

Green, Donald, Bradley Palmquist and Eric Schickler. 2002. *Partisan Hearts and Minds.* New Haven, CT: Yale University Press.

Gutmann, Amy, and Dennis F. Thompson. 1998. *Democracy and Disagreement.* Cambridge, MA: Harvard University Press.

Huckfeldt, R., J. M. Mendez, and T. Osborn. 2004. "Disagreement, Ambivalence and Engagement: The Political Consequences of Heterogeneous Networks." *Political Psychology* 25(1): 65–95.

Huckfeldt, Robert and John Sprague. 1987. "Networks in Context: The Social Flow of Political Information." *American Political Science Review* 81(4): 1197–1216.

Huckfeldt, Robert, Paul E. Johnson and John Sprague. 2004. *The Survival of Diverse Opinions within Communication Networks.* Cambridge: Cambridge University Press.

Hwang, Hyunseo, Youngju Kim, and Yeojin Kim. 2016. "Influence of Discussion Incivility on Deliberation: An Examination of the Mediating Role of Moral Indignation." *Communication Research* 45(2): 213–240.

McClurg, Scott D. 2006. "The Electoral Relevance of Political Talk: Examining Disagreement and Expertise Effects in Social Networks on Political Participation." *American Journal of Political Science* 50(3): 737–754.

Mill, J. S. 1869. *On Liberty.* Longmans, Green, Reader, and Dyer.

Miller, Patrick R., and Pamela Johnston Conover. 2015. "Red and Blue States of Mind: Partisan Hostility and Voting in the United States." *Political Research Quarterly* 68(2): 225–239.

Mutz, Diana C. 2002. "The Consequences of Cross-cutting Networks for Political Participation." *American Journal of Political Science* 46: 838–855.

Mutz, Diana C. 2006. *Hearing the Other Side: Deliberative versus Participatory Democracy.* Cambridge: Cambridge University Press.

Mutz, Diana C. 2015. *In-your-face politics: The Consequences of Uncivil Media.* Princeton, NJ: Princeton University Press.

Price, Vincent, Joseph N. Cappella, and Lilach Nir. 2002. "Does Disagreement Contribute to More Deliberative Opinion?" *Political Communication* 19(1): 95–112.

Rios, Kimberly, Kenneth G. DeMarree, and Johnathan Statzer. 2014. "Attitude Certainty and Conflict Style: Divergent Effects of Correctness and Clarity." *Personality and Social Psychology Bulletin* 40(7): 819–830.

Scheufele, Dietram A. 2000. "Talk or Conversation? Dimensions of Interpersonal Discussion and their Implications for Participatory Democracy." *Journalism & Mass Communication Quarterly* 77(4): 727–743.

Steele, Claude M., and Thomas J. Liu. 1983. "Dissonance Processes as Self-affirmation." *Journal of Personality and Social Psychology* 45(1): 5–19.

Wyatt, Robert O., Elihu Katz, and Joohan Kim. 2000. "Bridging the Spheres: Political and Personal Conversation in Public and Private Spaces." *Journal of Communication* 50(1): 71–92.

PART II
Taxing and Spending

6

SHOULD MEDICARE BE EXPANDED TO COVER ALL AMERICANS?

Health care is one of the most important and heated topics in American politics because it affects everyone in some way. It is not an exaggeration to say that for many, the issue of health care is a matter of life and death! Furthermore, anyone can face a serious health problem at any time, through no fault of their own. Perhaps the most stressful aspect of the American health care system is that it requires many people to balance mental and physical well-being with financial hardship. The high cost of health care puts many Americans one injury or illness away from bankruptcy. Yet the debate over health care is wide-ranging and complex because it involves a variety of issues such as: taxes, debt, hospitals, treatment options, prescription drugs, mental health, reproduction, contraception, end-of-life decisions, etc.

The importance of the health care issue puts it front and center on the agenda of most newly elected presidents. Indeed, from Franklin Roosevelt to Donald Trump, presidents have frequently made health care reform a central priority in their administrations. Franklin Roosevelt proposed a second bill of rights that would have included access to health care for all Americans. Harry Truman pushed for a single-payer health care system—where the federal government pays all health care costs for all Americans—but was sidetracked by the Korean War and public concern over communism. Since it was first proposed, single-payer health care has been equated with socialism by those looking to prevent it from being enacted.

Another factor that weakened the case for single-payer health care was the rise of employer-sponsored health insurance. During World War II, the federal government imposed restrictions on wages in order to prevent inflation. Since they were prohibited from offering more salary, many businesses began offering free health care in order to attract high-quality employees. As a larger portion of

Americans received health care from their employer, there was less of a need for government to provide health care. In order to cover groups that were unlikely to be employed, and therefore unlikely to have employer-based insurance, the federal government stepped in to cover the poor and elderly. Specifically, in 1965 Congress established the Medicare and Medicaid programs to provide government funded health care for senior citizens and low income Americans, respectively. While Medicare pays most of the medical costs for the elderly and disabled, Medicaid provides free emergency care to those living in poverty. Both Medicare and Medicaid are funded through a payroll tax on current workers, with higher income Americans paying more than lower income workers. Additionally, Medicare is not entirely free, as recipients have to pay deductibles and copays on many of its benefits.

Some have argued that the federal government should expand the current Medicare program to provide health care to all Americans. In 2017, Senator Bernie Sanders (VT) proposed a plan that would provide nation-wide Medicare coverage. Although the Sanders plan would not eliminate private insurance, it would prevent any insurance company from providing the same benefits covered under Medicare (Sanders n.d.). Sanders would pay for the plan with tax increases on individuals and employers, but most of the cost would be paid by the wealthy.

Public opinion polls suggest that a majority of Americans support expanding Medicare to cover everyone. In 2017, a Quinnipiac poll asked "Do you think that an expansion of Medicare that would make it available to any American who wanted it, also known as universal health care, would be a good idea or a bad idea?" Overall, 60 percent of Americans said it was a good idea, 33 said it was a bad idea, and the rest had no opinion (Malloy 2017). These results are similar to other polls that ask similar questions (Economist/You Gov Poll 2017). Support is split along partisan lines however, with 83 percent of Democrats saying Medicare for all is a good idea compared to only 33 percent of Republicans.

Whether someone would benefit from Medicare for all depends on their position in society. The United States has the best health care in the world, if you can afford quality insurance. For those who are unable to afford quality insurance, Medicare for all would provide them better health care at a far lower cost. Conversely, those who currently have quality health care are likely to pay more money in taxes and receive lower quality health care as a result. Additionally, people who have preexisting health problems would benefit from Medicare for all, while people who are healthy for most of their life will pay for health care for other people. There is also an element of personal responsibility involved in this issue as people who make good choices—such as eating right, not smoking, and drinking alcohol in moderation—have to pay to subsidize the health care of people who make poor choices. As with many public policies, whether Medicare for all is a good or bad idea depends on your individual circumstances.

Is Health Care a Right?

An important point of disagreement in the Medicare for all debate is whether health care is a *right* that the government must provide to every person. Consider the other rights that Americans receive when they are accused of a crime, such as the right to a lawyer and a trial by jury. These rights cost the government enormous sums of money, but they are essential to protect people's life, liberty, and property against wrongful convictions. Or consider the fact that states treat education as a fundamental right (see Chapter 7) that every young person must be provided with. Many people argue that health care is even more important to people's lives than education because for some it is literally a matter of life and death. Without public education, people could still find low-skilled jobs and poor parents would be able to teach their children. In contrast, health care requires a high level of expertise, expensive equipment, and often costly prescription drugs. If the government does not deny people an education because they are poor, they should not deny them health care for the same reason. Supporters of Medicare for all argue that it is the most effective way to assure that Americans will not die because they cannot afford quality health care.

Those in favor of Medicare for all also argue that the private market is an unjust and inefficient way to provide health care. The free-market health care system provides care to people based on their ability to pay for the treatment, and not necessarily the health needs of the patient. In fact, the people who need health care the most are usually in the low income brackets. Low income Americans are more likely to be overweight and to smoke cigarettes, both of which are factors that drastically increase one's probability of needing health care (World Health Organization n.d.; Drewnowski and Specter 2004; Goszkowski 2008; Hyman 2010). Moreover, people with preexisting medical problems, often inherited from their parents, spend so much on health care—through copays and deductibles—that they can become poor and even enter bankruptcy. Supporters of Medicare for all argue that people should not be made to choose between health care, and whether to buy food or pay the rent.

An important benefit of expanding Medicare for all is that more Americans would have access to preventive medicine without the concern that it will cut into their budgets. For many Americans, the decision to see a doctor for routine checkups is deterred by the cost of their visits. Additionally, even Americans with health insurance avoid preventive tests and treatments if their insurance plans have high deductibles. Preventive medicine and routine checkups are effective ways to reduce overall health care costs because they prevent much more costly illnesses in the future. The earlier a health problem is identified, the better the chances of survival and the lower the costs of health care.

Of course, opponents of Medicare would point out that many people have poor health because they made bad decisions. People need to have incentives to engage in more healthy behaviors. In a private market health care system, people have a financial incentive to stay healthy in order to avoid expensive health care.

When people engage in unhealthy behaviors, they are more chronically sick, and as a result their personal health insurance is more costly. Meanwhile, someone who eats well, exercises regularly, never smokes, and drinks in moderation, will likely have fewer costly illnesses, and therefore would pay less for insurance. In other words, people are responsible for their own behaviors. Expanding Medicare to cover all Americans would force healthy people to pay for the health care of people who make bad decisions in regards to their personal health. It would also reduce the incentive for people to live healthier lives, because they know health care will not cost them any additional money.

Expanding Medicare to cover all people is also unnecessary given that current government programs cover the most vulnerable in society. Those with low incomes are already provided free emergency care by Medicaid, while the children from poor and lower-middle class families can get health care through the Children's Health Insurance Program. Let us not forget that Medicare already covers senior citizens. Although people with preexisting conditions may have to pay more for health care through deductibles and copays, the Affordable Care Act already prevents insurance companies from denying them coverage or hiking their premiums. Medicare for all would simply expand health care coverage to Americans that can afford insurance, but choose not to buy it.

The Cost and Quality of Health Care

Supporters argue that expanding Medicare to cover all Americans will cost less money than the current health care system. Specifically, Bernie Sanders argues that his Medicare for all plan would cost $6 trillion *less* over 10 years (Sanders n. d.). Medicare for all would reduce administrative costs and eliminate the profits going to insurance company shareholders. The private health insurance industry runs like a business, with high pay for corporate executives, advertising, profit, and far too many administrators that do not improve the health care that patients receive. Expanding Medicare would provide cheaper health care because the managers would be paid less, there would be little need for advertising, and all profits would be put back into improving health care.

Of course, whether people pay more or less for health care would depend on how the program is funded. Under the Sanders plan, wealthy people would face large tax increases, but most Americans would receive better quality coverage and at a much cheaper cost. Specifically, the Sanders plan would impose a 6.2 percent tax on employers, a 2.2 percent tax on individuals, while increasing taxes on capital gains, raising income taxes on the wealthy, and expanding the estate tax (Sanders n.d.). While people would pay more in taxes, for most of them it would be offset by the money they save on health insurance premiums. According to Sanders, his Medicare for all plan would save people money because "a family of four earning $50,000 would pay just $466 per year to the single-payer program, amounting to a savings of over $5,800 for that family each year" (Angell 2017).

Sanders also argues that his plan would save businesses money. "The average annual cost to the employer for a worker with a family who makes $50,000 a year would go from $12,591 to just $3,100" (Sanders n.d.). In short, supporters of Medicare for all argue that the program would lower the cost of health care, ensure everyone has coverage, and would be paid for mostly by tax increases on the wealthy.

Opponents of expanding Medicare point out that the current system is already too costly, and expanding it would require more taxes than Sanders estimates. The cost of the current Medicare program is likely to increase in the near future as more people enter the program, health care costs continue to rise, and recipients live longer. In 2016, Medicare provided health coverage to roughly 57 million people, at a cost of 15 percent of total government spending (Desilver 2017; Peter G. Peterson Foundation 2017). The Medicare board of trustees estimates that the Medicare program will expand to cover 78 million people by 2028, and by 2042 Medicare will account for *21 percent* of the entire federal budget. Seniors are also living longer, which further drives up Medicare costs.

In 1970, the average 65-year-old male was expected to live until age 79; today, he is expected to live until 84. The comparable life expectancies for women are 84 in 1970 and 87 today. While this is a welcome trend, it means that Medicare recipients will receive benefits for longer than they have in the past. In addition, medical costs typically increase with age, further driving increases in costs.

(Board of Trustees 2017)

Finally, the cost of health care has nearly tripled over the last forty years. Adding more people to the already bloated Medicare system would result in runaway debt and eventually much higher taxes.

Another problem with the current Medicare system is that it involves a great deal of inefficiency and waste. Under the current Medicare program, a small fraction of doctors receive roughly a quarter of the total Medicare spending. For example, in 2012, $1 billion dollars was spent to cure a common eye problem on only 143,000 patients (Abelson and Cohen 2014). If doctors and patients know that the federal government will pay the bill, they are more willing to pay for treatments that may not be completely necessary. Opponents of Medicare for all argue that it would lead to even more wasteful spending on unnecessary procedures. A private health insurance market forces people to make choices regarding what remedies are worth the money, which effectively drives down overall costs.

How much would it cost to expand the Medicare program to cover all Americans? One analysis found that the *annual* costs of Bernie Sanders' Medicare for All plan would be $2.5 trillion, which is a steep price considering that in 2016, the *entire federal government* spent $3.9 trillion on everything (Millhiser

2017). The cost of Medicare for All would far exceed current national expenditures on health care. These results are echoed in a study by the Urban Institute, which found that "Together, national health expenditures would increase by a total of $518.9 billion (16.9 percent) in 2017, and by 6.6 trillion (16.6 percent) between 2017 and 2026" (Holahan et al. 2016, p. 2). According to another estimate, "over 70 percent of working privately insured households would pay more under a fully funded single-payer plan than they do for health insurance today" (Millhiser, 2017). Once again, who would pay more under Medicare for all depends on how the program would be funded. Bernie Sanders intends to put most of the cost on the wealthy, who would also be the most likely to seek health care in the private market, meaning they would pay the most and get the least, which is not very fair to high-income people.

Opponents of Medicare for all also argue that such a single-payer system would drastically alter the current health care system. The United States health care industry evolved in a private market and adapted to its demands. A private health care market incentivizes technological innovation, better medical facilities, and specialization among doctors (Starr 2016). According to health care policy expert Paul Starr,

> The financing arrangements [...] created incentives for high-cost specialized care and protected much of the public from the full, direct cost of that system. As a result, starting from 4 percent of GDP, health care grew to 17.5 percent, far more than in any other country. That level of costs is reflected in investments in medical technology, the physical infrastructure of hospitals and other facilities, the patterns of medical training and specialization, and the size and structure of the health-care labor force.
>
> *(Starr, 2016)*

Moving to a government funded system would fundamentally alter the financial incentives of hospitals, doctors, and medical researchers.

A government run system would also weaken the incentives for doctors to become highly specialized if they do not expect to be rewarded for their services. In other words, doctors would have less incentive to become highly specialized if they would not be able to charge more money for their treatments. Consequently, Americans who needed specialized treatments would be less likely to receive it because the few remaining specialists would be too busy and would be unlikely to accept Medicare patients. As a result, most Americans would get care from general physicians, while specialists would only treat the wealthy. Although the current system certainly favors the wealthy, ordinary Americans have access to specialists because their insurance will usually cover the cost, which is unlikely to remain under a Medicare for all system.

Review Questions

1. Why was the Medicare program first enacted?
2. How might Medicare for all reduce the overall cost of health care?
3. How does free health care potentially undermine personal responsibility?
4. What groups of people stand to benefit the most from a Medicare for all program?
5. In what specific ways would Medicare for all potentially reduce the quality of health care?

Discussion Questions

1. Do Americans have a right to health care coverage?
2. Should the federal government raise the retirement age?
3. Should the government provide free health insurance for people with pre-existing conditions?
4. What are some ways to reduce the costs of health care?

Sources for Further Inquiry

Books

Cogan, John F. 2017. *The High Cost of Good Intentions: A History of US Federal Entitlement Programs.* Stanford, CA: Stanford University Press.

Giaimo, Susan. 2009. *Markets and Medicine: The Politics of Health Care Reform in Britain, Germany, and the United States.* Ann Arbor, MI: University of Michigan Press.

Jacobs, Lawrence, and Theda Skocpol. 2015. *Health Care Reform and American Politics: What Everyone Needs to Know.* New York, NY: Oxford University Press.

Marmor, Theodore R. 2017. *The Politics of Medicare.* New York, NY: Routledge.

Smith, David G., ed. (2017). *Entitlement Politics: Medicare and Medicaid, 1995–2001.* New York, NY: Routledge.

Journal and Newspaper Articles

Conover, Chris. 2017, September 28. "The #1 Reason Bernie Sanders' Medicare-for-all Single-Payer Plan is a Singularly Bad Idea." Forbes.com. Retrieved from https://www.forbes.com/sites/theapothecary/2017/09/28/the-1-reason-bernie-sanders-medicare-for-all-single-payer-plan-is-a-singularly-bad-idea/#2b979cf85502

Hacker, Jacob S. 2005. "Dismantling the Health Care State? Political Institutions, Public Policies and the Comparative Politics of Health Reform." *British Journal of Political Science* 34(4): 693–724.

Jensen, Carsten, and Michael Bang Petersen. 2017. "The Deservingness Heuristic and the Politics of Health Care." *American Journal of Political Science* 61(1): 68–83.

Obama, B. H. 2017. "Repealing the ACA without a Replacement—the Risks to American Health Care." *New England Journal of Medicine,* 376(4): 297–299.

Schneider, Eric C., and David Squires. 2017. "From Last to First—Could the US Health Care System Become the Best in the World?" *New England Journal of Medicine* 377(10): 901–904.

Scott, Kirstin W., Robert J. Blendon, and John M. Benson. 2016. "Sick of Health Care Politics? Comparing Views of Quality of Care between Democrats and Republicans." *Journal for Healthcare Quality* 38(6): 39–51.

References

Abelson, Reed, and Sarah Cohen. 2014, April 9. "Sliver of Medicare Doctors Get Big Share of Payouts." *The New York Times*. Retrieved from http://www.canceradvoca cy.org/wp-content/uploads/2014/10/Abelson-and-Cohen-Sliver-of-Medicare-Doc tors-Get-Big-Share-of-Payments.pdf

Angell, Marcia. 2017, September 21. "The Benefits of Bernie Sanders' 'Medicare for All' Plan." *The Boston Globe*. Retrieved from https://www.bostonglobe.com/opinion/2017/09/20/the-benefits-bernie-sanders-medicare-for-all-plan/SAnYu2aEu6xcphx5eh809N/story.html

Board of Trustees. 2017, July 13. *Annual Report of the Federal Hospital Insurance and Federal Supplemental Medical Insurance Trust Fund*. Retrieved from https://www.cms.gov/Resea rch-Statistics-Data-and-Systems/Statistics-Trends-and-Reports/ReportsTrustFunds/Downloads/TR2017.pdf

Desilver, Drew. 2017, April 4. "What Does the Federal Government Spend your Tax Dollars on? Social Insurance Programs, Mostly." The Pew Research Center. Retrieved from http://www.pewresearch.org/fact-tank/2017/04/04/what-does-the-federal-gov ernment-spend-your-tax-dollars-on-social-insurance-programs-mostly/

Drewnowski, Adam, and S. E. Specter. 2004. "Poverty and Obesity: The Role of Energy Density and Energy Costs." *The American Journal of Clinical Nutrition* 79(1): 6–16.

Economist/You Gov Poll. 2017, April 2–4. *The Economist*. Retrieved from https://d25d2506sfb94s.cloudfront.net/cumulus_uploads/document/divhts7l9t/econTabReport.pdf

GoszKowski, Rob. 2008, March 21. "Among Americans, Smoking Increases as Income Decreases." Gallup. Retrieved from http://news.gallup.com/poll/105550/among-am ericans-smoking-decreases-income-increases.aspx

Holahan, John, Lisa Clemans-Cope, Matthew Buettgens, Melissa Favreault, Linda J. Blumberg, and Siyabonga Ndwandwe. 2016. "The Sanders Single-Payer Health Care Plan: The Effect on National Health Expenditures and Federal and Private Spending." The Urban Institute. Retrieved from https://www.urban.org/sites/default/files/alfres co/publication-pdfs/2000785-The-Sanders-Single-Payer-Health-Care-Plan.pdf

Hyman, Mark. 2010, September 18. "The Link Between Poverty, Obesity and Diabetes." *The Huffington Post*. Retrieved from https://www.huffingtonpost.com/dr-mark-hyman/not-having-enough-food-ca_b_721344.html

Malloy, Tim. 2017, June 28. "U.S. Voters Reject GOP Health Plan More than 3–1, Quinnipiac University National Poll Finds; Voters Support Gun Background Checks 94–95 Percent." Quinnipiac University Poll. Retrieved from https://poll.qu.edu/na tional/release-detail?ReleaseID=2470

Millhiser, Ian. 2017, September 13. "7 Tough Questions Single-payer Advocates Must Answer before their Ideas Can Become Law." Think Progress. Retrieved from https://thinkprogress.org/tough-questions-single-payer-7a5daec51693/

Peter G. Peterson Foundation. 2017, July 14. "Medicare Trustees Warn of Serious Financial Shortfalls." Retrieved from https://www.pgpf.org/analysis/2017/07/medicare-trustees-warn-of-serious-financial-shortfalls

Sanders, Bernie. n.d. "Medicare for All: Leaving No One Behind." Berniesanders.com. Retrieved from https://live-berniesanders-com.pantheonsite.io/issues/medicare-for-all/

Starr, Paul. 2016, February 1. "The False Lure of the Sanders Single-Payer Plan." The American Prospect. Retrieved from http://prospect.org/article/false-lure-sanders-single-payer-plan

World Health Organization. n.d. "Tobacco Free Initiative." Retrieved from http://www.who.int/tobacco/research/economics/rationale/poverty/en/

7

SHOULD COLLEGE TUITION BE FREE FOR ALL AMERICANS?

Education is one of the most important factors in the well-being of modern societies. While it is commonly accepted that governments play an important role in promoting public education, it is questionable whether that responsibility should extend beyond providing basic skills and competencies. In the United States for example, state and local governments have long worked to ensure that all children have access to public education. Meanwhile, *higher education* has traditionally been a private industry, with little government involvement beyond providing land-grants to build colleges and universities. To the extent that universities were regulated and funded, it was state governments that led the way rather than the federal government.

The role of the federal government in higher education expanded during World War II when Congress passed the Servicemen's Readjustment Act (1944), which established the G.I. Bill for military veterans. Specifically, the G.I. bill provided funding to cover the cost of tuition and housing while military veterans attended college. Largely because of the G.I. Bill, college attendance increased by *50 percent* in the years following World War II (U.S. Department of Education, 2016a). Subsequent wars in Korea and Vietnam further increased the number of Americans who could attend college with government funding. As more workers gained a college degree, it became increasingly necessary for new workers to attend college to compete for quality jobs. In the early 1970s, nearly one quarter of young Americans (18–24 years old) attended college, but by 2016 that number increased to 40 percent (U.S. Department of Education, 2016a). Increasing rates of college attendance resulted in a rapid expansion of public colleges and universities across the country.

The federal government began offering funding to *non-veterans* in 1972 when Congress established the Basic Educational Opportunity Grant, which later became known as Pell Grants. To this day, Pell Grants continue to provide direct funding to college students to defray the costs of higher education. Importantly, Pell Grants are need-based, such that students from lower-income households receive more funding than students from high-income families. The assumption behind need-based funding is that parents are responsible for saving for their children's college education. Most college students do not receive sufficient funds from their parents, or government funding, to cover the *entire* cost of college. As a result, most college students take out loans to cover tuition, fees, books, housing, and food. In 1965, the federal government began subsidizing student loans for the children of low and middle income parents. Although students still must pay back subsidized loans, the interest rates are substantially lower than unsubsidized loans. Similar to government grants, which do not have to be repaid, the amount of subsidized loans students could borrow was inversely related to their parents' income. In short, the federal government now plays an important role in providing financial assistance to Americans attending college through both grants and low-interest student loans.

Some have argued that the federal government should expand higher education funding to provide free college tuition to all Americans. During the 2016 presidential primaries, both of the main competitors for the Democratic nomination supported free college for most Americans. Vermont Senator Bernie Sanders made free college for all a central part of his policy platform, while his opponent Hillary Clinton supported free college for children of low and middle income Americans, but excluded children of wealthy parents. Given the importance of young voters to the Democratic Party's coalition, it is likely that future Democratic candidates will pursue free college in some form.

There is some precedent for this idea on the state level, as Tennessee and Oregon provide free tuition for students attending community colleges. In 2017, New York became the first state to provide free college tuition at four-year colleges, though the program is only available for middle and lower income families. Another approach is to use state lottery funds to provide merit-based scholarships to college students. For example, Georgia provides *nearly free* college to students that maintain a high grade point average. Of course, funding is contingent on the availability of lottery revenue, which certainly is a gamble. In short, it is not unprecedented for governments to provide free college and it occurs in both liberal leaning (New York) and conservative leaning (Georgia) states.

What do the American people think about free college? In a 2016 Gallup poll, Americans were about evenly divided on this issue, with 47 percent supporting, and 45 percent opposing, free college tuition (Saad 2016). These results were similar to a YouGov poll conducted in 2015, in which 46 percent said they supported using taxes to pay for college tuition, compared to 41 percent who were opposed (Moore 2015). Whether people support free college has a lot to do with their age, income, and party identification. In the 2016 Gallup poll, two-thirds (67%) of Democrats *supported* free college, while 70 percent of Republicans *opposed* the idea (Saad 2016). Perhaps not surprisingly, young people are more likely to support free college than older Americans. Among those aged 18–34, 63 percent supported free college, compared to only 37 percent of Americans who were 55 and older (Saad 2016). Additionally, wealthier Americans are less likely to support free college than middle class or poorer workers (*ibid.*).

Ultimately, the debate over free college is a microcosm of the larger debate over government entitlements. Those supporting government entitlements, such as Medicaid, public schools, or welfare, argue that they provide poor citizens opportunities to enjoy their freedom by pursuing their goals. Free college in particular, would allow students from middle-class and poor families the opportunity to get a quality education, which will help them find their desired job and become productive members of society. Of course, free college is not really *free* because someone has to pay the bill. Similar to other entitlements, free college would take a lot of money from people who may not directly benefit, especially if they do not have children. A related concern is that government entitlements, in general, reward dependence and laziness, rather than hard work and personal responsibility. As for free college, there are concerns about whether it would encourage inefficiency and waste in higher education institutions. Most Americans support equality of opportunity in the abstract, but also oppose government dependence and wasteful spending. The main question is whether the benefits of free college outweigh the costs.

Free College Promotes Opportunity

Support for equality of opportunity is a core value in American culture. In the abstract, Americans believe that people ought to have the opportunity to succeed regardless of their parents' wealth or where they were born. A core principle of the American dream is that people can succeed through hard work and determination. In order to promote equal opportunity, the United States government has instituted numerous programs such as welfare, unemployment, Pell Grants, and Medicaid. These *entitlement* programs—so-called because American citizens are entitled to them if they meet certain requirements—provide many opportunities for citizens to achieve their goals in life even if they come from a disadvantaged background, made a few poor decisions, or simply had a run of bad luck. Welfare is designed to make sure children in poor families have food and shelter, Medicaid prevents people from dying because they can't afford medical care, while Pell Grants provide recipients with the opportunity to attend college.

In the United States, public education is easily the largest and most expensive entitlement program. In fact, states treat education as a *right*, rather than a freedom. For example, Article VIII, Section 1 of the Georgia state Constitution establishes that "Public education for the citizens prior to the college or post-secondary level shall be free and shall be provided for by taxation" (Georgia

Constitution, art. 8, sec. 1). Treating education as a right requires the government to provide it to all citizens. Public education is an essential component of freedom because it removes barriers to success. While public education is often considered a right, higher education has traditionally been considered a freedom and privilege.

Supporters of free college tuition argue that a college education should now be treated like public education. The main argument in favor of free college is that a typical high school education does not provide students adequate skills to be competitive in the modern economy. Indeed, a college education provides numerous benefits to those who attain one. In 2015, roughly 85 percent of college graduates were employed compared to two-thirds of high-school graduates (Rugaber 2017). College graduates also make more money than high-school graduates. The median household income of four-year college graduates is roughly *50 percent more* than someone with only a high-school diploma (*ibid.*). Over the course of an entire career, the typical college graduate earns roughly $1.2 million *more* than a high-school graduate (Hershbein and Kearney 2014). Furthermore, college graduates are more likely to own a home and invest money in retirement accounts, both of which shorten the amount of time that college graduates have to remain in the workforce compared to those who never attend college (Rugaber 2017).

At the same time that college has become increasingly important for young people's economic futures, the cost of attending college has skyrocketed. Since the early 1980s, tuition and fees at four-year public colleges have steadily increased far beyond the rate of inflation. In *current dollars*, average tuition and fees at four-year public colleges was $2,211 in 1980, compared to $8,778 in 2016, which represents a nearly 400 percent increase (U.S. Department of Education, 2016b). As college costs have risen, students have become increasingly reliant on loans to cover these costs. Average total debt per student in the class of 2016 was $37,172, which is a 6 percent increase over just the previous year (U.S. Federal Reserve 2018). Since the early 1990s, college graduates have become more likely to hold student loan debt after college, and the amount of debt they owe has more than tripled—from about $10,000 to $35,000—in a little over twenty years (Kantrowitz 2016). After graduation, the average monthly student loan payment for 20–30-year-olds is roughly $351, and the student loan delinquency rate is 11 percent (U.S. Federal Reserve 2018).

Student loan debt has long-term consequences for individuals and society. Following college, more students are saddled with debt, which prevents them from investing in their future, buying a home, and starting a family. In order to pay down debt, parents may work more hours, or take a second job, rather than have children or spend time with their families. Supporters of free college argue that it would reduce overall student loan debt, strengthen families, and allow people to lead happier, and more fulfilling lives.

Free College Promotes Inefficiency and Irresponsibility

Opponents of free college argue that it would result in wasteful spending, encourage irresponsible behavior, and do nothing to reduce inefficiencies in higher education. As is the case with many entitlement programs, free college redistributes money from the rich to the poor. The wealthy can already afford college, but are now forced to subsidize the education of other people's children. While this situation may be acceptable for public education, college students are adults who are perfectly capable of paying for their own higher education. If an adult wants to attend college, they should have the responsibility of paying for it either by having a part-time job, serving in the military, or by taking out loans.

On a related point, free college is unnecessary because there are already many paths for hard-working individuals to attain a college education without taking on excessive debt. Between federal and state grants, students from low-income families get most of their college costs paid for, and the rest can be made up with existing academic scholarships, work study, or part-time jobs. If students are not willing to work while they attend college, they should be responsible for paying for their education (through loans) after they graduate. Another route to attain a quality education is through the military. Although it does not cover all college costs, the G. I. Bill pays for tuition and books, and provides a housing stipend. In other words, joining the military allows young people to serve their country and attend college while accumulating very little debt.

Another complaint about government entitlements in general, and free college in particular, is that they encourage laziness and dependence instead of promoting personal responsibility. When people are provided a free entitlement from the government, they have little incentive to work hard if they are assured continued support. If students know that the government will pay for college, they have less incentive to perform well in high school in order to attain scholarships and grants for academic performance. Furthermore, when students have to pay for college, they take it more seriously, and try to graduate as soon as possible. Conversely, if college students know that they have four years of free college, they have less incentive to finish earlier.

If the government provides free college, it will likely encourage many young people to attend college even if it is not necessary for their desired careers. Opponents of free college argue that not everyone needs to attend college to get a good job. In fact, most jobs in the United States do not require a four-year college degree (Samuelson 2012). Furthermore, there are a variety of skill-based jobs, such as plumbers, electricians, and mechanics, that require attendance at a vocational or trade school instead of a more costly four-year university. Providing free college at four-year institutions will attract far too many students who would be better off at a trade school, or entering the workforce right after high-school. Forcing students to pay for college requires them to think seriously about whether attending college is worth the time and money required. As more people abuse the system, free college would become more costly to American taxpayers.

In short, providing free college would likely result in Americans paying billions of dollars for many students to waste four years of their life in a college classroom.

Another problem with free college is that it completely ignores, and possibly facilitates, inefficiencies in the higher education system. The main driver of increased college costs is labor, including faculty and administrative salaries. From 1993 to 2007, the amount universities spent on administration per student rose 66 percent, with most of that due to paying for administrative personnel (Odland 2012). In other words, college students are paying more money for college largely because the administrations of American universities are inefficient. Treatment of faculty in universities is another source of inefficiency. Tenure policies allow faculty at most universities to remain in their jobs long after they became ineffective classroom instructors. Furthermore, research universities provide faculty release time for research projects, while their classes are staffed with graduate students or adjuncts. Forcing faculty to actually teach, and teach more classes, would go a long way to bringing down costs. Making college free would provide no incentive for universities to implement reforms that would drive down costs. Instead, higher education would continue to be inefficient, with the excessive costs passed on to the taxpayers.

What is Fairness?

On a concluding note, I would like to point out that both sides of the free college debate are using the shared value of fairness to support their position. Supporters of free college argue that it is *unfair* that educational opportunity depends on where one happens to be born rather than hard work and natural talents. Moreover, they argue that it is *unfair* to force low-income individuals to serve in the military, or work during college, while children of wealthy families can attend college without such burdens. Wealthy students get to focus entirely on their academic work, without a part-time job, and graduate debt-free, simply because they were lucky enough to be born into wealthy families. Meanwhile, children from low-income families have to work extra-hard, hold a part-time job, or risk their lives in the military, in order to get the same benefits as wealthy children. This dual system of higher education stands in stark contrast to the ideals of a meritocracy where individuals succeed or fail based on their hard work and natural talents. Supporters of free college argue that if Americans really want to equalize the classes, it is time to provide children of low-income families with similar opportunities to those who are lucky enough to be born to wealthy parents.

Opponents of free college also invoke fairness to support their arguments. They argue that requiring higher taxes is unfair to wealthy families that must pay for their children to attend college and for the education of other people's children. One of the benefits of working hard is to provide one's children with the best education possible, and parents should not be financially penalized for trying to help their children achieve their dreams. Opponents of free college argue that it is *unfair* to penalize parents who work hard to provide their children a better education, which free college would do by taxing wealthy parents, and providing reduced benefits. Both sides believe in fairness, but simply look at it from different perspectives. In order to make the system fair to the poor, it has to unfairly tax the rich. This difference of opinion does not necessarily mean that rich people are selfish and poor people are moochers. Instead, both sides have a different perspective on what constitutes *fairness* because they have different backgrounds and self-interests. Consequently, they feel that some conceptions of fairness are more important or relevant to the debate over free college. This debate provides an excellent example of how life experiences and framing can lead people to see the same issue from different perspectives.

Review Questions

1. How did the federal government take on a larger role in funding higher education?
2. How does higher education promote equality of opportunity?
3. How might free college promote irresponsible behavior?
4. How might free college create more waste in higher education spending?

Discussion Questions

1. Is a college education worth the cost?
2. What are some ways to lower the costs of college education?
3. Is it fair that government assistance for college is based on parental income?
4. What would be the best way to fund free college? Who should have to pay?

Sources for Further Inquiry

Books

Bok, Derek. 2015. *Higher Education in America*. Princeton, NJ: Princeton University Press.
Dougherty, Kevin J., Sosanya M. Jones, Hana Lahr, Rebecca S. Natow, Lara Pheatt, and Vikash Reddy. 2016. *Performance Funding for Higher Education*. Baltimore, MD: Johns Hopkins University Press.
Palfreyman, David, Ted Tapper, and Scott Thomas, eds. 2017. *Towards the Private Funding of Higher Education: Ideological and Political Struggles*. New York, NY: Routledge.
Stevens, Mitchell, and Michael W. Kirst, eds. 2015. *Remaking College: The Changing Ecology of Higher Education*. Stanford, CA: Stanford University Press.

Journal and Newspaper Articles

Elliott, William, and Melinda Lewis. 2015. "Student Debt Effects on Financial Well-being: Research and Policy Implications." *Journal of Economic Surveys* 29(4): 614–636.

Houle, Jason N., and Cody Warner. 2017. "Into the Red and Back to the Nest? Student Debt, College Completion, and Returning to the Parental Home among Young Adults." *Sociology of Education* 90(1): 89–108.

Jongbloed, Ben, and Hans Vossensteyn. 2001. "Keeping up Performances: An International Survey of Performance-based Funding in Higher Education." *Journal of Higher Education Policy and Management* 23(2): 127–145.

Kelly, Andrew P. 2015. "High Costs, Uncertain Benefits: What Do Americans without a College Degree Think about Postsecondary Education?" American Enterprise Institute for Public Policy Research. Retrieved from https://eric.ed.gov/?id=ED557611

Kim, Kyung-Nyun, and Rose M. Baker. 2015. "The Assumed Benefits and Hidden Costs of Adult Learners' College Enrollment." *Research in Higher Education* 56(5): 510–533.

Leonhardt, David. 2014, May 27. "Is College Worth it? Clearly, New Data Say." *The New York Times.* Retrieved from https://www.nytimes.com/2014/05/27/upshot/is-college-worth-it-clearly-new-data-say.html

Looney, Adam, and Constantine Yannelis. 2015. "A Crisis in Student Loans?: How Changes in the Characteristics of Borrowers and in the Institutions they Attended Contributed to Rising Loan Defaults." *Brookings Papers on Economic Activity* 2: 1–89. Retrieved from https://muse.jhu.edu/article/616850/summary

Marcus, Jon. 2015, June 10. "Where Free College Isn't a Cure-All." *The Atlantic.* Retrieved from https://www.theatlantic.com/education/archive/2015/06/free-college-tuition-not-a-cure/395504/

References

Hershbein, Brad, and Melissa S. Kearney. 2014, September 29. "Major Decisions: What Graduates Earn over their Lifetimes." The Hamilton Project. Retrieved from http://www.hamiltonproject.org/papers/major_decisions_what_graduates_earn_over_their_lifetimes/

Kantrowitz, Mark. 2016, January 11. "Why the Student Loan Crisis is Even Worse than People Think." *Time.* Retrieved from http://time.com/money/4168510/why-student-loan-crisis-is-worse-than-people-think/

Moore, Peter. 2015, August 20. "Three-fifths Want Taxes to Fund Debt-free College." YouGov.com. Retrieved from https://today.yougov.com/news/2015/08/20/three-fifths-want-debt-free-college/

Odland, Steve. 2012, March 24. "College Costs Out of Control." Forbes. Retrieved from https://www.forbes.com/sites/steveodland/2012/03/24/college-costs-are-soaring/#6f55eadb1f86

Rugaber, Christopher S. 2017, January 12. "Pay Gap between College Grads and Everyone Else at a Record." *USA Today.* Retrieved from https://www.usatoday.com/story/money/2017/01/12/pay-gap-between-college-grads-and-everyone-else-record/96493348/

Saad, Lydia. 2016, May 2. "Americans Buy Free Pre-K; Split on Tuition-Free College." Gallup. Retrieved from http://www.gallup.com/poll/191255/americans-buy-free-pre-split-tuition-free-college.aspx

Samuelson, Robert J. 2012, May 27. "It's Time to Drop the College-for-all Crusade." *Washington Post.* Retrieved from https://www.washingtonpost.com/opinions/its-time-to-drop-the-college-for-all-crusade/2012/05/27/gJQAzcUGvU_story.html?utm_term=.78779122035f

U.S. Department of Education. 2016a. "Percentage of 18- to 24-year-olds Enrolled in Degree-granting Postsecondary Institutions, by Level of Institution and Sex and Race/ethnicity of Student: 1970 through 2015." National Center for Education Statistics. Retrieved from https://nces.ed.gov/programs/digest/d16/tables/dt16_302.60.asp?current=yes

U.S. Department of Education. 2016b. "Average Undergraduate Tuition and Fees and Room and Board Rates Charged for Full-time Students in Degree-granting Postsecondary Institutions, by Level and Control of Institution: 1963–1964 through 2015–2016." National Center for Education Statistics. Retrieved from: https://nces.ed.gov/programs/digest/d16/tables/dt16_330.10.asp?current=yes

U.S. Federal Reserve. 2018. "Consumer Credit-G.19." Board of Governors of the Federal Reserve System. Retrieved from https://www.federalreserve.gov/releases/g19/current/default.htm

8

SHOULD CONGRESS INCREASE FUNDING FOR THE MILITARY?

One of the primary purposes of the federal government is to provide for the national defense. Ever since World War II, the United States government has maintained a large standing army even during periods of relative peace. Currently, spending on national defense makes up a large portion of the annual budget of the U.S. Government. In 2015, the budget for the department of defense was $598 billion, which accounts for roughly 16 percent of all money spent by the federal government (U.S. Government Spending 2015). During the height of the Afghanistan and Iraq Wars (2001–2009), defense spending increased nearly 70 percent from $412 billion to $699 billion (Zakaria 2011). By comparison, China takes second place in military spending at only $146 billion, while the U.S. spends more than the next seven countries combined (Taylor and Karklis 2016).

Whether the U.S. spends too much on national defense has long been a recurring topic in American politics. In his farewell address, President Dwight Eisenhower warned of the dangers of the military industrial complex, which is the defense industry as well as the non-governmental contractors manufacturing military weapons. During the Cold War with the former Soviet Union, Ronald Reagan pushed for a large defense buildup, while his opponent in 1984 argued that defense funds should be spent on other national priorities. More recently, President Barack Obama advocated for cutting overall military spending to focus on strategic defense and tactical forces rather than the more costly ships and planes that are not required to fight modern battles. In other words, Obama argued that the military needs to adapt to current circumstances, which will cost less taxpayer money. Following Obama, President Donald Trump has promised a return to high levels of military spending, and most Republicans in Congress support his efforts (Rubio and Cotton 2015).

In contrast to Congress, public opinion polls suggest that most Americans do not have a strong desire for more military spending. In 2017, a Gallup survey showed that only 37 percent of Americans believed the U.S. spent too little on defense, while 31 percent thought it spent too much and 28 percent thought spending was about right (Gallup n.d.). In other words, nearly two-thirds of Americans believe that defense spending should *not* be increased. These results are similar to a 2016 survey from the Pew Research Center in which 35 percent of Americans thought the U.S. should increase defense spending, while another 24 percent wanted to decrease spending. There was a partisan divide as well, with 61 percent of Republicans supporting increased defense spending, compared to only 20 percent of Democrats (Pew Research Center 2016).

Of course, these surveys asking about general support for military spending rarely make people confront the hard choices involved in the issue. For example, it is easier for people to say that the U.S. should increase defense spending when they are not thinking about the corresponding tax increases or cuts to other government services that would be required. In an innovative survey design, voters were offered arguments supporting and opposing military funding and then asked to allocate funds to government departments (Chadwick 2016). This study helps people make a more informed decision about military spending than traditional surveys. The study found that most registered voters favored substantial cuts to military spending. Furthermore, this study suggested that majorities of both *Republicans and Democrats* opposed increases to defense spending. In short, when voters are confronted with the tradeoffs involved in government spending, there is widespread support for reducing military spending.

Ultimately, the debate over military spending involves two long-standing conflicts in American politics. One conflict is over the appropriate role of the United States in international affairs. While some believe the U.S. should stay out of international conflicts, others argue that it must defend itself and fight for its principles and interests around the world. Another conflict centers on government spending on the federal bureaucracy. The military is the largest part of the federal bureaucracy, which makes it a prime target for those looking to reduce federal spending. As is often the case with government spending in general, reducing government spending has a negative impact on the economy. Of course, whether people see military spending as wasteful or a good use of government funds largely depends on their foreign policy goals and economic self-interest.

Isolationism vs. Internationalism

Should the United States get involved in conflicts between foreign nations? This question has been one of the most important issues throughout American history. In his farewell address, President George Washington argued that the U.S. should generally avoid meddling in the conflicts between European countries. Washington expressed the general stance of isolationism, wherein the country avoids foreign conflicts that do not have a substantial and direct effect on America's economic interests. In contrast, internationalism is the theory that America must be involved in world affairs to promote security, peace, and human rights. Of course, these two positions are general guidelines as few would say the U.S. should *never* be involved in foreign conflicts, nor should we get involved in *every* conflict around the world.

Public opinion regarding the role of the United States in foreign affairs has ebbed and flowed over time in response to international events. Recent polls suggest that Americans lean in favor of isolationism. In a 2016 survey, 37 percent of Americans believed the U.S. should "help other countries deal with their problems" while a majority (57%) agreed the U.S. should "deal with its own problems, while letting other countries get along the best they can." Interestingly, Republicans were more likely than Democrats to support isolationism in foreign policy, though the partisan divide is rather small. "Roughly six-in-ten Republicans (62%) say the United States should deal with its own problems and let other countries deal with their problems as best they can, compared with 47% of Democrats" (Pew Research Center 2016). In short, it appears that most Americans lean toward isolationism and this sentiment largely cuts across partisan lines.

These polling results reflect a recent split in the Republican Party between isolationists and internationalists. Much of this sea change is due to the long-running wars in Iraq and Afghanistan, but also to the emergence of popular Republican politicians who express isolationist views, such as Ron Paul, his son Rand, and President Donald Trump. Once Republican elites started framing foreign policy around budgets and government spending, many Republicans in the general public started supporting a more isolationist perspective as well. Consequently, public opinion about the role of the U.S. in the world is not easily divided along partisan lines.

Not surprisingly, military spending plays a central role in this debate because internationalism requires more military funding than isolationism. Following the attack on Pearl Harbor in 1941, internationalism was the dominant foreign policy approach. Supporters of military spending argue that the main lesson of World War II is that conflicts abroad will spread if left unattended. It is better to engage in military conflict early than to deal with its consequences after the conflict is already out of control. A large military is also necessary to promote freedom and human rights around the world. Since World War II, the U.S. military has engaged in conflicts to stop the spread of communism, overthrow oppressive dictators, and prevent human rights abuses. Cutting military spending would weaken America's ability to help promote peace and prosperity around the world.

Supporters of increased military spending also argue that having a large standing army deters potential enemies from attacking the United States and its allies. The more powerful military a nation has, the more likely it is that adversaries will seek peaceful resolutions rather than armed conflict. President Theodore Roosevelt was echoing this deterrence theory, when he said the U.S. Navy has been "an infinitely more potent factor for peace than all the peace societies of every kind and sort" (Inboden 2016). Having a large and well-funded army that is spread around the world can help prevent conflicts from starting and incentivize peaceful solutions. A large military presence also facilitates international trade because the U.S. protects shipping lanes and maintains security for economic trading partners. The military plays an important role in facilitating economic growth in the modern world-wide economy.

Opponents of military spending do not see America's role in the international arena in such positive terms. Instead, isolationists argue that America spends too much money defending other countries and causes more conflicts than it solves. Those opposing military spending point to a long history of wars that only seem to cause more conflict in the future. Moreover, some argue that intervening in other countries causes anger and resentment toward the United States. In a bipartisan opinion piece, Representatives Barney Frank (D) and Ron Paul (R) argue that "the idea that as a superpower it is our duty to maintain stability by intervening in civil disorders virtually anywhere in the world often generates anger directed at us and may in the end do more harm than good" (Frank and Paul 2010). Isolationists argue that the U.S. has gotten involved in far too many unnecessary military conflicts that cost the lives of American soldiers and increased the national debt. Many opponents of military spending simply believe that the U.S. should let other countries handle their own problems.

On a related note, opponents of military spending argue that many allies of the U.S. have become dependent on its protection. The U.S. military has bases all over the world and secures key shipping lanes. Many isolationists argue that other countries should take on more responsibility for defending themselves and their economic interests, rather than being dependent on the U.S. to protect them. Currently, Americans are paying high taxes to secure most of the world, while other countries are getting a free ride. Cutting military spending would force other nations to take on a larger role in keeping the world safe.

Cutting military spending is also a way to potentially restrain elected leaders from invading other countries or getting involved in conflicts around the world. Having a large standing army at their disposal may result in leaders resorting to armed conflicts even when peaceful solutions are possible. In contrast, having a weaker military may act as a restraint on leaders who might otherwise choose war over peace. Simply put, it is far easier to attack someone that you know you can beat. Reducing the military budget may restrain leaders from engaging in armed conflicts, and instead incentivize peaceful solutions to international problems.

Wasteful Spending or Good Jobs? Maybe Both

The issue of military spending also involves the long-standing debate in American politics over spending on the federal bureaucracy. Many Democrats and Republicans argue that military spending should be reduced in order to cut taxes, shift spending to other areas, or reduce the national debt. They argue that America does not need to invest so heavily on defense given that the country already far outspends other nations. Defense spending has been central to the debate over national priorities following the military buildup during World War II and the maintenance of a large standing army ever since. Former President and general Dwight Eisenhower put the tradeoffs of military spending in real terms during his "The Chance for Peace Speech" when he said:

> Every gun that is made, every warship launched, every rocket fired signifies, in the final sense, a theft from those who hunger and are not fed, those who are cold and are not clothed. This world in arms is not spending money alone. It is spending the sweat of its laborers, the genius of its scientists, the hopes of its children. The cost of one modern heavy bomber is this: a modern brick school in more than 30 cities. It is two electric power plants, each serving a town of 60,000 population. It is two fine, fully equipped hospitals. It is some 50 miles of concrete highway. We pay for a single fighter plane with a half million bushels of wheat. We pay for a single destroyer with new homes that could have housed more than 8,000 people.
>
> *(Eisenhower 1953)*

As Eisenhower makes clear, the more money spent on the military, the less money is available for other important priorities of the American people. Opponents of military spending argue that those funds would be put to better use helping the poor, maintaining roads, or cutting taxes on American businesses and workers.

Supporters of defense spending argue that it creates good jobs for American workers and provides a ladder to success for individuals from disadvantaged backgrounds. Defense spending also involves many entrenched interests that would directly suffer if military spending were cut. The military provides direct pay to soldiers and other defense personnel, but also creates jobs indirectly through defense contractors. Moreover, the defense contractors are based in the U.S., meaning that jobs cannot be outsourced for cheaper labor in other countries. Cutting military spending would threaten the country's ability to defend itself, while also sending many Americans to the unemployment line. Additionally, the military provides a ladder to success for poor and underprivileged young people, who cannot afford college or cannot find a job right out of high school. In short, cuts to the military would likely lower the number of soldiers, which would disproportionately affect young adults from poor families.

Opponents of increased military spending also argue that the military is exceptionally wasteful in how they spend money. One of the main factors leading to military inefficiency stems from the close, often insular, relationship between the Department of Defense, defense contractors, and members of congressional sub-committees that determine defense funding. The close association of this trifecta of institutions is commonly called the "military-industrial complex" (MIC) that Dwight

Eisenhower warned about in his farewell address. A particularly costly consequence of the military-industrial complex is that certain defense contractors can attain virtual monopolies over defense contracts. For example, a 2014 report from the Center for Strategic and International Studies found that half of the Department of Defense proposals had *only one* defense contractor issue a bid (Schatz 2017). Competition among contractors incentivizes each company to maximize efficiency, resulting in lower priced contracts and less cost to taxpayers. If a company is assured to get a defense contract, they have no incentive to reduce costs.

Within the military-industrial complex, Congressmen are tasked with the responsibility of keeping costs low. Members of Congress are often reluctant to cut military spending however, especially when it would affect the economy in their state or district. Defense contractors build ships and planes within the U.S., while military bases support the economy of the areas where they reside. Any efforts to reduce the size of defense contracts or to close military bases will cost American jobs. Congressmen typically do whatever is in their power to keep military money flowing to their constituents, even when it may not be in the best strategic interests of the military. There is a seemingly endless supply of examples of Congressmen adding funding to their home districts and states, even when the Department of Defense never asked, and in some cases rejected, such funding. For just one example, the 2016 defense budget included an earmark from Mississippi Senator Thad Cochran, which "directed the Coast Guard to build a $640 million National Security Cutter in Mississippi that the Coast Guard says it does not need" (Tiefer 2016). Ironically, congressmen commonly call for an end to government waste, as long as that waste is not located in their district or state.

As a member of the Senate Armed Services Committee, which oversees defense spending, Arizona Senator John McCain routinely pointed out wasteful projects and abuse in the Department of Defense budget. For example, McCain argued that development of the Littoral Combat Ships cost over $12 billion, and yet has never been approved for combat, and may never be operational. "In other words, U.S. taxpayers have bought 26 ships and 13 mission packages that have demonstrated next-to-no combat capability" (McCain 2016). Perhaps the best example of military waste is the F-35 fighter jet that cost over a *trillion dollars* and produced no actual benefits for national defense (Schaffer and Shaer 2015). In short, the current military funding system creates wastes that are financed by taxpayers. Cutting military spending would force the government to become more efficient in how it spends money.

Review Questions

1. What is the difference between internationalism and isolationism?
2. How does military spending affect foreign policy?
3. How does military spending affect local economies?
4. What is the military-industrial complex?

Discussion Questions

1. Would cutting military spending threaten America's national security?
2. If military spending is reduced, where should the money be spent?
3. Does having a large military make the U.S. more likely to engage in military conflicts around the world?
4. If the U.S. reduced its military presence around the world, would other countries spend more on defense or would the world be less safe?
5. Since World War II, has the American military been a force for good in the world, or has it caused more problems than it has solved?

Sources for Further Inquiry

Books

DeGrasse, Robert W. 2016. *Military Expansion, Economic Decline: Impact of Military Spending on U.S. Economic Performance*. New York, NY: Routledge.
Fisher, Louis. 2015. *Presidential Spending Power*. Princeton, NJ: Princeton University Press.
Preble, Christopher A. 2009. *The power problem: How American military dominance makes us less safe, less prosperous, and less free*. Ithaca, NY: Cornell University Press.
Rubin, Irene S. 2016. *The Politics of Public Budgeting: Getting and Spending, Borrowing and Balancing*. Washington, D.C.: CQ Press.
Thorpe, Rebecca U. 2014. *The American Warfare State: The Domestic Politics of Military Spending*. Chicago, IL: University of Chicago Press.

Journal and Newspaper Articles

Johnson, Justin. 2015, November 6. "Assessing Common Arguments for Cutting National Security Spending: Informing Current and Future Budget Debates." The Heritage Foundation. Retrieved from http://www.heritage.org/defense/report/assessing-comm on-arguments-cutting-national-security-spending-informing-current-and
Moyn, Samuel. 2017. "Beyond Liberal Internationalism." *Dissent* 64(1): 116–122.
Preble, Christopher A. 2010. "Cut (Really Cut) Military Spending." CATO Institute. Retrieved from https://www.cato.org/publications/commentary/cut-really-cut-military-spending
Rathbun, Brian C., Joshua D. Kertzer, Jason Reifler, Paul Goren, and Thomas J. Scotto. 2016. "Taking Foreign Policy Personally: Personal Values and Foreign Policy Attitudes." *International Studies Quarterly* 60(1): 124–137.
Thompson, William R. 2016. "The 1920–1945 Shift in US Foreign Policy Orientation: Theory, Grand Strategies, and System Leader Ascents." *Foreign Policy Analysis* 12(4): 512–532.

References

Chadwick, Lauren. 2016, March 10. "Most Voters Favor Defense Cuts. Most Politicians Do Not." *Time.com*. Retrieved from http://time.com/4253842/defense-spending-obama-con gress-poll-voters/

Eisenhower, Dwight D. 1953, April 16. "Transcript of Speech: The Chance for Peace. " Retrieved from https://www.eisenhower.archives.gov/all_about_ike/speeches/chance_ for_peace.pdf

Frank, Barney, and Ron Paul. 2010, July 6. "Why we Must Reduce Military Spending." *The Hill.* Retrieved from http://www.huffingtonpost.com/rep-barney-frank/why-we-must-re duce-milita_b_636051.html

Gallup. n.d. "Military and National Defense." Retrieved from http://www.gallup.com/p oll/1666/military-national-defense.aspx

Inboden, William. 2016. "The Role of a Strong National Defense." The Heritage Foundation. Retrieved from http://index.heritage.org/military/2016/essays/role-of-a-strong-na tional-defense/#rf18-1379

McCain, John. 2016, December 19. "Senator John McCain Presents: America's Most Wasted." Senate.gov. Retrieved from https://www.mccain.senate.gov/public/_cache/ files/9f435670-9a18-4362-9ff0-294540a13cb7/americas-most-wasted-indefen sible-12-19-16.pdf

Pew Research Center. 2016, May 5. "Public Uncertain, Divided Over America's Place in the World." Retrieved from http://www.people-press.org/2016/05/05/public-uncerta in-divided-over-americas-place-in-the-world/

Rubio, Marco, and Tom Cotton. 2015, March 26. "Why Defense Budget Must Grow." CNN.com. Retrieved from https://www.cnn.com/2015/03/26/opinions/ rubio-cotton-defense-cuts/index.html

Schaffer, Tony, and Susan Shaer. 2015, October 21. "The Sorry Saga of the F-35: when the Pentagon wastes money, we all get a Vegas hangover." Fox News.com. Retrieved from http://www.foxnews.com/opinion/2015/10/21/sorry-saga-f-35-when-pentagon-wastes -money-all-get-vegas-hangover.html

Schatz, Thomas A. 2017, February 17. "Battling Wasteful Spending." *U.S. News and World Report.* Retrieved from https://www.usnews.com/opinion/articles/2017-02-17/how- donald-trump-can-curb-wasteful-department-of-defense-spending

Taylor, Adam, and Laris Karklis. 2016, February 9. "This Remarkable Chart Shows how U.S. Defense Spending Dwarfs the Rest of the World." *Washington Post.* Retrieved from https://www.washingtonpost.com/news/worldviews/wp/2016/02/09/this-rema rkable-chart-shows-how-u-s-defense-spending-dwarfs-the-rest-of-the-world/

Tiefer, Charles. 2016, January 1. "The 10 Most Blatantly Wasteful Defense Items in the Recent $1.8 Trillion Spending Bill." Forbes. Retrieved from https://www.forbes.com/ sites/charlestiefer/2016/01/01/the-10-most-blatantly-wasteful-defense-items-in-the-r ecent-1-8-trillion-spending-bill/2/#7c181a617a07

U.S. Government Spending. 2015. "U.S. Government Spending." Retrieved from http:// www.usgovernmentspending.com/year_spending_2015USbn_17bs2n_30#usgs302

Zakaria, Fareed. 2011, August 3. "Why Defense Spending Should be Cut." *Washington Post.* Retrieved from https://www.washingtonpost.com/opinions/why-defense-spend ing-should-be-cut/2011/08/03/gIQAsRuqsI_story.html?utm_term=.4d6ef811111b

PART III

Social Policy

9

SHOULD THE FEDERAL GOVERNMENT LEGALIZE MARIJUANA?

One of the fundamental questions in American politics is the extent to which government should regulate individual freedom in order to promote the public good. The debate over drug use strikes at the heart of this conflict between the widely-shared values of freedom and public safety. Some believe that government has no business punishing people for consuming mind-altering drugs. After all, if I want to screw up my body by consuming drugs, that is my choice, and not anyone else's business. Others argue that drug use has victims beyond the user because it destroys families, increases crime, and threatens social order. Legalization of drugs is a classic conflict between individual freedom and the ability of the government to maintain social order.

Right in the middle of this drug legalization debate is marijuana, which is made from the dried flowers, seeds, and leaves of the hemp plant. For most of American history, marijuana was sold legally and had very little regulation over its production or use. In 1619, Virginia *required* that every farmer grow hemp, which was widely used to make products such clothing and rope. In the late 1800s, marijuana was commonly used in medicine and sold in pharmacies (Public Broadcasting Service n.d.). Public opposition to marijuana grew during the 1920s, leading most states to outlaw the drug within the next decade. The Marihuana (sic) Tax Act of 1937 made the drug effectively illegal for recreational use. Although federal laws weakened some in the 1960s, President Ronald Reagan's anti-drug campaign in the 1980s resulted in the Comprehensive Crime Control Act (1984), which established strict federal penalties for the sale and possession of marijuana. The fight against marijuana was part of the larger war on drugs, which was fought during the last few decades of the 20th century.

Recently, Americans have grown more supportive of legalizing marijuana for both medicinal and recreational use. According to Gallup, only 12 percent of

Americans supported legalizing marijuana in 1969, but that number increased to 34 percent in 2001, and by 2017 a *substantial majority* (64%) of Americans supported legalization (McCarthy 2017). There is a slight partisan divide on this issue, with 72 percent of Democrats supporting legalization, compared to 51 percent of Republicans. Support for legalizing marijuana has increased among all partisan groups in a short period of time. From 2004 through 2017, support for legalization increased 37 percent among Democrats and 31 percent among Republicans. Some of this change is likely due to the large generational divide over legalization however, as young people are much more likely to support legalizing marijuana than older Americans. In a 2015 poll, 71 percent of those aged 18–34 supported legalization compared to only 35 percent of Americans aged 65 and over (Jones 2015). As older Americans are replaced in the population with younger generations, public support for legalizing marijuana is likely to continue growing.

Increasing public support for legalizing marijuana has resulted in states softening their anti-marijuana laws. Following the 2016 election, eight states have voted to legalize small amounts of marijuana for recreational use, while other states have decriminalized the drug, making possession punishable by only a small fine. The states that have legalized marijuana cut across the political spectrum, such as Colorado, Alaska, Washington, and Nevada. If public support for marijuana continues to intensify, more states are likely to experiment with legalization and taxation of the drug.

The debate over legalization of marijuana involves questions of freedom versus social good, but also questions about the dangers of the drug for individuals, families, and society. Those opposing marijuana legalization argue that it is addictive, lowers motivation, and serves as a "gateway" to even more dangerous drugs such as cocaine and methamphetamines. Advocates for marijuana legalization argue that the fears about all of these supposed effects of marijuana are vastly overblown. Furthermore, supporters argue that marijuana is far less dangerous than legal substances such as cigarettes and alcohol. In fact, marijuana is less addictive than cigarettes, and unlike alcohol, there is little risk of overdosing. Supporters of legalization also argue that the prohibition of marijuana has caused more problems than the supposed dangers of the drug. The prohibition of marijuana has destroyed the lives of those arrested for possession, resulted in overcrowded prisons, and facilitated the growth of drug cartels.

Freedom vs. Order

The question of whether to legalize marijuana centers on one of the main conflicts facing government policy. In order for the government to maintain order in society, they must infringe on some people's freedom to live their life the way they desire. The government must take away freedom to protect individuals against other citizens. Some might suggest that government should only restrict individual freedom when it causes harm to other people, but even this requires a standard for what counts as a "harm" to someone else. Certainly physical harm to another person such as murder or rape should be illegal, but a person's actions can also indirectly harm others. If I decide to drive a car while intoxicated, or run a red light, it increases the risk of an accident for other citizens even if my car is not involved. Similarly, if I take a mind-altering drug that makes me more dangerous, it increases the threat to other people who had no part in my decision.

Furthermore, what happens when hurting myself also harms my family or threatens social order? For example, what if a father smokes marijuana, and as a consequence lacks the motivation to hold a job? This personal decision will harm his life, along with his wife and children, and they will have to rely more on government benefits. Even if this person is single, they may end up homeless, desperate, and more likely to steal from others to survive. In other words, personal decisions can harm people other than the individual making the choice. If personal decisions are harmful to the larger society, the government may be justified in limiting or banning that behavior.

Of course, this line of reasoning potentially leads down a slippery slope to government oppression. There is little doubt that regular physical exercise is good for people, and that high-calorie foods are less healthy than vegetables. Is the government justified in *banning* fast food, and forcing people to eat vegetables and exercise regularly? Such a policy may make individuals healthier and happier, while reducing overall health care costs, but the cost would be some people's freedom to live their lives as they desire. Freedom requires that people have the ability to make poor decisions. As a society, we must allow people the freedom to make choices, even when we personally believe that their choice is wrong.

The challenge for policymakers is to balance individual freedom with social good. It is not enough to say that taking a drug is bad. To make the drug illegal, one has to show that it has a negative effect on others or society at large. That is precisely where the marijuana legalization debate resides. Opponents of legalization argue that marijuana has risks beyond the user, while supporters argue that those risks are minimal, and that marijuana even benefits some people. Thus, the question of whether to legalize marijuana depends on the effects of the drug on users. Unfortunately, there is a great deal of uncertainty regarding how marijuana affects individuals and its ramifications for society.

The Effects of Marijuana

There are certainly times when it is appropriate for the government to ban drugs, but only when they have a substantially negative effect on society. For example, it is understandable to ban drugs that are highly addictive or could cause death from overdose. But marijuana is not highly addictive, and there has never been a reported death from marijuana overdose. Opponents argue that marijuana use acts as a gateway to more dangerous drugs. That is, using marijuana gets young people accustomed to the high it creates, which cause them to move on to more dangerous and addictive drugs. If marijuana is a gateway drug, it may worsen the nationwide drug epidemic.

Supporters of marijuana legalization dispute the gateway effect hypothesis, arguing that there is very little solid evidence that marijuana *causes* people to use more drugs. Although marijuana users are more likely to use other drugs (Fergusson et al. 2006), this may simply stem from a proclivity to use drugs rather than marijuana causing wider drug use (Morral et al. 2002). If marijuana did not exist, would those people have moved on to the harder drug anyway? The prohibition of marijuana also helps explain evidence for the gateway effect because marijuana users enter into situations where more dangerous drugs are available and encouraged (Hall and Lynskey 2005). Marijuana prohibition pushes many users to find a drug dealer, who often offers them more dangerous drugs. More scientific evidence is needed to sort out whether marijuana is a gateway drug, but as it stands the evidence is not conclusive in either direction.

Opponents of marijuana legalization argue that use of the drug has negative consequences beyond the gateway effect. Marijuana could potentially lower long-term motivation, which could increase unemployment and decrease worker productivity. Supporters of legalization argue that marijuana only lowers motivation when people are high on the drug, but does not affect long-term motivation in users. In fact, many collegiate athletes have chosen to use marijuana over alcohol because the former does not cause a hangover. Few would consider professional athletes to be lazy, at least compared to ordinary Americans.

Another side effect of marijuana is its potential to cause mental disorders and reduce intelligence. Opponents point to studies showing that smoking marijuana makes users less intelligent, and the effects remain even after people stop using. Using marijuana is associated with an 8–10 point drop in I.Q. over the course of 20 years, which is sufficient to move someone from the 50th to the 30th percentile (Evins 2014). Marijuana use also increases the likelihood of schizophrenia and psychosis among those with genetic predispositions. Finally, roughly 9 percent of marijuana users become addicted to the drug, while many others suffer withdrawal symptoms that can include cravings, insomnia, anxiety and depression (Evins 2014).

Another point of contention in the legalization debate is the potential effects on minors who may be more likely to use the drug if it is legalized. Supporters of legalization point out that marijuana will still be illegal to anyone under 21 years of age. Indeed, all of the states that have legalized marijuana still prohibit its possession to minors. Additionally, supporters argue minors already use the drug, and will likely use it regardless of its legality. These assurances aside, opponents of legalization argue that removing the ban would normalize marijuana use, sending a message to young people that it is acceptable to use the drug. The danger in this scenario is that marijuana has its most negative health effects on adolescents, whose brains are still developing.

Supporters of legalization argue that marijuana has minimal consequences for users, especially compared to drugs that are already legal, such as tobacco and alcohol. When it comes to personal health, tobacco is more addictive and poses more dangers than marijuana (Boffey 2014). Additionally, alcohol abuse can result in overdose, drunk driving, and long-term dependence at a far greater rate than marijuana. Supporters of legalization argue that it makes no sense for people to be thrown in jail for using a drug that is, by all accounts, safer than tobacco and alcohol. One could imagine someone wishing to use marijuana to cope with high anxiety, but since it is illegal, they end up relying on alcohol to self-medicate. Granted, neither drug is a good option, but shouldn't individuals have the option to choose a safer drug to deal with their anxiety or depression?

Prisons, Schools, and Taxes

Supporters also argue that legalizing marijuana would help to reduce the over-crowded prisons across America. If marijuana were legal, fewer citizens would be put in jail for possession of the drug, and current prisoners could possibly be released. Reducing prison populations would lower the cost for taxpayers and would keep families together. Too often families are ripped apart when one of them is sent to prison for marijuana possession. Although many states have decriminalized marijuana—making it a crime punishable by a fine, but not jail time—other states still put citizens in jail for possession. When a young person goes to jail for possession, it has lifelong effects, because they will have a harder time getting a job with a felony on their record. If a parent is sent to jail, they will not be around for their children, which can have long-term developmental consequences.

Opponents of legalization argue that many of the people in prison for marijuana are repeat violent offenders. Rarely are people in jail for possession of a small amount of marijuana. Instead, jails are filled with dealers who would be selling other drugs if marijuana were legal. Furthermore, marijuana legalization could increase prison populations in the long term because it will increase high school dropouts and unemployment, which in turn will lead users to a life of crime and dependence on more addictive drugs.

Legalizing marijuana also has potential economic benefits. Marijuana has the potential to increase government revenue if it were taxed at a high rate, as alcohol and cigarettes currently are (Caputo and Ostrom 1994). The more money that comes in through marijuana taxes, the more money it will free up to pay for public education, law enforcement, and possibly lower income and sales taxes. In 2015, taxes and fees from the marijuana industry added $135 billion to Colorado's state revenue (Miller 2016). Legalizing marijuana could also boost the economy by creating jobs for marijuana growers and distributers. If marijuana were legal, it would create a boon in job growth across the country. In 2016, the marijuana industry is expected to contribute roughly $17 billion to the U.S. economy, and that is expected to grow to as much as $44 billion by 2020 (Schepp 2016). Perhaps more importantly, legalizing marijuana would shift the drug into the legal market and away from the black market. Instead of drug dealers profiting off of the drug, entrepreneurs would have the ability to create jobs and spur economic growth. Taking marijuana out of the black market would also make the drug safer because drug dealers would not be able to lace marijuana with more addictive drugs, nor would it force users to interact with drug dealers which may facilitate access to more dangerous drugs.

Opponents of marijuana legalization argue that the economic benefits described above are fool's gold. Marijuana may bring in additional revenue initially, but increased use of the drug among the populace will increase demand for unemployment benefits, welfare, prisons (as discussed above), foster care, and health care. The costs of these long-term strains on social services will dwarf any short-term benefits to state budgets. Once again, the debate over marijuana legalization depends on the consequences of its use, which can potentially be answered by future empirical research on the states that have already legalized it.

Federalism

Regardless of one's opinion about whether marijuana should be legal, there is a separate question about which level of government should make that decision. Currently, the federal Controlled Substance Act classifies marijuana as a schedule I drug, and therefore prohibits its sale or possession in any state. Although states have legalized marijuana for recreational use, it is still illegal under federal law. Supporters of legalization have called for Congress to legalize marijuana on the federal level, which would allow every state to decide the question. In a similar fashion, prostitution is not illegal under federal law, but instead is left to each individual state to decide its legality. With the exception of Nevada, every state has chosen to make prostitution illegal. Many argue that marijuana legalization should be decided in the same manner, by the voters of each state. Another benefit of repealing the federal ban would be that states could act as *laboratories of democracy*. Some states could legalize marijuana and other states could monitor whether the policy was a success. States can experiment with different policies, with successful policies getting adopted by other states. Conversely, if marijuana legalization turns out to have all the negative consequences that opponents predict, it will only affect citizens in one state rather than the entire country.

Opponents of federal legalization argue that legalizing marijuana in one state will make it more difficult for every other state to control the drug. If marijuana can be grown legally in Colorado, it will be easier to transport the drug to neighboring states such as Wyoming, Kansas or Nebraska. Since it is impractical to set up checkpoints on every road crossing state lines, it would be very easy for citizens to cross state lines to buy the drug and then return home. Additionally, citizens in Wyoming could cross the border into Colorado to legally smoke marijuana and then return to Wyoming while high. Opponents argue that a federal marijuana ban is needed to prevent the laws in one state from affecting citizens in other states. Once again, there is a conflict between freedom of choice and harm to others. In theory, states should have the freedom to set their own policies, but those policies usually have consequences for other states, which potentially makes it a national issue.

Review Questions

1. What types of people are more likely to support legalizing marijuana?
2. What are the benefits of legalizing marijuana?
3. How does marijuana affect the health of users?
4. How does marijuana legalization play into the larger debate over federalism?

Discussion Questions

1. Why have Americans become more supportive of legalizing marijuana in recent years?
2. Do you believe marijuana use poses a substantial harm to users?
3. Should the federal government ban drug possession or should it be left up to the states?
4. Should people be sent to prison for drug possession?
5. Is there a racial bias in drug laws in this country?

Sources for Further Inquiry

Books

Boggs, Carl. 2015. *Drugs, Power, and Politics: Narco Wars, Big Pharma, and the Subversion of Democracy*. New York, NY: Routledge.

Caulkins, Jonathan P., Beau Kilmer, and Mark A.R. Kleiman. 2016. *Marijuana Legalization: What Everyone Needs to Know?* New York, NY: Oxford University Press.

Gaines, Larry K., and Janine Kremling. 2013. *Drugs, Crime, and Justice: Contemporary Perspectives*. Long Grove, IL: Waveland Press.

Gerber, Rudolph J. 2004. *Legalizing Marijuana: Drug Policy Reform and Prohibition Politics*. Westport CT: Praeger Publishers.

Tate, Katherine, James Lance Taylor, and Mark Q. Sawyer, eds. 2013. *Something's in the Air: Race, Crime, and the Legalization of Marijuana*. New York, NY: Routledge.

Journal and Newspaper Articles

Bloom, Max. 2017, June 19. "A Bad Argument for Legalizing Marijuana." *National Review*. Retrieved from http://www.nationalreview.com/article/448757/legalizing-marijuana-debate-shouldnt-revolve-around-pots-prohibition

Gwynne, Kristen. 2013, June 27. "Five Reasons Cops Want to Legalize Marijuana." *Rolling Stone*. Retrieved from http://www.rollingstone.com/politics/news/five-reason s-cops-want-to-legalize-marijuana-20130627.

Hamblin, James. 2018, June 22. "The New Model for a Health-First Approach to Legalizing Weed." *The Atlantic*. Retrieved from https://www.theatlantic.com/health/a rchive/2018/06/what-canada-is-doing-right-with-marijuana/563279/

Kerr, David CR, Harold Bae, Sandi Phibbs, and Adam C. Kern. 2017. "Changes in Undergraduates' Marijuana, Heavy Alcohol and Cigarette Use Following Legalization of Recreational Marijuana Use in Oregon." *Addiction* 112(11): 1992–2001.

Nemko, Marty. 2014, Nov. 7. "Legalize Pot? You Must Be High." *Time*. Retrieved from http://time.com/3573394/legalize-pot-you-must-be-high/

Lowrey, Annie. 2018, August 20. "America's Invisible Pot Addicts." *The Atlantic*. Retrieved from https://www.theatlantic.com/health/archive/2018/08/americas-invisi ble-pot-addicts/567886/

Miron, Jeffrey. 2014, Nov. 19. "Why Congress should legalize pot." CNN. Retrieved from http://www.cnn.com/2014/11/19/opinion/miron-marijuana-legalization/

Schwadel, Philip, and Christopher G. Ellison. 2017. "Period and Cohort Changes in Americans' Support for Marijuana Legalization: Convergence and Divergence across Social Groups." *The Sociological Quarterly* 58(3): 1–24.

References

Boffey, Philip M. 2014, July 30. "What Science Says About Marijuana." *New York Times*. Retrieved from http://www.nytimes.com/2014/07/31/opinion/what-science-says-a bout-marijuana.html?opinion-series

Caputo, Michael R., and Brian J. Ostrom. 1994. "Potential Tax Revenue from a Regulated Marijuana Market a Meaningful Revenue Source." *The American Journal of Economics & Sociology* 53(4): 475–490.

Evins, Eden. 2014, June 5. "Marijuana is a Risky Habit We Shouldn't Encourage." *New York Times*. Retrieved from http://www.nytimes.com/roomfordebate/2013/05/22/ how-can-marijuana-be-sold-safely/marijuana-is-a-risky-habit-we-shouldnt-encourage

Fergusson, David M., Joseph M. Boden, and John Horwood. 2006. "Cannabis Use and Other Illicit Drug Use: Testing the Cannabis Gateway Hypothesis." *Addiction* 101(4): 556–569.

Hall, Wayne D., and Michael Lynskey. 2005. "Is Cannabis a Gateway Drug? Testing Hypotheses about the Relationship between Cannabis Use and the Use of Other Illicit Drugs." *Drug and Alcohol Review* 24(1): 39–48.

Jones, Jeffrey M. (2015, Oct. 21). In U.S., 58% Back LegalMarijuana Use. *Gallup*. Retrieved from http://www.gallup.com/poll/186260/back-legal-marijuana.aspx

McCarthy, Justin. 2017, October 25. "Record-High Support for Legalizing Marijuana Use in the U.S." Gallup.com. Retrieved from http://news.gallup.com/poll/221018/record-high-supp ort-legalizing-marijuana.aspx?g_source=POLITICS&g_medium=topic&g_campaign=tiles

Miller, Joshua. 2016, February 22. "In Colorado, a Look at Life after Marijuana Legalization." *Boston Globe*. Retrieved from https://www.bostonglobe.com/metro/2016/02/21/from -colorado-glimpse-life-after-marijuana-legalization/rcccuzhMDWV74UC4IxXIYJ/story. html

Morral, Andrew R., Daniel F. McCaffrey, and Susan M. Paddock. 2002. "Reassessing the Marijuana Gateway Effect." *Addiction* 97(12): 1493–1504.

Public Broadcasting Service. n.d. "Marijuana Timeline." Retrieved from http://www.pbs. org/wgbh/pages/frontline/shows/dope/etc/cron.html

Schepp, David. 2016, March 18. "Legal Marijuana: A $44 Billion Business by 2020?" CBS News. Retrieved from http://www.cbsnews.com/news/legal-marijuana -a-44-billion-business-by-2020/

Sullum, Jacob. 2014, Apr. 3. "More Pot, Safer Roads: Marijuana Legalization Could Bring Unexpected Benefits." Forbes. Retrieved from http://www.forbes.com/sites/jacobsullum/ 2014/04/03/more-pot-safer-roads-marijuana-legalization-could-bring-unexpected-bene fits/print/

10

SHOULD UNIVERSITIES ENCOURAGE AFFIRMATIVE ACTION POLICIES?

The Declaration of Independence states that all men are created equal, but throughout the history of the United States, all men and women have not been *treated* equally. The U.S. Constitution protected slavery for at least 20 years after ratification, mandated the extradition of runaway slaves, and rewarded states with high populations of slaves with more representation in the House of Representatives. After the 13th Amendment abolished slavery, state governments enacted systematic policies of discrimination toward blacks and other minorities. Racial segregation of public schools was legal until 1954, when the U.S. Supreme Court issued their ruling in *Brown v. Board of Education* that banned segregation of all public facilities. Of course, blacks are not the only group to face discrimination from federal and state governments. Women did not get the right to vote nationwide until the 19th Amendment in 1920. Government policies have also discriminated against racial and ethnic groups including Native Americans, Chinese, Mexicans, and Japanese Americans. For some, these acts of discrimination perpetuated inequalities for particular social groups.

Affirmative action is the intentional policy of encouraging diversity in hiring and college enrollment. The purpose of affirmative action policies is to help overcome past injustices towards minorities, which continue to diminish opportunities for those groups. The term "affirmative action" was used by President John F. Kennedy, who signed executive order 10925 that required federal contractors to take "affirmative action to ensure that applicants are treated equally without regard to race, color, religion, sex, or national origin." Following Kennedy, President Lyndon Johnson signed executive order 11246, which required government contractors to "take affirmative action" to promote equality in their hiring practices and to provide documentation of these efforts. In a speech to Howard University, President Lyndon Johnson famously said the following:

You do not take a person who, for years, has been hobbled by chains and liberate him, bring him up to the starting line of a race and then say you are free to compete with all the others, and still just believe that you have been completely fair. Thus it is not enough just to open the gates of opportunity. All our citizens must have the ability to walk through those gates.

(Johnson 1966)

The affirmative action policies of many universities came under scrutiny from students who felt they were denied acceptance to their preferred school simply because of the color of their skin. The United States Supreme Court stepped into this conflict with its landmark decision in the case *Regents of the University of California v. Bakke* (1978), in which the court ruled that race could be used as one of many factors in college admissions, but universities could not reserve a set number of seats for minority students—otherwise known as quotas. Years later, the Court's decision in *Gratz v. Bollinger* (2003) ruled that universities could not award points based on race, but in the same year the court ruled in *Grutter v. Bollinger* (2003) that graduate schools could consider race if their goal was to ensure diversity. In the majority opinion in the *Grutter* case, Justice Sandra Day O'Connor argued that universities have a compelling interest to ensure that students have exposure to the perspectives of minority groups, and therefore, affirmative action policies were constitutional as long as the policy was narrowly tailored to establish a critical threshold of diversity.

Do affirmative action policies discriminate against white applicants? Does affirmative action do more harm than good for minorities? Supporters of affirmative action argue that it helps overcome past injustices towards racial minorities and promotes diversity on college campuses. Opponents argue that affirmative action is less necessary today than in the past, and it constitutes discrimination against whites. In this chapter, I first explain how disagreement over affirmative action stems from opposing conceptions of equality. I then discuss how unconscious and unintentional prejudices can create inequalities in how people are treated in college admission, the workforce, and society more broadly.

Formal and Substantive Equality

In the disagreement over affirmative action, each side invokes the principle of equality, but they define it in very different ways. Opponents of affirmative action argue that it is enough to provide *formal equality* to women and racial minorities. That is, formal equality occurs when the law treats everyone the same regardless of their race, religion or sex. Striving for formal equality demands a level playing field that is not intentionally favorable toward any one group. As an analogy, formal equality is the goal when designing the rules for athletic competitions. The rules are not supposed to systematically favor one person or team over another. Of course, some people will be born with more athletic ability than others, and they will perform better. Some teams will be from larger markets and will be able to attract better players through free agency. Even weather advantages some teams over others. Would you rather play half your games in southern California or Wisconsin? Formal equality ignores all of those factors that might advantage some teams or groups over others, and simply provides the same *opportunity* to everyone.

Supporters of affirmative action argue that formal equality is insufficient because it ignores social inequalities that advantage some groups of people. The problem with formal equality is that it is largely blind to existing inequalities in society that make it more difficult for members of some groups to compete on a level playing field. In other words, treating everyone as if they are equal is actually unfair to those groups from unequal backgrounds. Supporters of affirmative action argue that the government should promote a more *substantive equality* by helping minorities to overcome social inequalities. Formal equality ignores the inequality in the current playing field, and thus puts minorities at a disadvantage. If whites have existing advantages that make them more likely to succeed, formal equality will inevitably result in inequality in social outcomes such as college admissions and employment opportunities.

There is little doubt that groups advanced by affirmative action face more difficult paths to success. For most of this country's history, blacks were subjected to systematic oppression by both laws and social norms. State laws affecting public schools and employment created economic disparities between men and women, and blacks and whites. Even today, there is an abundance of evidence that women and racial minorities do not have the same economic opportunities as white males. For example, public schools with higher percentages of blacks receive less funding than predominantly white schools (Spatig-Amerikaner 2012; White 2015). As a result, blacks are less likely to attend college after high school and less likely to graduate within six years (Cook 2015). Although women have made recent advances in educational attainment, they still face systematic discrimination in the workplace.

Opponents of affirmative action also believe in equality of opportunity, but they support a meritocracy where jobs and college admissions are awarded to the most deserving candidate. Although it may be tempting for affirmative action supporters to label opponents as heartless and blind to existing inequalities, this would be a straw-man argument. Opposing affirmative action does not require denial of existing inequalities between blacks and whites. It is perfectly consistent to support improving opportunities for poor and disadvantaged children, while opposing affirmative action for adults.

Not all minorities are from impoverished backgrounds, nor are all whites born into privilege. For example, some research suggests that affirmative action at elite institutions mostly benefits minorities from upper-middle-class backgrounds, who are unlikely to face the same challenges as *whites* from low-income families (Sander and Taylor 2012). The main problem with affirmative action is that it treats race and ethnicity as the defining characteristic rather than hard work and merit. Affirmative action punishes whites for the color of their skin, regardless of how hard they worked or how much adversity they had to overcome. White students are being punished for the actions of their ancestors, when they may or may not have benefited from their skin color. Keeping skin color as the defining characteristic of affirmative action continues to treat people as members of racial groups rather than as equal human beings.

Stereotypes and Prejudice

One of the difficulties in talking about affirmative action, or civil rights more broadly, is that few people believe that they are racist or prejudiced. What we often fail to understand is that prejudice can result from perfectly normal mental processes that our minds developed to help us survive. We are prejudiced anytime we prejudge someone, but the human mind is naturally inclined to make judgments about other people based on their superficial characteristics. Our minds classify objects into groups, and we use what we know about the groups to understand the individual object. For example, imagine you are walking through the woods and noticed a furry animal. Assuming that you have never seen this particular animal before, your mind will first seek to classify it into a group of animals that you know something about. You will then use your knowledge of the group of animals to predict its behavior, and then determine your best course of action. Whether you classify this animal as a bear, deer, rabbit, or wolf, will make a huge difference to how you react.

Stereotypes are simply our set of stored knowledge about a group of people or a classification of objects. We may have varying stereotypes about people with dark skin, blue eyes, who are tall, short, attractive, thin, etc. When we meet a new person that holds one of these characteristics, our minds automatically attribute our knowledge of the group to the individuals. As we saw in the example above, this is usually a useful process, and our stereotypes allow us to make good judgments without much information about the particular individuals.

Of course, stereotypes can also be very destructive when they are based on incorrect or insufficient information, or when we overgeneralize group stereotypes to individual members. While it is fairly safe and cautious to assume that a bear is dangerous until learning otherwise, it is altogether different to assume that anyone with a tattoo is dangerous because you have some preconceived notion that bad people have tattoos. Likewise, if someone believes that black people are more likely to be felons, they are not justified in assuming that any new black person they meet is a felon. Indeed, stereotypes are often based on incomplete and incorrect information about the group, which is then applied to the next individual we meet that holds that characteristic. Altogether, stereotypes of other social groups are the basis for prejudice, racism and religious intolerance.

Now imagine a police officer who encounters a person who reaches into their jacket pocket. The police officer must make a prediction about whether that person is reaching for a gun or a cell phone. The officer is likely to make different predictions about their intentions depending on whether the person is a wearing a suit, is young, looks poor, or is black, white or Hispanic. Our predictions of other people's behavior occur largely outside of our conscious awareness. It is naïve to think that people encounter each new individual without making any prejudgments based their similarities to other groups of people. This is what causes prejudice in everyday life. Of course, some people will say that they treat everyone equally, but we cannot possibly know this for sure, because it happens largely outside of our conscious awareness.

We also rarely recognize when we benefit from the prejudices of others. Wealthy people *want to believe* that they got ahead because of hard work and determination, and by implication the poor just need to work harder. Physically attractive people rarely seem to recognize how their looks benefit them, and some even complain that their appearance is a burden because people do not take them seriously. Rarely do we acknowledge, or even recognize, how we benefit from our natural advantages. If someone from a wealthy school district never attends a poor school, they will have a hard time understanding just how much they benefit from their situation. Instead, we tend to focus on the ways we may be disadvantaged, without ever acknowledging how we may benefit from our race, sex, height, economic background, or natural intelligence.

As an example, consider how stereotypes associated with someone's name can affect their economic opportunities. An interesting study sent out identical applications with either traditional white-sounding names or African-American sounding names (Bertrand and Mullainathan 2004). Applications with white-sounding names received *50 percent* more calls for interviews than the identical applications with African-American sounding names. Supporters of affirmative action argue that ignoring existing racial divisions in American society is to pretend that racial prejudice has not existed and does not exist. Affirmative action policies are meant to help overcome some of the social inequalities that are faced by minorities.

What are we to do? If we carry implicit prejudices, should we never make judgments? Of course not! We all have to do our best to recognize our own misconceptions and stereotypes; but ultimately, we may never know if we discriminated against someone because of the characteristics they hold. Supporters of affirmative action argue that the only way to counteract discrimination is to understand the groups that are most likely to suffer from it, and enact policies and programs that promote equal outcomes for disadvantaged groups. If people in society hold stereotypes that cause them to unwittingly discriminate against people based on their skin color, affirmative action is the best way to ensure equality.

Of course, many opponents of affirmative action would argue that it increases implicit biases by stigmatizing successful blacks. When a black person succeeds, there will be those who think that she was an affirmative action hire, which implies that she did not deserve the job or admission to a prestigious university. On a related note, affirmative action can lower the self-esteem of minorities by treating them as if they need help to succeed. Treating everyone equally allows minorities to feel pride that they succeeded on a level playing field, without any advantages given to them simply because of their sex or the color of their skin. Affirmative action serves to perpetuate negative stereotypes about minorities by suggesting that they need help and cannot succeed without government assistance.

The Mismatch Problem

Another prominent argument against affirmative action is that it actually hurts the very people it is supposed to benefit. Some research suggests that affirmative action creates a mismatch between students and their educational environment. In brief, affirmative action helps minority students get admitted to schools that they would not have been admitted to based entirely on academic merit. Consequently, many minority students are entering colleges with rigorous educational standards that they are not prepared to meet, and they find themselves unable to keep up with their fellow students. The mismatch problem results in minority students failing to complete college at the top universities when they probably would have done well at different colleges that did not assume a high level of academic preparation.

Affirmative action can also cause long-term damage to the self-esteem of minority students, and perpetuate the myth that they are not as intelligent as whites. When affirmative action policies place students with a lower level of academic preparation into a college that assumes they have a high level of preparation, they are setting them up for failure. After minority students cannot keep up with others, they assume that they are less intelligent than the white students, who happen to come from better high schools. Sanders and Taylor (2012) make this point well in the following example:

> Think back to high school and recall a subject at which you did fine but did not excel. Suppose you had suddenly been transferred into an advanced class in that subject with a friend who was about at your level and 18 other students who excelled in the subject *and* had already taken the intermediate course you just skipped. You would, in all likelihood, soon be struggling to keep up. The teacher might give you some extra attention but, in class, would be focusing on the median student, not you and your friend, and would probably be covering the material at what, to you, was a bewildering pace.

Wouldn't you have quickly fallen behind and then continued to fall farther and farther behind as the school year progressed? Now assume that you
and the friend who joined you at the bottom of that class were both black
and everyone else was Asian or white. How would that have felt? Might you
have imagined that this could reinforce in the minds of your classmates the
stereotype that blacks are weak students?

(Sander and Taylor 2012)

Opponents of affirmative action argue that this is an all too common situation
whenever universities use admissions criteria other than academic merit. A better
idea is to place students in colleges where they have the best chance to succeed,
which is precisely the purpose of merit-based admissions systems. Instead of
affirmative action, a more effective policy would be to provide minorities with a
better education prior to the university level. Trying to fix inequality at the university level is far too late in the process.

Review Questions

1. What did the Supreme Court rule about the constitutionality of affirmative
    action?
2. How can a policy be unequal if it treats everyone equally?
3. Why do stereotypes often create unintentional and unconscious prejudices?
4. How might eliminating affirmative action help change stereotypes of
    minorities?
5. What is the mismatch problem in higher education?

Discussion Questions

1. Do you believe that racial quotas are unconstitutional?
2. Would an income-based affirmative action program be preferable to a
    race-based program?
3. What kinds of stereotypes do people probably hold about you?
4. Have you ever been disadvantaged because of other people's stereotypes?
5. How might stereotypes help explain racial disparities in police shootings?

Sources for Further Inquiry

Books

Ibarra, Robert A. 2001. *Beyond Affirmative Action: Reframing the Context of Higher Education.*
Madison, WI: University of Wisconsin Press.
Lauren, Paul Gordon. 2018. *Power and Prejudice: The Politics and Diplomacy of Racial Dis-
crimination.* New York, NY: Routledge.

Reay, Diane, Miriam E. David, and Stephen J. Ball. 2005. *Degrees of Choice: Class, Race, Gender and Higher Education*. Stoke on Trent: Trentham Books.

Reich, Michael. 2017. *Racial Inequality: A Political-economic Analysis*. Princeton, NJ: Princeton University Press.

Sowell, Thomas. 2004. *Affirmative Action around the World: An Empirical Study*. New Haven, CT: Yale University Press.

Sterba, James P. 2009. *Affirmative Action for the Future*. Ithaca, NY: Cornell University Press.

Journal and Newspaper Articles

Harris, Angel L. 2014, April 27. "Wealth-based Affirmative Action May Be the Best Alternative to Racial Preference." *New York Times*. Retrieved from https://www.nytimes.com/roomfor debate/2014/04/27/should-affirmative-action-be-based-on-income/wealth-based-affirma tive-action-may-be-the-best-alternative-to-racial-preference

Higginbotham, F.Michael. 2014, April 27. "Race-based Affirmative Action Is Still Needed." *New York Times*. Retrieved from https://www.nytimes.com/roomfordebate/ 2014/04/27/should-affirmative-action-be-based-on-income/race-based-affirmative-action- is-still-needed

Kahlenburg, Richard D. 2012, October 3. "A New Kind of Affirmative Action Can Ensure Diversity." *The Chronicle of Higher Education*. Retrieved from https://www. chronicle.com/article/A-New-Kind-of-Affirmative/134840

Kateri-Hernández, Tanya. 2014, April 27. "'Stereotype Threat' Is Not Easily Countered Without Affirmative Action." *New York Times*. Retrieved from https://www.nytimes. com/roomfordebate/2014/04/27/should-affirmative-action-be-based-on-income/stereo type-threat-is-not-easily-countered-without-affirmative-action

Navarrette, Ruben. 2014, April 24. "Why a Minority Opposes Affirmative Action." CNN.com. Retrieved from https://www.cnn.com/2014/04/24/opinion/navarrette-a ffirmative-action/index.html

Sander, Richard, and StuartTaylor Jr. 2012, October 2. "The Painful Truth about Affir- mative Action." *The Atlantic*. Retrieved from https://www.theatlantic.com/national/a rchive/2012/10/the-painful-truth-about-affirmative-action/263122/

Strauss, David A. 2016. "Fisher v University of Texas and the Conservative Case for Affirmative Action." *The Supreme Court Review* 1: 1–24.

Strauss, Valerie. 2017, August 2. "Actually, we Still Need Affirmative Action for African Americans in College Admissions. Here's Why." *The Washington Post*. Retrieved from https://www.washingtonpost.com/news/answer-sheet/wp/2017/08/02/actua lly-we-still-need-affirmative-action-for-african-americans-in-college-admissions-her es-why/?utm_term=.697cc1194672

References

Bertrand, Marianne, and Sendhil Mullainathan. 2004. "Are Emily and Greg more Employable than Lakisha and Jamal? A Field Experiment on Labor Market Discrimina- tion." *American Economic Review* 94(4): 991–1013.

Brown v. Board of Education, 347 U. S. 483(1954).

Cook, Lindsey. 2015, January 20. "U.S. Education: Still Separate and Unequal. "*U.S. News and World Report*. Retrieved from http://www.usnews.com/news/blogs/data -mine/2015/01/28/us-education-still-separate-and-unequal

Gratz v. Bollinger, 539 U.S. 244(2003).

Grutter v. Bollinger, 539 U. S. 306(2003).

Johnson, Lyndon B. 1966. "Commencement Address at Howard University: 'To Fulfill These Rights,' June 4, 1965." In *Public Papers of the Presidents of the United States: Lyndon B. Johnson, 1965*, Vol. 2. Washington D.C.: Government Printing Office, 635–640.

Regents of Univ. of Cal. v. Bakke, 438 U. S. 265(1978).

Sander, Richard, and StuartTaylor Jr. 2012, October 2. "The Painful Truth about Affirmative Action." *The Atlantic.* Retrieved from https://www.theatlantic.com/national/archive/2012/10/the-painful-truth-about-affirmative-action/263122/

Spatig-Amerikaner, Ary. 2012. "Unequal Education: Federal Loophole Enables Lower Spending on Students of Color." Center for American Progress. Retrieved from https://cdn.americanprogress.org/wp-content/uploads/2012/08/UnequalEduation.pdf

White, Gillian B. 2015, September 30. "The Data are Damning: How Race Influences School Funding. "*The Atlantic.* Retrieved from https://www.theatlantic.com/business/archive/2015/09/public-school-funding-and-the-role-of-race/408085/

11

SHOULD ILLEGAL IMMIGRANTS BE GRANTED WORK VISAS?

America has had a complicated history when it comes to immigration. On the one hand, America was founded by immigrants and has been a melting pot of different races, cultures, ethnicities, and religions. For generations, immigrants have embodied the American spirit of hard work and individualism. On the other hand, U.S. history books are filled with examples of prejudice and discrimination against immigrants. Many of the founding fathers were concerned about the dangers immigration posed to America's national identity. For example, Alexander Hamilton argued that foreigners would not embody the love of liberty that a Republican form of government requires (see Rampell 2015; "Alexander Hamilton" 2010). Only a few years after the Constitution was ratified, Congress passed the *Naturalization Act* of 1790, which limited immigration to "free white persons [of] good moral character" (Smith 2002). Nearly a century later, Congress passed the *Chinese Exclusion Act* (1882) that banned Chinese laborers from immigrating to the United States (Chinese Exclusion Act 1882). In order to restrict immigration from Eastern Europe, Congress passed *The Immigration Act* of 1924, which limited new annual immigration to 2 percent of that country's population that already lived in the United States (Smith 2002). Although the target group frequently changes, the United States has repeatedly tried to restrict immigrants based entirely on their country of origin. This practice changed in 1965, when the *Immigration and Naturalization Act* made one's country of origin less important—in determining priority for legal immigration—than promoting family unification, attracting high-skilled workers, and allowing refugees from war-torn countries (History.com 2010).

More recently, the immigration debate has centered on how to handle the millions of people who entered the United States illegally or overstayed their temporary visas. In 1986, the *Immigration Reform and Control Act* was intended to limit the rise of illegal immigration (Immigration Reform and Control Act of

1986). The act granted amnesty to illegal immigrants already in the country, increased border security and imposed penalties on businesses that hired illegal workers (Plumer 2013; Nyce and Bodenner 2016). Implementation of the law fell short when it came to border security, while the penalties for businesses proved too weak and ineffective (Plumer 2013). Despite the intention of the law, illegal immigration more than *doubled* from roughly 3.5 million unauthorized immigrants in 1990 to over 7 million by the year 2000 (U.S. Immigration and Naturalization Service 2000). By 2010, there were 11.6 million illegal immigrants living in the United States (Baker 2014). What to do with the millions of illegal immigrants and their children—many of whom are now U.S. citizens—has become one of the most important questions in American politics.

One potential solution to the immigration problem is to establish a national guest worker program that would allow current illegal immigrants the ability to work in the country legally as long as they were employed. A guest worker program is by no means a new idea. During World War II, an agreement between the United States and Mexican governments established the *Bracero Program*, which was intended to alleviate labor shortages particularly in the farming industry. The Bracero Program lasted over two decades (1942–1964) and resulted in roughly 4.5 million Mexicans being admitted to the United States on temporary work visas (Rural Migration News 2006). The program was eventually ended because of strong objections from labor unions who argued that it resulted in fewer jobs and lower wages for American citizens.

In January 2004, President George W. Bush proposed a sweeping guest worker program that would grant legal status for immigrants who were currently residing in the United States illegally (Bush 2004). The program would allow workers to get a work visa that lasted three years, but was renewable as long as the worker could show proof of employment. Guest workers could also apply for citizenship while they were on a guest worker visa (Bush 2004). Although the Bush plan was never passed, it was one of the few sweeping immigration proposals that had sub-stantial support among both Democrats and Republicans (Smith 2007). In fact, a more comprehensive version of a guest worker program passed the U.S. Senate in 2013 with support among both Democrats and Republicans (Kim 2013). Although the bill may have had sufficient bipartisan support to pass the U.S. House of Representatives, the Speaker of the House never brought the bill for a vote because it lacked support from a majority of Republicans in the chamber (NBC News 2014).

Not surprisingly, the debate over a guest worker program mirrors the larger debate over immigration in the United States. Opponents have consistently argued that a guest worker program would amount to amnesty for immigrants who entered the country illegally or over-stayed their visas. Granting legal status to illegal immi-grants would reward people for breaking the law, and encourage future immigrants to break the law when seeking to enter the country (Rosenzweig, Carafano and Kephart 2005). Additionally, opponents argue that a guest worker program would take jobs from American citizens, while increasing the cost of government programs such as public education, welfare, and food stamps (Smith 2007; Bumiller 2006). Meanwhile, supporters of a guest worker program argue it will prevent businesses from denying unauthorized workers a minimum wage, health benefits or workers' compensation. Indeed, a guest worker program would place all workers on an equal playing field regardless of their country of origin.

Principles vs. Pragmatism

The most prominent conflict in the immigration debate more broadly is between principles and pragmatism. Sometimes the most effective approach to solve a problem will conflict with our ideas about the perfect law. For example, someone might strongly oppose drug use while simultaneously supporting a government program that provides free sterilized needles. Likewise, a person's morals might dictate that teenagers should remain abstinent, but they nonetheless support public schools providing free condoms as a way to prevent STDs and unwanted pregnancies. There are countless other instances when the most pragmatic approach may not be the ideal policy in every conceivable way.

When it comes to immigration, some people's core principles come into conflict with what they believe is the most pragmatic approach to solve a social problem. Those opposing a guest worker program take the principled stance that people must respect the rule of law, and granting amnesty to illegal residents would reward law-breakers (Wright, Levy and Citrin 2016). Meanwhile, supporters of a guest worker program argue that it is not practical or ethical to deport millions of undocumented immigrants. While it is not ideal to reward law-breakers, it is also not ideal to rip apart families and deport children to countries they do not even remember. Similar to other policies discussed in this book, disagreement over amnesty is based on a *conflict between shared values* that most people hold to some extent. Hopefully, recognizing that opposing opinions are based on values that you hold will alleviate at least some of the animosity that you might feel toward people who disagree with your perspective.

Both sides of the immigration debate should question the consistency of their views when it comes to amnesty for illegal immigrants. Those supporting amnesty should consider the message that it sends to potential criminals. When criminals are not punished for their crimes, it encourages other people to commit the same crime. Opponents of amnesty for illegal immigrants point to the aftermath of the *Immigration Reform and Control Act* of 1986 as evidence that amnesty will encourage more illegal immigration. When illegal immigrants were rewarded amnesty in 1986, it sent a signal to other foreign workers that they would not be punished for entering the United States illegally. After all, why wait out a lengthy *legal* immigration process if the government will simply grant amnesty if you break the law? Surely, supporters of amnesty can understand why some people think it is a bad idea to reward people who broke the law.

As for amnesty opponents, it is worth considering whether they would apply the same "law and order" standard to all laws. It is easy to say that criminals should always be punished, but are your views on law breakers consistent regardless of the crime they commit or why they commit the crime? Lots of people break the law! They cheat on their taxes, use illegal drugs, get in fist fights, drive faster than the speed limit, etc. Former presidents of both parties have admitted to breaking the law, yet they were elected to the highest office in the country. George W. Bush admitted to drunk driving and conservatives twice elected him president of the United States. Both Bill Clinton and Barack Obama admitted to using illegal drugs, yet were still elected. We seem to be willing to forgive people who break the law. What opponents of amnesty must ask themselves, and only they can answer, is what is it about this *particular law* that makes them so unforgiving?

In the meantime, amnesty opponents should be able to empathize with those who have genuine concerns about deporting people for a crime they committed years ago. According to the Department of Homeland Security, roughly *75 percent* of all unauthorized immigrants have lived in the United States for more than 10 years (Baker 2014). That is a long time for unauthorized immigrants to have children and build strong bonds with their communities. Even if you oppose amnesty, I hope you can understand how some people believe it is the most practical way to deal with the current problem.

More Competition on a Level Field

The most important benefit of a guest worker program is that it would create a level playing field for both workers and businesses in the United States. Capitalism works best when businesses and workers compete by the same rules. Under the current immigration system, some businesses get a competitive advantage from employing illegal immigrants. The fear of deportation allows companies to take advantage of immigrants, which puts the businesses at a competitive advantage against businesses that follow the rules. In contrast, businesses that follow the law spend more on labor costs, which forces them to charge more for their products and services. Businesses that employ low-skilled labor, such as the agricultural and service industry, have an *incentive* to break the law. If immigration opponents truly care about respect for the rule of law, they should support a guest worker program that would take away the financial incentive for employers to break the law.

The current system also disadvantages American workers because they are more costly to employ than illegal immigrants. A guest worker program would protect all workers, and force companies to treat them equally regardless of national origin. When workers compete on a level playing field, rewards are distributed based on hard work rather than country of origin. From this perspective, American citizens should welcome a guest worker program because it would allow them to compete in a fair system. In short, a guest worker program would create a fairer competition for both workers and businesses inside the United States.

It is also important to consider the consequences of worker abuse for the actual immigrant workers. Try to remember that immigrants are mostly decent people, who are simply trying to provide for themselves and their families. It is immoral to allow businesses to abuse immigrant workers by forcing them to work long hours in poor conditions, while withholding health benefits, and denying workers' compensation for on-the-job injuries (Southern Poverty Law Center 2013). Previous guest worker programs resulted in abuse of immigrant workers precisely because legal status was contingent on employment (Gonzalez 2017). Guest workers knew they would be deported if they lost their job, which allowed companies to deny them the same rights and privileges as American workers (Chen 2017; Gutierrez 2016). In order to prevent such abuse, guest workers must be granted amnesty and provided legal status that is not contingent on current employment (Binford 2013). If guest workers are being treated unfairly, they must be able to leave their job or seek legal assistance without the threat of deportation. Otherwise, a new guest worker program will fail to protect immigrant workers from abuse, or to create a level playing field for businesses and workers.

One of the best ways to reduce political hostility is to try to understand the perspective of those who hold an opposing perspective. In the case of immigration, it is important to understand that one's perspective on the issue is heavily influenced by their position in the current economy. Those who have high-skilled jobs are less likely to feel threatened by immigration than low-skilled laborers who genuinely fear that they will lose their jobs. The fact is, a guest worker program would probably harm the job prospects of low-skilled workers, who are already having trouble adjusting to a new high-tech economy. It is no coincidence that the intense reaction to immigration over the last few decades has corresponded with fundamental changes in the American economy that favor those with more formal education and technical skills. In many ways, workers who survived in the 20th century economy, such as factory workers, small farmers, and small retail shop owners, have been the hardest hit by the new economy where seemingly everything revolves around the internet. Before highly educated professionals cast aspersions on those who oppose immigration, it is important to try to understand the real anxiety they feel toward an influx of low-skilled laborers who will compete for their jobs.

Opponents of a guest worker program argue that increasing the supply of labor would take jobs away from American citizens and prevent them from bargaining for higher wages. New immigrants take jobs from Americans by increasing competition in the workforce. The easier it is for businesses to find low skilled labor, the less incentive they have to increase the pay for current workers in order to retain their services (Borjas 2016). It is difficult for workers to ask for higher wages when they know that there are thousands of people waiting for their jobs who are willing to get paid less money to do the same work. Many believe that good jobs should go to American citizens first, while immigrants can take jobs that Americans are either unwilling or unable to fill.

Why should American citizens have a competitive advantage over non-citizens in the job market? It seems that Americans often take this as an unquestioned assumption, a starting point in every discussion of immigration. The current immigration system is rigged in favor of people who were lucky enough to be born in the United States, and against people who did not inherit that same privilege. Is it right to give advantage to people based on luck rather than hard work and talent? A guest worker program is more consistent with American values because it does not give favor to people because they got lucky. Essentially, opponents of a guest worker program must argue that Americans are *entitled* to an advantage simply because they were born in the United States. How is this any different than affirmative action policies that give jobs to people simply because they were born black or female? Citizenship, skin color, and gender, are all determined at birth and have absolutely nothing to do with a person's qualification for most jobs. Why is it wrong to punish white people for their skin color, but perfectly acceptable to punish foreign workers because of where they were born? If you truly believe that jobs should be awarded based on merit, you should support a guest worker program.

Are Immigrants a Drain or Boon to Government Programs?

Opponents of a guest worker program argue that it is not only low-skilled workers who should fear an influx of legal immigrants. If a guest worker program provided legal status to the roughly 11 million people here illegally, it would put a strain on government programs that are already very costly. Currently, illegal immigrants are only eligible for a few of the many government programs that benefit low-income Americans, but that would change if unauthorized workers were made legal residents. One study in Texas found that "providing education, health care, law enforcement, and social and government services to illegal aliens and their dependents cost state taxpayers $12.1 billion a year, or about $1,200 a year per Texas household headed by a U.S. citizen" (McDonald 2015). There is no doubt that a guest worker program would increase demand for government services such as education, food stamps, and health care. Increased demand for government services will likely result in higher taxes and cuts to programs that benefit low-income Americans.

A large influx of legal immigrants would be especially problematic for the public education system in areas with high immigration. Immigrants tend to have more children than native-born Americans, which can place a large burden on school districts (McDonald 2015). Furthermore, immigrants are generally poorer than native-born Americans, resulting in lower tax revenue per student in public schools. For example, "of all public school students in poverty nationwide, 29 percent are from immigrant households" (McDonald 2015). States along the Mexican border are hit especially hard, with immigrant households accounting for 60 percent of the public school students in poverty in California, 43 percent in Arizona and 42 percent in Nevada (McDonald 2015). A guest worker program is likely to lower the quality of education in public schools because it will increase class sizes without adding enough additional revenue to hire more teachers or build more classrooms. Those living in school districts with higher levels of immigration have good reason to worry that they will have to pay higher taxes, while their children receive a lower quality education.

Supporters of a guest worker program argue that the fear over increased demand for public services is largely overblown. According to a study from the Cato Institute, the average immigrant gets *less* welfare benefits than the typical American citizen. "On average, each immigrant who is broadly eligible for welfare or entitlement programs costs $16,088 in 2016, about 27 percent less than the average native who costs $21,926" (Nowrasteh and Orr 2018). Immigrants also receive 39 percent less in benefits from welfare programs than American citizens, and "consume 27 percent fewer benefits relative to natives with similar incomes and ages" (Nowrasteh and Orr 2018).

While a guest worker program would increase the overall cost of government programs, it would also expand the number of workers paying taxes. Many illegal workers are paid under-the-table and therefore do not pay federal or state income taxes. A guest worker program would apply taxes to their wages, thereby increasing overall tax revenue for federal and state governments. In fact, some government programs may receive a needed boost in temporary funds to offset current deficits. Specifically, Medicare and Social Security are facing temporary shortfalls because the baby-boomer generation is currently increasing demand for services. Immigrants are less likely than American citizens to collect from Social Security or Medicare (Nowrasteh and Orr 2018). For example, "undocumented workers contribute about $15 billion a year to Social Security through payroll taxes" (Davidson 2013). Adding workers to the system would increase revenue for retirement programs at the very time they need it most. In short, while a guest worker program would increase tax revenue by including more workers, their families would be putting additional stress on government programs.

Dealing with Racism in the Immigration Debate

Throughout American history, racial prejudice has been an important part of the immigration debate. Benjamin Franklin complained about immigrants with darker skin tones changing the complexion of American culture. He argued that immigrants could not change their culture any more than they could change their skin tone (Rampell 2015). Opponents of excessive legal and illegal immigration have argued that it would weaken American culture by diluting it with the cultures of foreign nations. Even to this day, hostility toward immigration is increased by "assimilationist threat," which occurs when native-born Americans fear that new immigrants will not adopt the language, culture, and values of their new country (Paxton and Mughan 2006). Skin color has traditionally provided an easy way to divide up society into us versus them, and cause discrimination against blacks, Asians, eastern Europeans, and Hispanics. Although the specific race or ethnicity changed over time, the consistent fear among the dominant American culture was that new immigrants did not share American values, and were morally or intellectually deficient in some way.

The strong overlap between immigration and race has made it especially difficult to discuss the issue without feelings of anger and hostility. Indeed, pro-immigration supporters often accuse the other side of being motivated by racial prejudice, or more specifically a desire to keep America as a majority white country. To be clear, there is some empirical evidence that racism plays a large role in opinions about immigration. Research shows that opposition to immigration is strongest among white people with negative attitudes toward Hispanics (Brader, Valentino and Suhay 2008; Hartman, Newman and Bell 2014). There is also evidence that exposure to those speaking foreign languages can increase opposition to immigration (Newman, Hartman and Taber 2012). An interesting study even showed that white liberals were more likely to oppose immigration simply because they heard Hispanics speaking Spanish during their local public transit (Enos 2017). There is no denying that racists are much more likely to support policies that keep non-whites out of the country.

That being said, it is entirely unproductive to *assume people are racist* simply because they disagree with you about how to handle illegal immigration. As I hope this chapter has made clear, there are valid reasons to oppose a guest worker program that have nothing to do with racism. Assuming that a particular individual is racist is unproductive because it prevents any sort of meaningful exchange of ideas. Rather than assume the worst about people, it is more productive to give them the benefit of the doubt when it comes to their motivations. We tend to attribute negative motives to people who hold opposing perspectives, but doing so pretty much cuts off any chance of learning the actual reasons why they disagree. After all, if our goal is to learn the perspectives of others, it does not really matter why they hold their opinions. An argument is no more or less valid when it is used to cover up a nefarious motivation. In general, giving people the benefit of the doubt as to *why* they hold their opinions is necessary to reap the rewards of political discourse. In the end, assuming that everyone who disagrees with you is stupid and hateful will leave *you* both stupid and hateful.

Even if someone opposes immigration because they are overtly racist, they still might benefit from hearing reasons why immigration is a good thing. Learning *why* people hold opposing opinions can increase tolerance and reduce anger toward people who disagree. Furthermore, engaging in a productive discussion with minorities will help challenge racist stereotypes. Berating someone for being a racist, on the other hand, will only further strengthen their resolve and increase their hatred. Additionally, arguing with a racist might also benefit you! If someone opposes a guest worker program because they are racist, they still may provide strong arguments about its negative economic impact. Hearing those arguments can be enlightening for you even if persuasion is unlikely. Remember, political discussion can be very rewarding even when there is no chance either side will change their minds. After all, it is not as if talking with a racist will make you racist. What do you have to lose?

Review Questions

1. How did the 1965 *Immigration and Naturalization Act* change immigration policy?
2. Why is it problematic for a worker's legal status to be contingent on employment?
3. How could granting amnesty to illegal immigrants increase illegal immigration in the future?
4. How would a guest worker program affect public education?
5. How does immigration benefit retirement programs such as Medicare and Social Security?
6. What role does racism play in the immigration debate?

Discussion Questions

1. Is current opposition to immigration different from previous attempts to exclude people from certain nations and cultures?
2. Should American citizens get an advantage over foreign workers in the job market?
3. Does immigration benefit the economy?
4. What do you believe is the main reason people oppose immigration?
5. Should we be tolerant of people who espouse intolerant views about other groups of people?

Sources for Further Inquiry

Books

Bosworth, Mary, Alpa Parmar, & Yolanda Vázquez (Eds.). 2018. *Race, Criminal Justice, and Migration Control: Enforcing the Boundaries of Belonging*. New York, NY: Oxford University Press.

Cobas, José A., Jorge Duany, and Joe R. Feagin. 2015. *How the United States Racializes Latinos: White Hegemony and its Consequences*. New York, NY: Routledge.

Heer, David. 2018. *Immigration in America's Future: Social Science Findings and the Policy Debate*. New York, NY: Routledge.

Hollifield, James, Phillip Martin, and Pia Orrenius (Eds.). 2014. *Controlling Immigration: A Global Perspective*. Stanford, CA: Stanford University Press.

Nevins, Joseph. 2010. *Operation Gatekeeper and Beyond: The War on "Illegals" and the Remaking of the US–Mexico Boundary*. New York, NY: Routledge.
Pevnick, Ryan. 2011. *Immigration and the Constraints of Justice: Between Open Borders and Absolute Sovereignty*. New York, NY: Cambridge University Press.

Journal and Newspaper Articles

Borjas, George J. 2017, February 27. "The Immigration Debate We Need." *The New York Times*. Retrieved from https://www.nytimes.com/2017/02/27/opinion/the-immigra tion-debate-we-need.html
Calamur, Krishnadev. 2016, June 15. "Are Immigrants Prone to Crime and Terrorism?" *The Atlantic*. Retrieved from https://www.theatlantic.com/news/archive/2016/06/imm igrants-and-crime/486884/
Dinesen, Peter Thisted, Robert Klemmensen, and Asbjørn Sonne Nørgaard. 2016. "Attitudes toward Immigration: The Role of Personal Predispositions." *Political Psychology* 37(1): 55–72.
Garand, James C., Ping Xu, and Belinda C. Davis. 2017. "Immigration Attitudes and Support for the Welfare State in the American Mass Public." *American Journal of Political Science* 61(1): 146–162.
Gerber, Alan S., Gregory A. Huber, Daniel R. Biggers, and David J. Hendry. 2017. "Self-interest, Beliefs, and Policy Opinions: Understanding how Economic Beliefs Affect Immigration Policy Preferences." *Political Research Quarterly* 70(1): 155–171.
Mansur, Samier. 2017, September 13. "How Immigration Benefits Americans and Is Key to U.S. Leadership in the World." *Huffington Post*. Retrieved from: https://www.huf fingtonpost.com/entry/how-immigration-benefits-americans-and-is-key-to-us_us_ 59b6db42e4b02bebae75f071
Mutz, Diana. 2018. "Status Threat, not Economic Hardship, Explains the 2016 Presidential Vote." *Proceedings of the National Academy of Sciences* 115(19): 4330–4339.
Richwine, Jason. 2016, May 9. "The Cost of Welfare Use by Immigrant and Native Households." The Center for Immigration Studies. Retrieved from https://cis.org/Rep ort/Cost-Welfare-Use-Immigrant-and-Native-Households

References

"Alexander Hamilton on the Naturalization of Foreigners." 2010. *Population and Development Review* 36(1): 177–182.
Baker, Ryan. 2014. "Estimates of the Unauthorized Immigrant Population Residing in the United States." Office of Immigration Statistics. Department of Homeland Security. Retrieved from https://www.dhs.gov/sites/default/files/publications/Unauthorized% 20Immigrant%20Population%20Estimates%20in%20the%20US%20January%202014_1.pdf
Binford, Leigh. 2013. *Tomorrow we're All Going to the Harvest: Temporary Foreign Worker Programs and Neoliberal Political Economy*. Austin, TX: University of Texas Press.
Borjas, George J. 2016. "Yes, Immigration Hurts American Workers." *Politico Magazine*. Retrieved from https://www.politico.com/magazine/story/2016/09/trump-clinton-imm igration-economy-unemployment-jobs-214216
Brader, Ted, Nicholas A. Valentino, and Elizabeth Suhay. 2008. "What Triggers Public Opposition to Immigration? Anxiety, Group Cues, and Immigration Threat." *American Journal of Political Science* 52(4): 959–978.

Bumiller, Elisabeth. 2006, March 24. "Bush is Facing a Difficult Path on Immigration." *The New York Times.* Retrieved from https://www.nytimes.com/2006/03/24/politics/bush-is-facing-a-difficult-path-on-immigration.html

Bush, George W. 2004, January 7. "President Bush Proposes New Temporary Worker Program." Whitehouse Archives. Retrieved from https://georgewbush-whitehouse.archives.gov/news/releases/2004/01/20040107-3.htm

Chen, Michelle. 2017, November 9. "How Temporary Work Visas Hurt Migrant Women." *The Nation.* Retrieved from https://www.thenation.com/article/how-temporary-work-visas-hurt-migrant-women/

Chinese Exclusion Act. 1882. National Archives: Our Documents. Retrieved fromhttps://www.ourdocuments.gov/doc.php?flash=true&doc=47

Davidson, Adam. 2013, February 12. "Do Illegal Immigrants Actually Hurt the U.S. Economy?" *The New York Times.* Retrieved from https://www.nytimes.com/2013/02/17/magazine/do-illegal-immigrants-actually-hurt-the-us-economy.html

Enos, Ryan D. 2017. *The Space between us: Social Geography and Politics.* Cambridge: Cambridge University Press.

Gonzalez, Gilbert G. 2017. *Guest Workers or Colonized Labor?: Mexican Labor Migration to the United States.* New York, NY: Routledge.

Gutierrez, Laura D. 2016. *A Constant Threat: Deportation and Return Migration to Northern Mexico, 1918–1965.* San Diego, CA: University of California.

Hartman, Todd K., Benjamin J. Newman, and C. Scott Bell. 2014. "Decoding Prejudice toward Hispanics: Group Cues and Public Reactions to Threatening Immigrant Behavior." *Political Behavior* 36(1): 143–163.

History.com. 2010. "U.S. Immigration since 1965." History.com. Retrieved from https://www.history.com/topics/us-immigration-since-1965

Immigration Reform and Control Act of 1986. 8 U.S.C. 1101 note. Retrieved from https://www.eeoc.gov/eeoc/history/35th/thelaw/irca.html

Kim, Seung Min. 2013, June 27. "Senate Passes Immigration Bill." *Politico.* Retrieved from: https://www.politico.com/story/2013/06/immigration-bill-2013-senate-passes-093530

McDonald, Michael. 2015, November 16. "10 Ways Illegal Immigration Affects you Financially." Retrieved from https://www.gobankingrates.com/making-money/jobs/10-ways-illegal-immigration-affects-financially/

NBC News. 2014, July 1. "Why Immigration Reform Died in Congress." NBC News. Retrieved from https://www.nbcnews.com/politics/first-read/why-immigration-reform-died-congress-n145276

Newman, Benjamin J., Todd K. Hartman, and Charles S. Taber. 2012. "Foreign Language Exposure, Cultural Threat, and Opposition to Immigration." *Political Psychology* 33(5): 635–657.

Nowrasteh, Alex, and Robert Orr. 2018, May 10. "Immigration and the Welfare State: Immigrant and Native Use Rates and Benefit Levels for Means-Tested Welfare and Entitlement Programs." The Cato Institute. Retrieved from https://www.cato.org/publications/immigration-research-policy-brief/immigration-welfare-state-immigrant-native-use-rates

Nyce, Caroline Mimbs, and Chris Bodenner. 2016, May 23. "Looking Back at Amnesty under Reagan." *The Atlantic.* Retrieved from https://www.theatlantic.com/notes/2016/05/thirty-years-after-the-immigration-reform-and-control-act/482364/

Paxton, Pamela, and Anthony Mughan. 2006. "What's to Fear from Immigrants? Creating an Assimilationist Threat Scale." *Political Psychology* 27(4): 549–568.

Plumer, Brad. 2013, January 30. "Congress tried to fix immigration back in 1986. Why it didn't work." *Washington Post.* Retrieved from https://www.washingtonpost.com/news/wonk/wp/2013/01/30/in-1986-congress-tried-to-solve-immigration-why-didnt-it-work/?utm_term=.b5180f70fc25.

Rampell, Catherine. 2015, August 28. "Founding Fathers, Trashing Immigrants." *Washington Post.* Retrieved from https://www.washingtonpost.com/news/rampage/wp/2015/08/28/founding-fathers-trashing-immigrants/?noredirect=on&utm_term=.f036cb54462b

Rosenzweig, Paul, James Carafano and Janice Kephart. 2005, July 26. "The McCain-Kennedy Immigration Reform Bill Falls Short." The Heritage Foundation. Retrieved from https://www.heritage.org/report/the-mccain-kennedy-immigration-reform-bill-falls-short

Rural Migration News. 2006. "Braceros: History, Compensation." *Rural Migration News* 12(2). Retrieved from https://migration.ucdavis.edu/rmn/more.php?id=1112

Smith, Donna. 2007, June 28. "Senate Kills Bush Immigration Reform Bill." Thompson Reuters. Retrieved from https://www.reuters.com/article/us-usa-immigration/senate-kills-bush-immigration-reform-bill-idUSN2742643820070629

Smith, Marian L. 2002. "Race, Nationality, and Reality: INS Administration of Racial Provisions in the U.S. Immigration and Nationality Law since 1898." *National Archives: Prologue Magazine*, 34(2). Retrieved from https://www.archives.gov/publications/prologue/2002/summer/immigration-law-1.html

Southern Poverty Law Center. 2013. "Close to Slavery: Guest Worker Programs in the United States." Retrieved from https://www.splcenter.org/20130218/close-slavery-guestworker-programs-united-states

U.S. Immigration and Naturalization Service. 2000. "Estimates of the Unauthorized Immigrant Population Residing in the United States: 1990 to 2000." Retrieved from https://www.dhs.gov/sites/default/files/publications/Unauthorized%20Immigrant%20Population%20Estimates%20in%20the%20US%201990%20to%202000.pdf

Wright, Matthew, Morris Levy, and Jack Citrin. 2016. "Public Attitudes toward Immigration Policy across the Legal/illegal Divide: The Role of Categorical and Attribute-based Decision-making." *Political Behavior* 38(1): 229–253.

12

SHOULD STUDENTS BE ALLOWED TO CARRY GUNS ON COLLEGE CAMPUSES?

A well regulated militia, being necessary to the security of a free State, the right of the people to keep and bear arms, shall not be infringed.–

2nd Amendment to the U.S. Constitution

For much of its history, the 2nd amendment did not protect an individual's right to own a gun. The United States Supreme Court limited the power of the second amendment by ruling that it either only applied to the federal government (*U.S. v. Cruikshank*, 1876), or only served to protect militias (*U.S. v. Miller*, 1939). Not until 2008, in *District of Columbia v. Heller* did the Supreme Court change the interpretation of the 2nd Amendment to protect individuals' right to own firearms. Furthermore, the *D.C. v. Heller* (2008) ruling prevented the federal government from overly restricting one's ability to acquire a gun and use it for personal protection. In regards to the *Heller* case in particular, the court struck down the Washington D.C. law requiring guns to be either disassembled, or have a trigger lock when they were not being used. The Supreme Court ruled that the law infringed on the 2nd Amendment because it prevented the owners from using the gun for personal protection if someone broke into their house.

Two years later, the right to own a gun was further protected against state and local governments in the *McDonald v. Chicago* (2010) case, which struck down laws that made it overly burdensome for Chicago residents to legally acquire a handgun. In this case, the Supreme Court ruled that the right to own a gun for personal protection was an essential *liberty*, protected by the 14th Amendment, which states "nor shall any state deprive any person of life, liberty, or property, without due process of law." In other words, people have a right to own a gun for purposes of self-defense. It is important to point out that both *D.C. v. Heller* and *McDonald v. Chicago* were decided on a 5–4 basis, which means they could be overturned by the court in the future. In fact, the right to own a gun may disappear if only one of the justices in the majority of those cases were replaced by a justice with a different interpretation of the 2nd Amendment.

Although the Supreme Court has ruled that gun ownership is an essential liberty, every freedom listed in the constitution has restrictions. For instance, someone cannot shout fire in a crowded theater—or call in a bomb threat—and claim that they are practicing free speech. Governments have the power to regulate speech, religion, assembly, and voting rights, even though those regulations are not stated in the constitution. The government can regulate the type of gun people own in the interest of public safety, just as they can ban religious activity for the same reasons. Governments can pass laws preventing minors, felons, and the mentally ill from acquiring guns, just as they can prevent those groups from exercising the right to vote. In short, the right to own a gun is subject to reasonable restrictions, just like every other right. The key is to find the right balance between allowing citizens the ability to protect themselves and maintaining public safety.

Governments can also restrict the possession of firearms in certain places, such as government buildings, airports or public schools. In that regard, states have varying restrictions on where citizens can take their weapons, and some have decided to allow weapons in public buildings, churches, bars, and universities. As of 2016, 17 states *ban* concealed weapons on college campuses, while another 22 states allow each college and university to set policy on the matter. Two states allow faculty and staff to carry concealed weapons, but not students. Only eight states allow guns on campus including: Colorado, Georgia, Idaho, Kansas, Mississippi, Oregon, Texas, Utah and Wisconsin (National Conference of State Legislatures 2016). Even more states have come close to passing laws allowing guns on campus.

The few public opinion polls that exist on the issue of campus carry suggest a roughly equal split in support and opposition to the law. For example, a Huffington Post/YouGov poll in 2013 found that 43 percent supported, and 43 percent opposed, allowing guns on college campuses (Kingkade 2013). The overall numbers masked a large partisan split however, with 73 percent of Republicans supporting campus-carry compared to only 19 percent of Democrats. There is also a gender divide with 54 percent of men supporting campus-carry compared to only 33 percent of females. A 2014 survey of roughly 400 university presidents by the University of California at Santa Barbara found that 95 percent opposed allowing guns on campus (Jaschik 2014). In that survey, the most commonly cited concern was the danger posed by possible accidental discharge of the weapons around other students.

The question of whether guns should be allowed on college campuses is a nice example of the larger gun debate that is raging across the country. That is, the arguments in support and opposition to campus carry are similar to those used when debating other types of gun restrictions. The larger question of gun control pits two widely shared values against each other. The gun *rights* side argues that guns allow people to protect themselves in a dangerous world. Meanwhile, the gun *control* side argues that the government should make every effort to keep guns out of the hands of criminals and the mentally ill, while also minimizing risk when guns are misused by the general public. Another part of the debate focuses on the effectiveness of gun laws in stopping gun-related violence. While the gun rights side argues that gun restrictions only harm law-abiding citizens, gun control supporters point to evidence of gun restrictions that have proven effective at reducing violence. Unfortunately, debates over gun control often turn heated because of exaggerated fears on each side of the issue.

Guns, Protection, and Safety

Supporters of campus carry argue that students should have the ability to protect themselves in an increasingly dangerous world. Laws that ban guns on college campuses leave students vulnerable to criminals, who will disregard any gun restrictions. Criminals are going to bring concealed weapons on campus regardless of any laws that restrict them, so the gun ban only works to disarm citizens from protecting themselves. In fact, gun bans might actually increase campus crimes because criminals know that students and faculty will not have the means to protect themselves. Banning guns on college campuses is an invitation for criminals to take advantage of a vulnerable population.

There is also little evidence that students carrying concealed weapons on campus would make universities more dangerous. For one, more guns in society have not increased the rates of gun-related homicides. Instead, John Lott (2016) found that from 2007–2015 there was a substantial *decline* in murders and violent crimes, despite the fact that concealed weapons permits nearly doubled during that same time period. Supporters of campus carry also argue that students who have concealed weapons do not "commit weapons crimes at a higher rate than the general population" (Lyons 2017, p. 89). There is also no evidence that universities have become more violent after they allow concealed weapons on campus (Hennessy-Fiske 2015; Kopel 2015).

Allowing guns on campus may also deter mass shootings in universities. In 2007, a lone gunman killed 32 people on the Virginia Tech campus, while the very next year a student killed 5 people and wounded 21 on the campus of Northern Illinois University. Allowing guns on campus may deter potential mass shootings from ever occurring because shooters will have the knowledge that students and professors can fire back. Even if someone is so deranged that they are not deterred, mass shootings may claim fewer lives if students, faculty, and staff have the means to stop the gunman.

Opponents of campus carry argue that it would make universities more dangerous, and would potentially result in more casualties when shootings occur. If students bring guns on campus, it would threaten the safety of all other students in the classroom. One potential danger is guns going off by accident because students do not follow proper safety precautions when handling or storing their firearms. In a perfect world, all gun owners would be safe and cautious with their weapons, but people are far from perfect. Opponents of campus carry also argue that guns are especially dangerous in the hands of college-aged students who are more prone to bad decisions and immature behavior. In general, those under 25 years of age do not have a fully developed brain, and particularly the pre-frontal cortex is under-developed, meaning they are "compromised in their ability to think through what they're doing and what the consequences are" (Lyons 2017, p. 75). Additionally, college students are more likely to suffer from high anxiety, depression, and to engage in binge drinking—all of which increases the likelihood that students will use guns to harm to themselves or others (Webster et al. 2016).

When it comes to deterring mass shootings, it is worth considering that most of the deadliest university shootings ended with the gunman committing suicide. It is doubtful that the specter of getting shot and killed would deter a gunman who planned to kill themselves anyway. More importantly, allowing guns on campus might actually *increase* the death toll during a mass shooting or when a low-level crime occurs. When confronted with an active shooter, multiple students may fire back at the gunman, adding to the bullets flying around a densely populated area. Such a crossfire of bullets could potentially cause more fatalities and injuries than would result from a single gunman. Moreover, gun owners are not necessarily expert marksman, and the more shots that miss the target, the more bullets that might hit innocent bystanders. Even on a smaller scale, wide-spread gun ownership might result in low-level crimes escalating to gun fights. For example, if someone tries to steal a car at gun-point, the car owner may be more likely to fire at the attempted thief, which would threaten the lives of the car owner and any other people that may be in the area. In short, allowing guns on campus would increase the risk of injury and death for gun owners and all other members of the campus community.

Allowing guns on campus could also have a chilling effect on the free exchange of ideas in classrooms. Universities are supposed to be a marketplace of ideas where students are challenged to question their preconceptions and consider new ideas and perspectives. The knowledge that students are carrying guns may motivate faculty to avoid emotionally charged issues and make students fearful of disagreeing with their classmates. For example, after Texas allowed guns on campuses, the University of Houston faculty senate advised instructors to "be careful discussing sensitive topics" and to considering dropping "certain topics from your curriculum" (Hannon 2016). Even if gun owners are unlikely to use guns for intimidation, the fear of guns among students and faculty could threaten the free exchange of ideas.

Are Gun Laws Effective?

The argument over gun control is also fought on empirical grounds, with each side pointing to research or anecdotes that support their preferred policy. Supporters of campus carry point to studies showing that allowing concealed weapons reduces violent crimes and property theft (Lott and Mustard 1997). If criminals fear that their potential victims might have guns, they may be more hesitant to commit crimes. Areas with stricter gun control laws typically have more gun-related crimes, while states with weaker gun laws have less crime. For example, large cities have some of the strictest gun laws, but also have some of the highest rates of gun-related homicides. Of course, this does not necessarily mean that weakening gun laws would reduce crime. Areas with high rates of gun-related homicides are more likely to pass restrictive gun control policies. In other words, it could be that gun crimes cause state and local legislatures to pass more restrictive gun policies, and not the other way around.

Opponents of campus carry point to their own research that shows gun control works in reducing violent crime (Ludwig 1998). Laws that restrict gun ownership when citizens are under a restraining order reduce intimate partner homicide rates (Vigdor and Mercy 2006). According to one study, allowing police to confiscate guns of suspected criminals reduced violent gun-related crimes by nearly 50 percent (Sherman and Rogan 1995). Opponents of campus carry could also point to Australia as a good case study of the power of gun restrictions to reduce violent crime and mass shootings. Australia banned rapid-fire rifles and instituted gun buy-back programs starting in 1996. Following the gun reforms, Australia saw reductions in gun-related crimes and homicides. Moreover, there has not been a single mass shooting since 1996, while there were 13 mass shootings with 104 fatalities in the 18 years prior to the assault rifle ban (Davy 2016). Was Australia just lucky or did gun restrictions actually reduce mass shootings?

Perhaps the biggest roadblock to productive discussion of gun control is the tendency for each side to engage in *motivated reasoning* when evaluating research on the effectiveness of gun control policies. Recall from Chapter 3 that motivated reasoning is an unconscious bias that causes people to be more critical of evidence that contradicts their preferred policy, while uncritically accepting research that supports their viewpoint. Motivated reasoning leads each side of the gun debate to accept research supporting their side, no matter how poor the methods, or untenable its assumptions. Conversely, if research contradicts their preferred policy, they begin with the assumption that there is something wrong, and go looking for a weakness in the methods. Consequently, each side of the gun debate believes that research supporting their view stands on solid empirical grounds, while research on the other side is politically motivated and simply bad science. Indeed, a common charge is that research is funded by the gun lobby, or the researcher is a liberal professor, and for these reasons alone, we can dismiss their findings. Of course, empirical research stands on its own merits regardless of who performs the research! The only way to dispute research is to replicate it, not by attacking the person doing the analysis.

Obstacles to Compromise

The gun control debate seems more resistant to compromise than the other issues discussed in this book. One reason for this paralysis in the gun control debate is that each side suffers from largely unsubstantiated fears of what will happen if the other side gets their way. Some in the gun control side seem to truly believe that weakening gun laws will bring back the old west—that they saw in movies—where everyone has guns and they frequently fire at each other. Indeed, many on the gun control side seem to be overly fearful of guns and people who own them. They believe that gun owners are less responsible than they actually are, and shoot people a lot more than reality suggests. In areas that allow citizens to open carry, it is very rare for governments to revoke those licenses due to irresponsible behavior. Of course, there are examples of guns escalating benign conflicts into deadly confrontations, but those situations are more the exception than the rule. Gun rights advocates argue that most gun owners are responsible with their firearms, and their ability to protect themselves should not be restricted because a few people act irresponsibly.

Of course, gun control advocates are not alone in holding unsubstantiated fears. Those opposing gun control seem to have an irrational fear of "the slippery slope" to government confiscation of all firearms. Many believe that any step toward the regulation of guns by the government will inevitably result in the government coming for their guns. This belief persists despite the absence of any evidence suggesting that politicians want to take away guns, or could do so even if they wanted. For example, many gun rights advocates were convinced that President Barack Obama wanted to ban guns despite the fact that he agreed with the *D.C. v. Heller* (2008) decision, and even signed legislation expanding gun rights in national parks. It is incredibly rare for any politician on the federal, state, or local level to openly advocate for the government to ban gun sales or confiscate guns. Just like irresponsible gun owners, politicians trying to ban guns are the exception rather than the rule.

Gun rights advocates might respond that "they really want to ban guns, but won't say it publically." First, there is no possible way to know someone else's motivations for sure. How would you feel if someone repeatedly told you what you were really thinking despite your constant pronouncements and actions to the contrary? Second, the gun rights side has been getting what they want for the past 20 years. Not only has there been no effort at gun confiscation, gun rights have been expanded in states all across the country. The Supreme Court has declared an individual right to own a gun for personal protection, meaning that attempts to confiscate guns would be ruled unconstitutional. Unfortunately, this unsubstantiated fear of some highly unlikely future confiscation prevents any small attempts by the government to reduce gun violence. In sum, until each side sees these unsubstantiated fears for what they are, political animosity will persist and compromise will be nearly impossible.

Review Questions

1.   How did the United States Supreme Court rule in the *District of Columbia v. Heller* (2008) and *McDonald v. Chicago* (2010) cases?
2.   What are the opposing arguments surrounding the effects of campus carry laws on the safety of college students?
3.   Why do opponents of campus carry laws argue that guns are especially dangerous in the hands of college students?
4.   What are the main obstacles to compromise on gun control policy?

Discussion Questions

1.   Do you believe allowing guns on campus will make students fearful of discussing controversial issues in the classroom?
2.   Should gun control be dealt with on the state and local level, or should there be a nationwide policy?
3.   What was the original purpose of the 2nd Amendment? Should we ignore the original intent and do what's best for our current circumstances?
4.   In general, do you trust college students to use guns in a responsible manner?
5.   Putting the campus carry issue aside, what are some other ways that universities can prevent gun violence?

Sources for Further Inquiry

Books

Cook, Philip J., and Kristin A. Goss. 2014. *The Gun Debate: What Everyone Needs to Know.* New York, NY: Oxford University Press.
Doherty, Brian. 2008. *Gun Control on Trial: Inside the Supreme Court Battle over the Second Amendment.* Washington D.C.: The Cato Institute.
Hemenway, David. 2004. *Private Guns: Public Health.* Ann Arbor, MI: University of Michigan Press.
LaFollette, Hugh. 2018. *In Defense of Gun Control.* New York, NY: Oxford University Press.
Lott, John R. 2010. *More Guns, Less Crime: Understanding Crime and Gun Control Laws* (3rd ed.). Chicago, IL: University of Chicago Press.
Spitzer, Robert J. 2016. *The Politics of Gun Control* (6th ed.). New York, NY: Routledge Press.

Journal and Newspaper Articles

Ayres, Ian, and John Donohue. 2003. "Shooting Down the 'More Guns, Less Crime' Hypothesis". *Stanford Law Review* 55: 1193–1312.
Black, Dan A., and Daniel S. Nagin. 1998. "Do Right-to-carry Laws Deter Violent Crime?" *The Journal of Legal Studies* 27(1): 209–219.

Bogost, Ian. 2016, Mar. 9. "The Armed Campus in the Anxiety Age." *The Atlantic*. Retrieved from https://www.theatlantic.com/education/archive/2016/03/campus-ca rry-anxiety-age/472920/

Duggan, Mark. 2001. "More Guns, More Crime." *Journal of Political Economy* 109(5): 1086–1114.

Kleck, Gary, Tomislav Kovandzic, and Jon Bellows. 2016. "Does Gun Control Reduce Violent Crime?" *Criminal Justice Review* 41(4): 488–513.

Lund, Nelson. 2016, May 31. "The University Police Can't Prevent Violent Crimes." *The New York Times*. Retrieved from http://www.nytimes.com/roomfordebate/2016/05/ 31/should-guns-be-permitted-on-college-campuses/the-university-police-cant-prevent-violent-crimes

Michaels, Samantha. 2016, Nov. 2. "New Research Confirms Guns on College Campuses are Dangerous." Mother Jones. Retrieved from http://www.motherjones.com/politics/ 2016/10/campus-carry-laws-guns-mass-shooters

Reilly, Katie. 2016, Feb. 26. "How Guns on Campus Could Change What Texas Teaches." *Time*. Retrieved from http://time.com/4237638/campus-carry-texas-universities/

Skorton, David and Glenn Altschuler. 2013, Feb. 21. "Do We Really Need More Guns On Campus?" Forbes. Retrieved from http://www.forbes.com/sites/collegeprose/ 2013/02/21/guns-on-campus/#78010557264c

References

Davy, Mellissa. 2016, June 22. "Australia's Gun Laws Stopped Mass Shootings and Reduced Homicides, Study Finds." *The Guardian*. Retrieved from https://www.thegua rdian.com/world/2016/jun/23/australias-gun-laws-stopped-mass-shootings-and-redu ced-homicides-study-finds.

District of Columbiav.Heller, 554 U. S. 570(2008).

Hannon, Elliot. 2016, Feb. 23. "University of Houston Faculty Devises Pointers on How to Avoid Getting Shot by Armed Students." The Slatest. Retrieved from: http://www. slate.com/blogs/the_slatest/2016/02/23/university_of_houston_faculty_reacts_to_texa s_campus_carry_gun_law.html

Hennessy-Fiske, Molly. 2015, June 10. "Gun Rights Advocates' Push for Campus-Carry Measures like Texas' is Slow Going." *Los Angeles Times*. Retrieved from http://www.la times.com/nation/la-na-guns-campus-20150610-story.html

Jaschik, Scott. 2014, June 4. "Presidents vs. Guns." Inside Higher Ed. Retrieved from http s://www.insidehighered.com/news/2014/06/04/poll-finds-most-college-leaders-opp ose-concealed-carry-campus

Kingkade, Tyler. 2013, Jan. 8. "Guns on College Campuses Divides Americans' Opinion in New Poll." *Huffington Post*. Retrieved from http://www.huffingtonpost.com/2013/ 01/08/poll-guns-on-campus_n_2428443.html.

Kopel, David. 2015, Apr. 20. "Guns on University Campuses: The Colorado Experience. "*The Washington Post*. Retrieved from https://www.washingtonpost.com/news/ volokh-conspiracy/wp/2015/04/20/guns-on-university-campuses-the-colorado-experi ence/?utm_term=.5286b83fc41b

Lott, John R. 2016, July 26. "Concealed Carry Permit Holders Across the United States: 2016." Retrieved from https://papers.ssrn.com/sol3/papers.cfm?abstract_id=2814691

Lott, John R., and David B. Mustard. 1997. "Crime, Deterrence, and Right-to-Carry Concealed Hand Guns." *The Journal of Legal Studies* 26(1): 1–68.

Ludwig, Jens. 1998. "Concealed-Gun-Carrying Laws and Violent Crime: Evidence from State Panel Data." *International Review of Law and Economics* 18(3): 239–254.

Lyons, Christina L. 2017, Jan. 27. "Guns on Campus." *CQ Researcher*, 27(4): 73–96.

McDonaldv.Chicago, 561 U. S. 742(2010).

National Conference of State Legislatures. 2016, May 31. "Guns on Campus." Retrieved from http://www.ncsl.org/research/education/guns-on-campus-overview.aspx

Sherman, Lawrence W., and Dennis P. Rogan. 1995. "Effects of Gun Seizures on Gun Violence: 'Hot Spots' Patrol in Kansas City." *Justice Quarterly* 12(4): 673–693. *United Statesv.Cruikshank*, 92 U. S. 542(1876).

United Statesv.Miller, 307 U. S. 174(1939).

Vigdor, Elizabeth Richardson, and James A. Mercy. 2006. "Do Laws Restricting Access to Firearms by Domestic Violence Offenders Prevent Intimate Partner Homicide?" *Evaluation Review* 30(3): 313–346.

Webster, Daniel W., John J. Donohue, Lois Klarevas, et al. 2016, Oct. 16. "Firearms on College Campuses: Research Evidence and Policy Implications." Johns Hopkins Bloomberg School of Public Health. Retrieved from http://www.jhsph.edu/research/centers-and-in stitutes/johns-hopkins-center-for-gun-policy-and-research/_pdfs/GunsOnCampus.pdf

PART IV
Government Reforms

13

SHOULD CONGRESS HAVE TERM LIMITS?

Article I of the United States Constitution established the legislative branch of the federal government, including the qualifications for members of the Senate and House of Representatives. The constitution requires all members of the U.S. House of Representatives and roughly one-third of Senators to come up for reelection every two years. Additionally, members of Congress must be at least 25 years old to serve in the House of Representatives, while Senators must be at least 30 years old. When writing the qualifications for office in the new constitution, the framers considered, but decided against, including limits on the number of terms congressmen could serve. Term limits were not a new idea at the time, as they existed in some of the colonies prior to the American Revolution, and the Articles of Confederation limited the number of years Congressmen could serve. In *Federalist 53*, James Madison (1788) argued in favor of the two-year term for House members, as opposed to a one-year term, by pointing to the benefits of having experienced policy makers in the House of Representatives. Term limits would likewise reduce the number of experienced legislators and deprive Congress of essential knowledge. After all, if voters wanted to impose term limits, all they have to do is vote out the incumbent.

In the late 20th century, support for congressional term limits gathered steam, resulting in reforms in state legislatures across the country. The movement for congressional term limits was driven largely by high reelection rates and public dissatisfaction with Congress. It is an understatement to say that incumbent congressmen are *very* likely to win reelection. In the U.S. House of Representatives, over 85 percent of incumbents have been reelected in every national election since 1990, and most years over 90 percent were reelected (Open Secrets.org n.d.). At the same time, reelection rates for senators never dropped below 75 percent.

Although there are occasional "wave" elections, they are more the exception than the rule in congressional races, and even wave elections still reelect an overwhelming majority of the 535 sitting congressmen. High reelection rates allow congressmen to serve as career politicians, something that the public largely opposes (Hibbing and Theiss-Morse 1995).

Public opinion polls show that there is fairly strong support for term limits among the general public. In 2013, a Gallup poll found that 75 percent of Americans supported term limits, while only 21 percent opposed the idea (Saad 2013). These results are similar to polls taken roughly 20 years earlier, suggesting that public support for term limits is pretty stable over time. Additionally, there is not a partisan divide on this issue as 65 percent of Democrats and 82 percent of Republicans support instituting term limits on Congress. Research suggests that public support for legislative term limits is driven largely by general cynicism and negativity toward government (Karp 1995).

Responding to overwhelming public pressure, many state legislatures moved to impose limits on the number of terms members of Congress could serve. By the early 1990s, nearly half (23) of the states had imposed congressional term limits of some kind. In 1995, the Supreme Court struck down congressional term limits in *U.S. Term Limits, Inc., v. Thornton* (1995). Writing for the majority of the court, Justice John Paul Stevens argued that the U.S. Constitution sets qualifications for congressional office, and the framers decided not to impose term limits. Consequently, if qualifications are to be imposed, it must come through a constitutional amendment. Additionally, Stevens argued that term limits violated a fundamental democratic principle that the people shall choose their representatives. Although a majority of the House voted to approve a term limits amendment, it did not receive the required two-thirds vote to pass. Given that congressmen are unlikely to vote against their own interests, some have suggested holding a constitutional convention to bypass congress and pass an amendment with only the approval of three-fourths of state legislatures (Sabato 2007).

The debate over congressional term limits involves both theoretical and practical considerations. On the theoretical end of the debate, there is the divide between individuals' trust in themselves versus the collective. If people trusted others as much as themselves, there would be no need for term limits. Term limits represent a self-imposed limitation on Americans' options in the voting booth, which is only rational if people do not trust other voters to make good decisions. This chapter examines empirical evidence regarding the ability of voters to make good decisions, which should help inform the need for Congressional term limits. The practical side of the term limit debate centers on how term limits affect the behavior of elected legislators. As such, the second part of this chapter examines the real world implications of term limits by looking at evidence from state legislatures, where some states have term limits while others allow unlimited reelection.

Can Voters Make Good Decisions?

Whether people believe that term limits are a good idea ultimately comes down to their trust in the decisions of others. Individuals tend to believe that they make informed and rational decisions when they step into the voting booth, while most other people are subject to manipulation. This distinction between faith in oneself versus the collective underlies the debate over many laws that limit human behavior. For example, you will be hard pressed to find an individual who believes that they personally need a limit on how fast they can drive. I am perfectly capable of regulating how fast I drive without government regulation. At the same time, I oppose eliminating speed limits on everyone because I do not trust other drivers to act responsibly. We have speed limits because each individual has far less confidence in other people than they do in themselves. There would be no need for speed limits if people trusted other drivers to the same extent that they trust themselves. Likewise, there would be no need for term limits if people had faith in other voters' ability to make informed and rational decisions. Essentially, term limits simply *limit the options available to voters* when choosing who will represent them in Congress. It makes no sense for an individual to limit their own options in the voting booth. If I like a candidate, and think she has done a good job, I would certainly want the opportunity to vote for her reelection. Support for term limits ultimately stems from individuals' lack of faith in other voters to make good decisions.

Do voters have sufficient information to vote correctly? On the one hand, there is abundant evidence that most Americans have very little knowledge about public affairs (Carpini and Keeter 1996). In fact, Americans have become even less knowledgeable about politics since the turn of the 21st century. Prior (2007) argues that changes in the media environment have resulted in a large portion of Americans tuning out of politics, resulting in low levels of political information. Some scholars have argued that this dearth of political information precludes voters from making decisions that effectively promote their own self-interest (Bartels 1996). When people have more political information, they are better able to vote consistently and correctly, but unfortunately, very few Americans meet this minimal threshold.

On the other hand, some scholars argue that Americans can make quality voting decisions without a great deal of specific knowledge about public affairs (Lau and Redlawsk, 1997). Voters frequently use information shortcuts, such as party identification and interest group support for policies, to infer how a candidate will act or a policy will affect them (Lupia 1994). For example, senior citizens may not understand the particular aspects of proposals to change Social Security, but if the American Association of Retired People (AARP) is opposed to the plan, they are likely to infer that it does not benefit the elderly. Likewise, if the National Rifle Association (NRA) is opposed to a plan to limit gun violence, both supporters and opponents of gun control can use the NRA's opposition as a shortcut to decide their own stance on the policy without knowing the particular aspects of the plan. Although not ideal, information shortcuts allow voters to make fairly informed decisions without remembering a large amount of detailed information (Lau and Redlawsk 2001).

There is also reason to believe that people are particularly well equipped to vote in a representative democracy, where most of their votes are for people and not policies. When people expect to make a choice at the voting booth, their minds automatically form impressions of political candidates (Lodge and Taber 2006). Impressions are simply positive and negative evaluations of the candidates running for office. When voters encounter new information about a candidate, they update their impression in a positive or negative direction, and then usually forget the particular piece of information (Lodge et al. 1989). By the time Election Day arrives, people have updated their impressions of the candidates with large amounts of information, but have probably forgotten most of the specific reasons why they like or dislike a candidate. As a result, voters may have well-informed opinions about the candidates even if they do not remember the specific facts that informed their opinion. If most people are able to make quality decisions regarding which candidate they support, then there is no need to impose term limits. Again, all term limits do is prevent voters from reelecting a representative that they would otherwise vote to keep in office.

Incumbency Advantages

Supporters of term limits argue that although many people have the *ability* to make informed decisions, there are structural factors that all but assure that most congressmen will get reelected. One factor leading to high reelection rates is party-line voting, where voters simply vote for all the candidates in the same party. Indeed, people often vote for fellow partisans even if they never heard of them before stepping into the voting booth. While party identification is a useful information shortcut, it is not hard to see how this approach to voting can result in people reelecting the same candidate every two or six years, regardless of how good a job they do. If voters simply vote for Democrats every two years, they may do so with little knowledge of the actions of that particular Congressperson. Most voters do not participate in party primaries—especially for non-presidential primaries—meaning they are presented with a binary choice in the general election between a Democrat and Republican. Most congressional districts in the House of Representatives are composed predominantly of either Republican or Democratic voters. As a result, for most members of Congress, the general election is a forgone conclusion.

Furthermore, most congressmen do not face serious challenges during the party primaries, and when they do, they usually have a sufficient fundraising advantage to defeat their challengers. Sitting members of congress usually have enormous financial advantages, allowing them to dominate the information environment with their message. Incumbents usually have a fundraising advantage because they are already in office and able to raise money for two to six years. Additionally, incumbents have an easier time getting money from lobbyists because they can affect policy while in office. Challengers can only raise money on the hope that they may one day be able to affect policy the way the incumbent can right now. If you were trying to influence policy, would you rather give money to someone with power to pass legislation right now, or someone who may or may not be able to pass policy in the future? It is easy to see why sitting congressmen are typically able to raise more money than challengers. Especially in low visibility House races, challengers must have a substantial store of campaign funds to get their message out to voters, otherwise the voters will only hear the message from incumbents. Consequently, even if an incumbent is doing a poor job of representing their constituents, their challenger probably lacks the money to explain to voters *why* the incumbent is doing a poor job.

Although it is possible that local media could help inform voters, they are usually more positive toward incumbents than challengers. Kahn and Kenney (2002) found that Senators running for reelection received more coverage than challengers, and when local media did cover challengers, it tended to be negative coverage. One reason for this media advantage is that incumbents have built relationships with local journalists, who rely on sitting senators to provide them with the local angle on national policy debates. Moreover, incumbents typically have more name recognition among the public than challengers, simply because they have already run for the office while the challenger is usually an unknown. This name recognition advantage allows the incumbent to use negative ads, and local media coverage, to define voter perceptions of the challenger. Meanwhile, the challenger has less ability to change perceptions of the incumbent since voters already have established impressions.

Altogether, these incumbency advantages make it very difficult for prospective challengers to defeat sitting members of Congress even if the incumbent is doing a poor job representing their constituents. Establishing term limits is one way to overcome the incumbency advantage because it allows new candidates the opportunity to make their case to voters on an equal playing field during open contests. Currently, the deck is stacked in favor of incumbents because they have more control over the information environment through both paid and free media. New candidates may have good ideas, but they lack the resources to adequately inform voters. Term limits would allow new candidates access to the political system, which would provide voters more options in the voting booth.

The Effects on Legislative Behavior

Many of the arguments for and against term limits are based on predictions about how they would affect the behavior of legislators. Since the Supreme Court ruled *Congressional* term limits unconstitutional, it is impossible to know for sure how term limits would affect members of the United States Congress. Fortunately, since some states have imposed term limits on state legislators, while other states allow unlimited reelection, it is possible to use evidence from state legislatures to predict the likely consequences of term limits on the federal level. Not surprisingly, both supporters and opponents of term limits find evidence from state legislatures that supports their position.

Supporters argue that term limits would eliminate career politicians who prioritize reelection over the public good. If congressmen knew they would only be in office a short time, they might care less about reelection and more about doing what is best for the country. Research supports this theory as state legislators in term limited states are more likely to act in the interests of the state rather than their particular constituents. For example, Carey and colleagues (1998) found that term limited legislators were less likely to devote time and resources to securing funding for district-level projects—also called *pork barrel spending*. Although such pork barrel spending is often popular among constituents, it can result in wasteful spending, bloated state budgets, and higher taxes. Pork barrel spending has been a particular problem on the federal level as Congress has difficulty controlling spending on projects that largely benefit people who live in their district or state. Term limits are likely to reduce wasteful spending among congressmen, which could help lower overall government spending, while shifting the cost of local projects to state and local governments.

Opponents of congressional term limits argue that they create ineffective and inexperienced legislators. The longer congressmen serve in office, the more they learn about the legislative process and the specifics of public policies. Career politicians become *policy experts* and more experienced at serving their constituents. It seems counter-productive to prevent experienced legislatures from returning to office in order for an inexperienced person to take their place. Furthermore, when state legislatures are less experienced and informed, it gives more power to lobbyists and the executive branch. Since inexperienced legislators lack information, lobbyists step in and provide guidance, but that guidance allows powerful state-level businesses to have greater power to shape legislation. Research also suggests that term limits weaken the ability of state legislators to act as a check on the executive branch (Carey et al. 2006). When state legislators are term limited, they are less willing to stand up for the institution of the legislature (Kousser 2005). Rather, term limits motivate legislators to seek new employment. Additionally, research suggests that term limits make it less likely that the policies from state legislatures will reflect public opinion in the state (Lax and Phillips 2012). In other words, term limits make it less likely that state legislatures will give the people what they want. Opponents argue that applying term limits to the United States Congress would likely give more power to the president, while also reducing democratic accountability in the national legislature.

Review Questions

1. What are the average reelection rates in the U.S. House of Representatives and the Senate?
2. Why did the U.S. Supreme Court rule Congressional term limits unconstitutional?
3. What are the main arguments against legislative term limits?
4. What are the specific advantages that incumbents in Congress have over challengers?
5. Why do term limits give more power to the executive branch?

Discussion Questions

1. Should states have the power to impose term limits on their congressional representatives?
2. How much do you trust other voters to make good decisions in the voting booth?
3. Can you think of any ways to reduce the incumbency advantage besides term limits?
4. Should we repeal the 22nd Amendment that imposes a two-term limit on the presidency?

Sources for Further Inquiry

Books

Bowler, Shaun, and Todd Donovan. 2013. *The Limits of Electoral Reform*. New York, NY: Oxford University Press.

Carey, John M., Richard G. Niemi, and Lynda W. Powell. 2009. *Term Limits in State Legislatures*. Ann Arbor, MI: University of Michigan Press.

Gaddie, Ronald Keith. 2003. *Born to Run: Origins of the Political Career*. New York, NY: Rowman & Littlefield Publishers.

Kousser, Thad. 2005. *Term Limits and the Dismantling of State Legislative Professionalism*. Cambridge, NY: Cambridge University Press.

Journal and Newspaper Articles

Broder, David S. 1994, February 9. "Why We'd Lose With Term Limits." *The Washington Post*. Retrieved from http://www.washingtonpost.com/wp-srv/politics/special/termlimits/stories/broder020994.htm.

Caress, Stanley M. 2015, Jan. 16. "Term Limits Don't Work." *U.S. News & World Report*. Retrieved from https://www.usnews.com/opinion/articles/2015/01/16/states-show-term-limits-wouldnt-work-for-congress

Carroll, Susan J., and Krista Jenkins. 2001. "Unrealized Opportunity? Term Limits and the Representation of Women in State Legislatures." *Women & Politics* 23(4): 1–30.

Cillizza, Chris. 2013, May 9. "People Hate Congress, but Most Incumbents Get Reelected. What Gives?" *The Washington Post.* Retrieved from https://www.washingtonpost.com/news/the-fix/wp/2013/05/09/people-hate-congress-but-most-incumbents-ge t-re-elected-what-gives/?utm_term=.5e6e7c78510b

Herrick, Rebekah, and Sue Thomas. 2005. "Do Term Limits Make a Difference? Ambition and Motivations among US State Legislators." *American Politics Research* 33(5): 726–747.

Lau, Richard R., David J. Andersen, and David P. Redlawsk. 2008. "An Exploration of Correct Voting in Recent US Presidential Elections." *American Journal of Political Science* 52(2): 395–411.

Lazarus, Jeffrey. 2006. "Term Limits' Multiple Effects on State Legislators' Career Decisions." *State Politics & Policy Quarterly* 6(4): 357–383.

Moncrief, Gary, and Joel A. Thompson. 2001. "On the Outside Looking in: Lobbyists' Perspectives on the Effects of State Legislative Term Limits." *State Politics & Policy Quarterly* 1(4): 394–411.

Nalder, Kimberly. 2007. "The Effect of State Legislative Term Limits on Voter Turnout." *State Politics & Policy Quarterly* 7(2): 187–210.

Steen, Jennifer A. 2006. "The Impact of State Legislative Term Limits on the Supply of Congressional Candidates." *State Politics & Policy Quarterly* 6(4): 430–447.

References

Bartels, Larry M. 1996. "Uninformed Votes: Information Effects in presidential Elections." *American Journal of Political Science* 40(1): 194–230.

Carey, John M., Richard G. Niemi, and Lynda W. Powell. 1998. "The Effects of Term Limits on State Legislatures." *Legislative Studies Quarterly* 23(2): 271–300.

Carey, John M., Richard G. Niemi, Lynda W. Powell, and Gary F. Moncrief. 2006. "The Effects of Term Limits on State Legislatures: A New Survey of the 50 States." *Legislative Studies Quarterly* 31(1): 105–134

Carpini, Michael X. Delli, and Scott Keeter. 1996. *What Americans Know about Politics and Why it Matters.* New Haven, CT: Yale University Press.

Hibbing, John R., and Elizabeth Theiss-Morse. 1995. *Congress as Public Enemy: Public Attitudes toward American Political Institutions.* New York, NY: Cambridge University Press.

Kahn, Kim F., and Patrick J. Kenney. 2002. "The Slant of the News: How Editorial Endorsements Influence Campaign Coverage and Citizen's Views of Candidates." *American Political Science Review* 96(2): 381–394.

Karp, Jeffrey A. 1995. "Explaining Public Support for Legislative Term Limits." *Public Opinion Quarterly* 59(3): 373–391.

Kousser, Thad. 2005. *Term Limits and the Dismantling of State Legislative Professionalism.* New York, NY: Cambridge University Press.

Lau, Richard R., and David P. Redlawsk. 1997. "Voting Correctly." *American Political Science Review* 91(3): 585–598.

Lau, Richard R., and David P. Redlawsk. 2001. "Advantages and Disadvantages of Cognitive Heuristics in Political Decision Making." *American Journal of Political Science* 45(4): 951–971.

Lax, Jeffrey R., and Justin H. Phillips. 2012. "The Democratic Deficit in the States." *American Journal of Political Science* 56(1): 148–166.

Lodge, Milton, and Charles S. Taber. 2005. "The Automaticity of Affect for Political Leaders, Groups, and Issues: An Experimental Test of the Hot Cognition Hypothesis." *Political Psychology* 26(3): 455–482.

Lodge, Milton, Kathleen M. McGraw, and Patrick Stroh. 1989. "An Impression-driven Model of Candidate Evaluation." *American Political Science Review* 83(2): 399–419.

Lupia, Arthur. 1994. "Shortcuts versus Encyclopedias: Information and Voting Behavior in California Insurance Reform Elections." *American Political Science Review* 88(1): 63–76.

Madison, James. 1788. Federalist No. 53. The Federalist Papers. Retrieved from https://www.congress.gov/resources/display/content/The+Federalist+Papers

OpenSecrets.org. (n.d.). "Re-Election Rates Over the Years." OpenSecrets.org Center for Responsive Politics. Retrieved from https://www.opensecrets.org/overview/reelect.php

Prior, Markus. 2007. *Post-Broadcast Democracy: How Media Choice Increases Inequality in Political Involvement and Polarizes Elections.* New York, NY: Cambridge University Press.

Saad, Lydia. 2013. "Americans Call for Term Limits, End to Electoral College." Gallup. Retrieved from http://www.gallup.com/poll/159881/americans-call-term-limits-end-electoral-college.aspx

Sabato, Larry. 2007. *A More Perfect Constitution: 23 Proposals to Revitalize our Constitution and Make America a Fairer Country.* New York, NY: Walker & Co.

U. S. Term Limits, Inc. v. Thornton, 514 U. S. 779(1995).

14

SHOULD SUPREME COURT JUSTICES BE ELECTED?

The Supreme Court of the United States is invested with a great deal of power over public policy. Federal courts can nullify state and local laws, while *Marbury v. Madison* (1803) gave the Supreme Court the power to strike down congressional legislation, which is referred to as judicial review. To be clear, the power of judicial review stems from the Supreme Court's ability to determine whether federal and state laws contradict the Constitution, and if so, the Court has the power to nullify those laws. The Supreme Court has used its power of judicial review to strike down both liberal and conservative legislation. Conservatives accuse the Supreme Court of judicial activism—meaning the courts make policy rather than interpret the law—for striking down limitations on abortion and legalizing gay marriage. Meanwhile, liberals accuse the court of activism for striking down laws that limit campaign spending and put restrictions on gun ownership.

As the Supreme Court has taken on a more activist role in public policy, it may be time to hold them accountable to the people through the electoral process. Article III of the U.S. Constitution gives the president the power to appoint Supreme Court justices with advice and consent of the Senate. The normal process is the president nominates a judge, and the Senate holds hearings and votes on confirmation. Although not required by the constitution, judges serving in federal courts are selected through the same confirmation process. It is important to notice that the American public is only included in the nomination process indirectly, through election of the President and Senators. The U.S. House of Representatives was not given any say over who sits on the Supreme Court, which is notable because it is the branch originally designed to be closest to the people. In fact, prior to ratification of the 17th Amendment in 1913, Senators were selected by state legislatures rather than the public, and of course the president is still selected by the

Electoral College and not the people. In other words, under the original constitution, Supreme Court justices were nominated and confirmed entirely by officials who were not subject to direct election by the people. Once they are confirmed, Supreme Court justices serve life terms, making them even less accountable to the people. Indeed, the Supreme Court was clearly designed to be the least democratic branch of government.

Many states have expanded the role of citizens in the judicial selection process by having some form of election for judges. On the state level, some judges are elected by the people in non-partisan elections where the judge's names appear on the ballot with no political party affiliation. Other states have partisan elections where judges have party labels on the ballots just like other politicians. Another way of electing judges is called the merit system, where the governor nominates a judge from a list created by a committee. After serving one term, judges are subject to a retention election, where voters simply vote on whether to keep the judge in office. One advantage of the merit system is that it weakens the governor's power to abuse the system by preventing them from stacking state courts with partisan allies. It also assures that judges will be qualified, while allowing the people to hold them accountable.

Should judicial elections be expanded to include members of the United States Supreme Court? The debate over judicial elections is a microcosm of the larger debate over the proper role of citizens in a democracy. Those supporting judicial elections favor more direct democracy by allowing the people to have a voice in the judicial branch. Opponents of judicial elections argue that most voters lack sufficient information to select the most qualified legal experts to serve as judges. Indeed, elections are more likely to produce popular judges, but not necessarily the most qualified. Additionally, electing judges is particularly problematic given their role in the American political system as a protector of individual rights, as well as a check on the executive and legislative branches of the federal government. Judicial elections threaten to undermine the independence of the Supreme Court by subjecting them to the public will.

An Uninformed Electorate

The framers of the United States constitution intentionally created a federal government that insulated officials from the general public. In fact, only members of the U.S. House of Representatives were directly elected by the people under the original constitution. Senators served six year terms and were selected by state legislatures, while presidents were elected by the Electoral College, and possibly Congress if no candidate received a majority. The least democratic of all institutions is the U.S. Supreme Court, where justices are nominated by the president and confirmed by the Senate. While the public has taken on a larger role in selecting Senators and the president, the Supreme Court remains separated from the public will.

If America is supposed to be a democracy, why are there so many barriers between the people and government officials? The answer lies in the framers' general distrust of the American public to make informed judgments, think rationally, and select the most qualified people to run the government. Instead, the framers feared the public because people are often irrational, short-sighted, uninformed, reactionary, and easily swayed by demagogues who appeal to emotion rather than reason. In the *Federalist* 10, James Madison (1787) argued that the constitution effectively restrained the masses from infringing on the rights of the minority, which he argued would naturally happen in a direct democracy. At the time, it was a *selling point* that the constitution limited the power of the public.

Over time, the public has taken on a larger role in governance both at the federal and state levels. The 17th Amendment gave the people the power to directly elect U.S. Senators, while reforms to the nominating process now allow the public to select presidential nominees instead of party officials. On the state level, the public has taken on an even larger role with many states allowing the public to vote for administrative officials such as lieutenant governors, transportation secretaries, and insurance commissioners. Many states also allow voters to select members of the legal system including: attorneys general, district attorneys, and judges. Although states vary in the types of judges they elect, 39 states have elections for at least some types of judges (Liptak 2008). The main problem with electing lower level administrative officials is that the public rarely has sufficient information to select the most qualified candidate. Elections help assure that the most popular candidate wins, but not necessarily the most qualified or experienced.

Judicial elections are especially problematic because they are usually non-partisan, meaning that judges' names appear on the ballot without any party affiliation. Party affiliation provides a strong message to voters regarding the judge's ideology and likely actions in office. Absent party affiliation, voters are usually staring at two names on the ballot that they likely have never heard of before they stepped into the voting booth. Opponents of judicial elections argue that most voters lack sufficient information to select the most qualified judge (Liptak 2008). Allowing governors to appoint judges is preferable because at least they have an incentive to appoint qualified individuals, and are subject to a check by state legislatures. Governors have staff and advisors that understand the law, are aware of the available pool of judges, and have time to consider each judge's qualifications and previous rulings. Altogether, the governor is in a position to make a much more informed decision than voters.

Judicial Independence

There is also an important difference between electing judges and electing other government officials. Unlike policy makers or district attorneys, judges are supposed to be independent and impartial. The role of judges in the judicial system is to assure that the government respects the rights of the citizens. Without judges, the government could lock up citizens without due process. Judges hear appeals that the government acted inappropriately, that a jury sentence was too harsh, or that a law is unconstitutional. In theory, judges are supposed to rule based on the law, and should not be influenced by public opinion, government officials, or concerns over reelection. Indeed, one of the purposes of the judiciary in general is to protect individual rights against the tyranny of the majority. If judges are elected by the public, it threatens their ability to remain independent and to base their decisions entirely on the rule of law. The desire to keep judges independent is why the constitution gives Supreme Court justices life terms in office, meaning they do not have to fear removal by Congress or the president, except in cases of impeachment.

Another problem with judicial elections is that judges must raise money to run for election and reelection. Given that the public usually has little information about judges, and elections are non-partisan, judges must increase name recognition by purchasing political advertisements on television, in newspapers, on billboards, and through direct mail. All of these advertisements cost substantial sums of money, especially if a judge is running for state-wide office on a state Supreme Court or appellate court. Indeed, imagine how costly a U.S. Supreme Court election would be if a judge were running a nationwide campaign. If judges are forced to raise money, it potentially results in a conflict of interest if they subsequently preside over cases involving donors. Additionally, Americans believe that judges collecting campaign donations represent a threat to the legitimacy of the judiciary (Gibson 2009). Raising money sets up a potential quid-pro-quo between the judge and donor. When judges are forced to raise money and cater to public opinion, it potentially threatens their independence and impartiality. Raising campaign funds may well threaten the independence of judges, whether or not they realize it.

Public Accountability

Supporters of judicial elections argue that it is necessary to hold judges accountable to the people given that the courts play such a large role in public policy. Why should judges be exempt from democratic governance when elected officials and prosecutors are accountable to the public will? If judges stray too far from the public will, the people should have the power to replace them. Indeed, this is the basic principle of representative democracy: that the will of the people prevails. Supporters of judicial elections argue that the best way to ensure that judges represent the people is to allow citizens to choose them, and to remove them from office if they do not serve in the public interest.

Furthermore, some argue that judges are merely politicians and therefore should be subject to popular election just like other politicians. On the Supreme Court, judges typically side with the ideology of the president that nominated them (Segal and Spaeth 2002). With a few exceptions, judges nominated by Republicans are consistently conservative in their rulings, while judges nominated by Democrats are consistently liberal. According to the attitudinal model of decision making, judges tend to make decisions that are consistent with their political ideology (Segal and Cover 1989). Judicial elections would allow voters to select judges that were liberal or conservative, and would subject judicial decisions to public scrutiny. Moreover, elected judges are more likely to fear punishment by voters if they stray too far from public opinion on an issue (Hall 1987). Consequently, the decisions of elected judges are more likely to follow public opinion than appointed judges (Brace and Boyea 2008). In short, knowing that they will have to face the voters will make Supreme Court justices more likely to give the people what they want.

Although judges would likely disagree, judicial decisions are not simply objective considerations of facts and evidence. Interpretations of laws and the constitution are subject to motivated reasoning and rationalizations (Braman and Nelson 2007). Even Supreme Court justices tend to engage in motivated reasoning in order to rule in ways that confirm their policy preferences. Indeed, given their extensive understanding of the law, judges are especially capable of rationalizing their decisions to fit some judicial ideology, even if they are merely voting on behalf of their preferred policies.

Judicial elections are also a way to reduce corruption because they prevent governors from stacking the courts with political allies. Many states have decidedly one party control, which allows governors to add partisans to the judicial branch. This process facilitates corruption because the judicial branch is going to oversee any trial that may involve the governor. It is unlikely that the judicial branch will be independent if most of the judges are allies of the governors. The main reason that many states initially adopted judicial elections was the belief that elected officials were more likely to be corrupted by self-interest and party faction than the public as a whole (Nelson 1993). The public may not be perfect, but they are far less susceptible to corruption than elected officials.

Review Questions

1.   Why did authors of the constitution desire to insulate public officials from the mass public?
2.   What are the different types of judicial elections?
3.   Why is electing judges different than electing representatives or senators?
4.   What is the attitudinal model of judicial decision making?

Discussion Questions

1.   Should judges be accountable to the public?
2.   Should there be a national ballot initiative where citizens can vote on federal policy?
3.   How might campaign donations affect judges' ability to be impartial in their rulings?
4.   Should Supreme Court judges serve a fixed number of years instead of a life term?

Sources for Further Inquiry

Books

Bonneau, Chris W., and Melinda Gann Hall. 2009. *In Defense of Judicial Elections*. New York, NY: Routledge Press.
Devins, Neal, and Lawrence Baum. 2019. *The Company They Keep: How Partisan Divisions Came to the Supreme Court*. New York, NY: Oxford University Press.
Gibson, James L. 2012. *Electing Judges: The Surprising Effects of Campaigning on Judicial Legitimacy*. Chicago, IL: University of Chicago Press.
Hall, Melinda Gann. 2014. *Attacking Judges: How Campaign Advertising Influences State Supreme Court Elections*. Stanford, CA: Stanford University Press.
Kahn, Paul W. 2002. *The Reign of Law: Marbury v. Madison and the Construction of America*. New Haven, CT: Yale University Press.
Lasser, William. 2017. *The Limits of Judicial Power: the Supreme Court in American Politics*. Chapel Hill, NC: UNC Press Books.

Journal and Newspaper Articles

Bonneau, Chris W. 2011, May 26. "Why we Should Keep Judicial Elections." *The Washington Post*. Retrieved from https://www.washingtonpost.com/opinions/why-we-should-keep-judicial-elections/2011/05/26/AGt08HCH_story.html?utm_term=.386d05e44479
Mishler, William, and Reginald S. Sheehan. 1996. "Public Opinion, the Attitudinal Model, and Supreme Court Decision Making: A Micro-analytic Perspective." *The Journal of Politics* 58(1): 169–200.
Unah, Isaac, and Ange Hancock. 2006. "US Supreme Court Decision Making, Case Salience, and the Attitudinal Model." *Law & Policy* 28(3): 295–320.
Watkins, William J. 2010, June 25. "A Role for the People in Judicial Selection." *Washington Examiner*. Retrieved from http://www.independent.org/news/article.asp?id=2817

References

Brace, Paul, and Brent D. Boyea. 2008. "State Public Opinion, the Death Penalty, and the Practice of Electing Judges." *American Journal of Political Science* 52(2): 360–372.
Braman, Eileen, and Thomas E. Nelson. 2007. "Mechanism of Motivated Reasoning? Analogical Perception in Discrimination Disputes." *American Journal of Political Science* 51(4): 940–956.
Gibson, James L. 2009. "'New-Style' Judicial Campaigns and the Legitimacy of State High Courts." *The Journal of Politics* 71(4): 1285–1304.
Hall, Melinda Gann. 1987. "Constituent Influence in State Supreme Courts: Conceptual Notes and a Case Study." *The Journal of Politics* 49(4): 1117–1124.
Liptak, Adam. 2008, May 28. "Rendering Justice, with One Eye on Re-election." *New York Times*. Retrieved from http://www.nytimes.com/2008/05/25/us/25exception.html
Madison, James. (1787). Federalist No. 10. The Federalist Papers. Retrieved from https://www.congress.gov/resources/display/content/The+Federalist+Papers
Marbury v. Madison, 1 Cranch 137(1803).

Nelson, Caleb. 1993. "A Re-Evaluation of Scholarly Explanations for the Rise of the Elective Judiciary in Antebellum America." *The American Journal of Legal History* 37(2): 190–224.

Segal, Jeffrey A., and Albert D. Cover. 1989. "Ideological Values and the Votes of US Supreme Court Justices." *American Political Science Review* 83(2): 557–565.

Segal, Jeffrey A., and Harold J. Spaeth. 2002. *The Supreme Court and the Attitudinal Model Revisited*. Cambridge: Cambridge University Press.

15

SHOULD VOTING BE MANDATORY IN NATIONAL ELECTIONS?

Every two years, a large portion of Americans do not show up to cast a ballot in national elections. In 2016, only 58 percent of eligible voters showed up to vote in the presidential election (Bialik 2016; Regan 2016). Turnout is even lower when a president is not at the top of the ballot; only 36 percent of eligible voters voted in the 2014 Congressional elections (Bialik 2016). In other words, 42 percent of eligible voters do not vote in national elections, while another 22 percent only show up during presidential elections. Comparatively, the United States lags behind many other industrialized democracies when it comes to citizens voting in national elections (see Desilver 2017).

When a large portion of Americans do not vote, it results in the under-representation of particular social and political groups. There are important differences between the types of people who show up to vote on Election Day and those who choose not to vote. Non-voters are more likely to be young, poor, non-white, and less educated (Pew Research Center 2014). If these groups are underrepresented in the electorate, their preferences will carry less weight in the policy-making process. Non-voters are also more likely to identify as independents and moderates, which potentially contributes to political polarization and legislative gridlock. The larger the gap between voters and non-voters, the less likely it is that government policies will reflect the will of the people. This is one reason why policymakers on the state level have tried numerous methods to increase voter turnout, such as same day registration, early voting, and even vote-by-mail in Oregon and Washington. Unfortunately, none of the common electoral reforms have caused large scale increases in voter turnout (Burden et al. 2014).

One way to increase turnout is to make voting *mandatory* by fining eligible voters who do not show up to voting stations. States already keep records of eligible voters, and which ones showed up at the polls. To establish mandatory voting, state governments would simply mail a small fine to eligible voters who did not show up in the previous election. Research suggests that mandatory voting would provide a sufficient incentive to increase turnout (Hirczy 1994). Compulsory voting is not unprecedented, as at least 18 other countries currently require eligible voters to show up to the polls, even if they do not cast a ballot. There are a wide variety of nations with compulsory voting "including Australia, Belgium, Egypt, Mexico and Turkey" (Corbin 2015). Based on the results in other countries, mandatory voting is very likely to increase the percentage of eligible voters that cast a ballot. For example, Australia enacted mandatory voting in 1924, and voter turnout increased from roughly 60 percent prior to the law to over 90 percent in the 1925 election (Galston and Dionne 2015). Another case is the Netherlands, who repealed their mandatory voting law in the late 1960s, after which turnout dropped from 95 percent to an average of 80 percent of eligible voters (Galston and Dionne 2015). Belgium also has mandatory voting and has the highest turnout of any nation (87%) among their voting-age population (Desilver 2017). In short, the existing evidence suggests that mandatory voting would be an effective way to increase turnout.

Although mandatory voting would likely increase turnout, it is questionable whether forcing people to vote would be ethical, or even beneficial for American democracy. The central question in the debate over mandatory voting is whether the right to vote is a freedom or a responsibility. Do American citizens have a civic duty to voice their preferences to the government? Does the right to vote include the freedom not to participate? Another important question in this debate is whether requiring people to vote will improve American democracy. Although compulsory voting would certainly increase the incentive to vote, democracy may not be strengthened by people voting with little interest in, and information about, the political system. In short, the debate over mandatory voting involves both the ethics of forcing people to vote, and its likely consequences for government effectiveness.

Is Voting a Right or a Responsibility?

Is citizenship a right or a responsibility? Currently, being a United States citizen does not require a great deal of service. Citizens are expected to obey laws, pay their taxes, and occasionally report for jury duty. Do we have a responsibility to serve our country to a greater capacity? The extent to which citizenship requires service is central to debates over the military draft, proposals for mandatory community service, and yes, mandatory voting.

Supporters of mandatory voting argue that Americans owe it to their fellow citizens to participate in the democratic process for the benefit of everyone. Does this require people to do something they might not otherwise do? Of course it does, but that does not mean it is unethical or without precedent. The United States has forced citizens into military service for the good of the country. The government requires people to file their tax returns, educate their children, serve in jury duty, and testify when they witness a crime. All of those things require more effort than showing up to a polling place once every two years! Sometimes it is acceptable to force people to do things if it promotes the overall good of society. Similar to jury duty and educating one's children, compulsory voting promotes a healthy and more representative democracy. Supporters of mandatory voting argue that requiring American citizens to show up at the polls for congressional elections every two years is the least they can do in service to their country. After all, being a United States citizen does not currently require a great deal of effort.

The primary line of opposition to mandatory voting is that people should have the freedom to choose whether to vote. In the U.S. Constitution, voting is labeled as a *right*, and as such, the government must provide people the opportunity to vote. Other rights allow people the option not to exercise their rights. People have a right to a jury trial and a lawyer, but they are not *forced* to have them. When people do not show up to vote, they are making a choice. Who knows why they are choosing not to vote. Perhaps they do not have the time, or they do not care who wins the election, or they are protesting the entire political system. Regardless of their motivation, each person should have the freedom to participate or to abstain. A democracy is supposed to give people what they want, and if they desire not to vote, then the government should allow them that freedom. Paradoxically, if the government started fining people who chose not to vote, they may end up voting for candidates that promise to repeal a mandatory voting law.

One could argue that mandatory voting violates the rights of certain religions and people who do not vote for political reasons. Most countries with mandatory voting get around this problem by not requiring people to cast a ballot, but instead they simply have to show up to the polls. For instance, Australia does not require citizens to vote, but they must show up to the polls or they receive a small fine, and the fines increase the more a person fails to show up. In other words, people could still show up and not cast a ballot. Would a similar system in the United States still violate people's freedom to be left alone?

Ultimately, whether mandatory voting is ethical may depend on its effects on government effectiveness. On the one hand, mandatory voting is more justified if it causes a substantial improvement in government representativeness. On the other hand, forcing people to vote is less justified if it has minimal or negative effects on government effectiveness. As with many government policies that prevents or forces behaviors, the question comes down to whether the potential benefits of the policy outweigh the imposition on individual freedom. Is it ever ethical for the government to force citizens to act in the public interest? Of course it is, but *only when the activity produces sufficient public benefit to outweigh the individual costs*. In short, whether one considers mandatory voting justified depends, to a large extent, on how much benefit it will bring to society. The next section examines the potential benefits and consequences of mandatory voting.

Mandatory Voting and Government Effectiveness

The debate over mandatory voting is an example of the larger question regarding public participation in government. Opponents of mandatory voting argue that democracy would be weakened if non-voters were forced to provide their input into the political system. Non-voters pay very little attention to political affairs, and are largely uninformed about government and public policy (Carpini and Keeter 1996; Brennan 2011; Gelman 2011). If people lack basic political information, one can only wonder about the basis for their voting decision. For example, those with less political knowledge are more likely to support policies that infringe on basic rights and liberties such as free speech or the right to jury trial (Chong 1993; Nelson, Clawson and Oxley 1997). If non-voters do not understand the principles protected in the bill of rights, they may be more willing to vote for candidates or policies that infringe on those rights.

The best argument *in favor* of mandatory voting is that elected representatives are less likely to pay attention to the concerns of non-voters. If non-voters were no different than voters, mandatory voting would be unnecessary because the decisions of voters would perfectly represent non-voters. Systematic inequalities in voting turnout create a government that serves some groups of people more than others. For various reasons, non-voters are more likely to be poor, unemployed, uneducated, and young (Hill 2011; Galston and Dionne 2015). Prior to the 2014 congressional elections, roughly a third (33%) of Americans made less than $30,000 a year, but that group made up only 19 percent of likely voters (Pew Research Center 2014). One reason that low-income Americans are less likely to vote is because they typically have hourly wage jobs and would lose money if they left work for one or two hours to stand in line at a voting booth. Compulsory voting would increase their financial incentive to vote, especially if the fines increased the more often people failed to vote. Perhaps this is one reason why countries with compulsory voting tend to have less income inequality than countries with voluntary voting (Hill 2011).

The voting population is also significantly older, whiter, and more educated than the actual population. According to the Pew Research Center, 18–29-year-olds made up 22 percent of the population in 2014, but only 10 percent of likely voters in the congressional elections that year (Pew Research Center 2014). Furthermore, whites made up roughly two-thirds of the population, but were 77 percent of likely voters. Meanwhile, a majority of non-voters have never attended college, while nearly three-fourths (72%) of likely voters have at least some college education (Pew Research Center 2014). There are important differences between voters and non-voters, which are likely to create inequalities in political representation. Mandatory voting may equal out those disparities, and create a government that is more responsive to all groups of people.

Another important benefit of compulsory voting is that it might reduce the partisan polarization of the electorate, which could result in a better functioning government. Especially at the federal level, a sharp ideological polarization has occurred among members of Congress. Over the last few decades, members of Congress have become more ideologically extreme and less likely to compromise with members of the opposing party (Poole and Rosenthal 2000; Theriault 2006; Mann and Ornstein 2016). The unwillingness to compromise has caused unprecedented gridlock and record levels of public dissatisfaction with the federal government (Binder 2014).

Part of the problem is that extreme partisans are more likely than moderates to show up to vote on a consistent basis, and this is especially true in party primaries where candidates are selected for the general election (Galston and Dionne 2015). According to the Pew Research Center, self-identified partisans—those saying they are either Democrats or Republicans—made up about 57 percent of the population in 2014, but made up over two-thirds (68%) of likely voters in the midterm congressional elections (Pew Research Center 2014). Consistent voters tend to be more partisan and ideologically extreme than infrequent voters (Abramowitz 2010 and 2013). Extreme partisans are the most likely to vote consistently, but they are also less likely to support legislative compromise (Harbridge and Malhotra 2011). Consequently, elected officials are reluctant to compromise with the opposing party because they are afraid of losing a primary where most voters are extreme partisans who hate compromise (Boatright 2013). Mandatory voting would increase the number of moderates and independents that vote, and because those types of voters desire legislative compromise, elected officials would have more incentive to reach across party lines (Harbridge and Malhotra 2011; Galston and Dionne 2015; Mann and Ornstein 2016). In short, mandatory voting could help reduce congressional gridlock, and in doing so, possibly increase public satisfaction with government.

On a related note, mandatory voting may also change how candidates campaign for office. Currently, candidates for elected office tend to devote most of their resources to getting their partisan base to the polls. That is, Republican candidates try to get fellow Republicans to vote, while the Democratic candidates focus on getting Democrats to the voting booths. In order to mobilize their partisan voters, elected officials tend to focus their attention on negative attacks and divisive issues. As a result, partisans end up voting out of fear of the opposing party's candidate, rather than enthusiasm for their candidate (Pew Research Center 2016; Abramowitz and Webster 2018). If mandatory voting increased turnout, candidates would have more incentive to speak to moderate and independent voters. Additionally, if candidates did not have to engage in costly get-out-the-vote campaigns, they would not have to raise as much money. Instead, elected officials could spend less of their time raising money, and more of their time serving their constituents.

Review Questions

1. What groups are less likely to consistently vote in national elections?
2. How might mandatory voting make government more responsive to all people?

3. What are some of the potential dangers posed by mandatory voting?
4. How might mandatory voting reduce congressional polarization and gridlock?

Discussion Questions

1. Is voting a right or a responsibility?
2. Would people become more informed about politics if they were forced to vote?
3. Should voters be forced to take a political competency test in order to register to vote?
4. What sorts of policies, besides mandatory voting, would increase turnout?
5. Should the United States allow citizens to vote over the internet?

Sources for Further Inquiry

Books

Elkink, Johan A., and David M. Farrell, eds. 2015. *The Act of Voting: Identities, Institutions and Locale.* New York, NY: Routledge.

Green, Donald P., and Alan S. Gerber. 2015. *Get out the Vote: How to Increase Voter Turnout.* Washington, D.C.: Brookings Institution Press.

Lupia, Arthur. 2016. *Uninformed: Why People Know so Little about Politics and what we Can Do about It.* New York, NY: Oxford University Press.

Malkopoulou, Anthoula. 2014. *The History of Compulsory Voting in Europe: Democracy's Duty?* New York, NY: Routledge.

Springer, Melanie Jean. 2014. *How the States Shaped the Nation: American Electoral Institutions and Voter Turnout, 1920–2000.* Chicago, IL: University of Chicago Press.

Journal and Newspaper Articles

Aly, Waleed. 2017, January 19. "Voting Should be Mandatory." *The New York Times.* Retrieved from https://www.nytimes.com/roomfordebate/2011/11/07/should-voting-in-the-us-be-mandatory-14/understanding-nonvoters

Dassonneville, Ruth, Fernando Feitosa, Marc Hooghe, Richard R. Lau, and Dieter Stiers. 2018. "Compulsory Voting Rules, Reluctant Voters and Ideological Proximity Voting." *Political Behavior* 41(1): 209–230. Retrieved from https://link.springer.com/article/10.1007/s11109-018-9448-6

Elliott, Kevin J. 2017. "Aid for our Purposes: Mandatory Voting as Precommitment and Nudge." *The Journal of Politics* 79(2): 656–669.

Hajnal, Zoltan, Nazita Lajevardi, and Lindsay Nielson. 2017. "Voter Identification Laws and the Suppression of Minority Votes." *The Journal of Politics* 79(2): 363–379.

Highton, Benjamin. 2017. "Voter identification laws and turnout in the United States." *Annual Review of Political Science* 20: 149–167.

Holbein, John B., and D. Sunshine Hillygus. 2016. "Making Young Voters: The Impact of Preregistration on Youth Turnout." *American Journal of Political Science* 60(2): 364–382.

Panagopoulos, C. 2008. "The Calculus of Voting in Compulsory Voting Systems." *Political Behavior* 30(4): 455–467.

Sheppard, Jill. 2016, January 8. "Compulsory Voting Results in More Evenly Distributed Political Knowledge." The London School of Economics and Political Science. Retrieved from http://blogs.lse.ac.uk/europpblog/2016/01/08/compulsory-voting-results-in-more-evenly-distributed-political-knowledge/

Singh, Shane P. 2016. "Elections as Poorer Reflections of Preferences under Compulsory Voting." *Electoral Studies* 44: 56–65.

Stephanopoulos, Nicholas. 2015, November 2. "A Feasible Roadmap to Compulsory Voting." *The Atlantic.* Retrieved from https://www.theatlantic.com/politics/archive/2015/11/a-feasible-roadmap-to-compulsory-voting/413422/

References

Abramowitz, Alan. 2010. *The Disappearing Center: Engaged Citizens, Polarization, and American Democracy.* New Haven, CT: Yale University Press.

Abramowitz, Alan. 2013. *The Polarized Public?: Why American Government is So Dysfunctional.* Upper Saddle River, NY: Pearson.

Abramowitz, Alan I., and Steven W. Webster. 2018. "Negative Partisanship: Why Americans Dislike Parties But Behave Like Rabid Partisans." *Political Psychology* 39(1): 119–135.

Bialik, Carl. 2016, November 15. "No, Voter Turnout Wasn't Way Down from 2012." Fivethirtyeight. Retrieved from https://fivethirtyeight.com/features/no-voter-turnout-was-nt-way-down-from-2012/

Binder, Sarah A. 2014, May 27. "Polarized We Govern?" Brookings Institute. Retrieved from https://www.brookings.edu/research/polarized-we-govern/

Boatright, R.G. 2013. *Getting Primaried: The Changing Politics of Congressional Primary Challenges.* Ann Arbor, MI: University of Michigan Press.

Brennan, Jason. 2011, November 7. "Mandatory Voting Would Be a Disaster." *The New York Times.* Retrieved from https://www.nytimes.com/roomfordebate/2011/11/07/should-voting-in-the-us-be-mandatory-14/mandatory-voting-would-be-a-disaster

Burden, Barry C., David T. Canon, Kenneth R. Mayer, & Donald P. Moynihan. 2014. "Election Laws, Mobilization, and Turnout." *American Journal of Political Science* 58(1): 95–109.

Carpini, Michael X. Delli, and Scott Keeter. 1996. *What Americans Know about Politics and why it Matters.* New Haven, CT: Yale University Press.

Chong, Dennis. (1993). "How People Think, Reason, and Feel about Rights and Liberties." *American Journal of Political Science* 37(3): 867–899.

Corbin, Cristina. 2015, March 20. "Constitution Experts on Obama Mandatory Voting Idea: Never Gonna Happen." Fox News.com. Retrieved from http://www.foxnews.com/politics/2015/03/20/mandatory-voting-experts.html

Desilver, Drew. 2017, May 15. "U.S. Trails Most Developed Countries in Voter Turnout." Pew Research Center. Retrieved from http://www.pewresearch.org/fact-tank/2016/08/02/u-s-voter-turnout-trails-most-developed-countries/

Galston, William A. and E.J. Dionne, Jr. 2015, September 25. "Should Voting be Compulsory?" *Newsweek.* Retrieved from http://www.newsweek.com/should-voting-be-compulsory-376905

Gelman, Andrew. 2011, November 7. "Understanding Nonvoters." *New York Times.* Retrieved from https://www.nytimes.com/roomfordebate/2011/11/07/should-voting-in-the-us-be-mandatory-14/understanding-nonvoters

Harbridge, Laurel, and Neil Malhotra. 2011. "Electoral Incentives and Partisan Conflict in Congress: Evidence from Survey Experiments." *American Journal of Political Science* 55(3): 494–510.

Hill, Lisa. 2011, November 7. "What We've Seen in Australia with Mandatory Voting." *The New York Times*. Retrieved from https://www.nytimes.com/roomfordebate/2011/11/07/should-voting-in-the-us-be-mandatory-14/what-weve-seen-in-australia-with-ma ndatory-voting

Hirczy, Wolfgang. 1994. "The Impact of Mandatory Voting Laws on Turnout: A Quasi-experimental Approach." *Electoral Studies* 13(1): 64–76. http://www.sciencedirect.com/science/article/pii/0261379494900094

Mann, Thomas E., and Norman J. Ornstein. 2016. *It's Even Worse than it Looks: How the American Constitutional System Collided with the New Politics of Extremism*. New York, NY: Basic Books.

Nelson, Thomas E., Rosalee A. Clawson, and Zoe M. Oxley. 1997. "Media Framing of a Civil Liberties Conflict and its Effect on Tolerance." *American Political Science Review* 91(3): 567–583.

Pew Research Center. 2014, October 30. "The Party of Non-Voters." Retrieved from http://www.people-press.org/2014/10/31/the-party-of-nonvoters-2/

Pew Research Center. 2016, June 22. "Partisanship and Political Animosity in 2016." Retrieved from http://www.people-press.org/2016/06/22/partisanship-and-political-a nimosity-in-2016/

Poole, Keith T., and Howard Rosenthal. 2000. *Congress: A Political-economic History of Roll Call Voting*. Oxford: Oxford University Press.

Regan, Michael D. 2016, November 20. "What Does Voter Turnout Tell Us about the 2016 Election?" PBS Newshour. Retrieved from https://www.pbs.org/newshour/poli tics/voter-turnout-2016-elections

Theriault, Sean M. 2006. "Party Polarization in the US Congress: Member Replacement and Member Adaptation." *Party Politics* 12(4): 483–503.

16

SHOULD A NATIONAL POPULAR VOTE REPLACE THE ELECTORAL COLLEGE?

In the United States, presidents are not technically elected by the people, but instead are elected by members of the Electoral College in each state. Following every presidential election, electors gather in their states to cast the votes that actually matter, at least according to the U.S. Constitution. The idea of a few individuals conducting elections on behalf of the many is nothing new. In fact, precursors to the Electoral College date all the way back to the 11th century! Elections of some princes, magistrates, and even the Pope, were conducted under rules similar to the Electoral College (Colomer 2016). Prior to the 17th Amendment, even U.S. Senators were elected by state legislatures rather than the people, and those legislatures were rarely apportioned based on equal representation. Prior to the *Reynolds v. Sims* (1964) decision, many state legislative districts were apportioned based on land rather than the number of people living in a district. In short, there is a long history of political leaders electing other political leaders, and frequently those electors represented disproportionate populations.

Although systems similar to the Electoral College are nothing new, the United States' version resulted from a compromise between delegates at the Constitutional Convention in 1787. During the convention in Philadelphia, the framers of the constitution debated the best way to elect the president. The first proposal was the Virginia plan, in which the president was selected by Congress, but this plan faced opposition on two fronts. First, small states objected to a presidential election by the *entire* Congress because larger states would have more power in selecting the president. Second, many convention delegates were concerned that the President would be beholden to the will of Congress if he relied upon them for reelection. A system of checks and balances required that the president be elected separate from Congress.

Some suggested that the president be elected by a popular vote among the people, but small states were once again concerned they would have little say in who became president (Rudalevige 2016). Southern states also objected to a popular vote because the three-fifths compromise counted slaves for representation in Congress even though they could not vote in any elections. Consequently, states with large numbers of slaves would have more say in Congress than in a popular vote, which motivated those states to oppose a popular vote for president. Additionally, many delegates did not believe the American people were sufficiently informed to select the most qualified candidate for president.

To satisfy all of these competing concerns, the framers created an Electoral College that would elect the president as a separate entity from Congress. Each state receives the same number of electors as they have representation in *both* houses of Congress—House seats plus Senate seats. Currently, there are 435 members of the House of Representatives and 100 Senators, equaling 535 total members of Congress. In 1961, ratification of the 23rd Amendment gave three electors to the District of Columbia, which brought the total number of electors to 538. There is also a majority requirement in the Electoral College, meaning that the winner must receive more than half (270) of all electors. If no candidate receives a majority of electors, the House of Representatives selects the president, with each state getting one vote. State legislatures decide how electors are allocated, but almost all states award their electors to the candidate getting the most state-wide votes. The only exceptions are Maine and Nebraska, which award two electors to the winner of the state-wide vote, and each congressional elector to the candidate who wins that specific Congressional district.

The Electoral College compromise satisfied the concerns of convention delegates. Large states were happy because they would have more power over the election than if only the Senate elected the president. Small states benefited from the requirement that the winning candidate receive a majority of Electoral College votes. Absent an Electoral College majority, the House of Representatives would elect the president with each state getting one vote. Since each state had equal representation, small states would carry greater weight in the outcome. States with a large number of slaves were satisfied because slaves would contribute to their number of Electors—by way of the House of Representatives—without requiring slaves to vote in the presidential election, which would be required under the popular vote plan. Finally, electors would not be members of congress, which allows the president to act as a separate institution and serve as a legitimate check on congressional power. In short, the best way to think of the Electoral College is the result of a compromise between competing interests at the *time of the convention*, rather than a master stroke of political genius (Rudalevige 2016).

Recent polls suggest that most Americans support replacing the Electoral College with a popular vote for president. For example, a Gallup poll in 2013 found that 63 percent of Americans supported a popular vote for president, while only 29 percent wanted to keep the Electoral College, and another 8 percent had no opinion (Saad 2013). Public support for a national popular vote has also been fairly stable over time (*ibid.*). Opposition to the Electoral College crosses partisan lines as well, with 61 percent of Republicans and 66 percent of Democrats supporting instituting a popular vote for President. In short, most Americans support the replacing the Electoral College with a popular vote.

The debate over the Electoral College centers on three key issues. On a theoretical level, there is a long-running debate in this country over whether the United States of America is one nation or a collection of states. Those believing that the *United States* is a collection of separate states would probably support retaining the Electoral College, while those seeing America as one nation would probably support a popular vote. On a practical level, both the Electoral College and the popular vote potentially weaken presidential mandates and the legitimacy of the electoral process. The third level of the debate concerns who benefits from the Electoral College and who benefits from the popular vote. The Electoral College benefits small, rural, and swing states. Conversely, large cities and more populous states would get most of the candidates' attention if the president were elected by a nationwide popular vote. Moreover, at any one time the Electoral College seems to benefit one political party or another, which makes it unlikely that a popular vote would garner enough support for a constitutional amendment. The remainder of this chapter deals with each of these broad issues.

Are We One Nation or a Collection of States?

Supporters of the Electoral College argue that it is consistent with the federal system of government established in the constitution. In no election do Americans vote as United States citizens, but instead they vote as members of the states where they reside. The federal government does not only represent the people, but also the economic interests of *regions* of the country. That is precisely the reason for the U.S. Senate, which represents the interests of states as an entity and is structured such that every state has equal representation, regardless of how many citizens reside in each state. The Senate allows *states* power to block legislation that is contrary to their interests. In other words, the constitution sets up a government in which states, rather than people, come together for a common purpose.

On the other hand, there are reasons to argue that the president uniquely represents all Americans, and therefore *should* be elected by a popular vote. The preamble to the constitution begins "we the *people*, in order to form a more perfect union" which suggests that the government serves the people and not the states. Perhaps the best argument against the "collection of states" argument is that times change! The 14th Amendment established individual rights as citizens of the United States, over and above the laws of particular states. In other words, the Supreme Court now recognizes individuals as having rights as U.S. citizens and places those rights above the laws of any particular state law. Furthermore, it makes no sense to cling to an electoral system because of a compromise that men made over *two hundred years ago*! Opponents of the Electoral College argue that the system is outdated and should be modified to the preferences of the modern populace. Given that opinion polls consistently show that the public supports a popular vote, the constitution should be amended to give the people what they want.

Practical Concerns

There are some practical reasons to oppose abolishing the Electoral College in favor of the popular vote. For one, the Electoral College makes it less likely that the entire country will go through a messy nationwide recount. If the popular vote is close, the Electoral College vote is usually decisive as it was in 1960—or isolates the recount to one state, as it did in Florida during the 2000 election. During the 2000 presidential election, the popular vote slightly favored Al Gore, but George W. Bush won the Electoral College. If there were a popular vote, Bush would have likely called for a nationwide recount. The Electoral College limited the messy recount to the state of Florida, since that was the only state that mattered to the result.

A related benefit of the Electoral College is that it provides a larger mandate for the winning candidate. In modern elections, presidents usually win by a small percentage of the popular vote, but that often turns into a large victory in the Electoral College. For example, in the 2012 presidential election, Barack Obama got 51 percent of the popular vote to beat Mitt Romney's 47 percent, but Obama won 332 electoral votes compared to only 206 for Romney. In other words, Obama won the popular vote by 4 percent, but won the Electoral College by 23 percent! Larger Electoral College victories provide presidents more legitimacy when they take office. Of course, opponents of the Electoral College are quick to point out that exaggerating the margin of victory only creates the illusion of a mandate, while the reality is that the country is very much divided.

Opponents of the Electoral College also point out that a president's legitimacy is weakened in cases where they win the Electoral College, but lose the popular vote. In those circumstances, the opposition party may see little reason to accept the new president, given that they only won because of an anachronistic electoral system. The Electoral College allows the will of the minority to defeat the will of the majority. While that works out well for the minority, it delegitimizes American democracy as well as the individuals holding the presidency. It is difficult for a president to declare a mandate when more people voted for someone else in the election.

Some States Benefit More than Others

Opponents of the Electoral College also argue that it benefits some states, while dis-advantaging others. First, the way electors are allocated gives greater weight to the voters in less populous states. For example, Wyoming has three Electoral College votes and (in the 2010 census) 563,626 people, meaning Wyoming gets one elector for every 187,875 citizens (U.S. Census 2010). Meanwhile, California has 37,253,956 people and 55 electors, which equates to one elector for every 677,344 people. In other words, votes cast in Wyoming carry roughly *three times* more weight than votes cast in California. This system gives voters in less populous states a distinct advantage in deciding who is elected president. It seems undemocratic to give some citizens more political power for *no other reason* than they happen to live in a less populous state.

Second, the Electoral College also affects which states get attention from the presidential candidates as well as sitting presidents running for reelection. During presidential elections, candidates focus their attention on only a small group of swing states that are electorally close. In recent elections, states such as Ohio, Florida, Virginia, and Pennsylvania have received the most attention from the candidates. Meanwhile, more populous states, such as California, Texas, New York, and Georgia, have been largely ignored because they are not considered competitive. Even after the election is over, presidents spend most of their first term travelling to swing states instead of safe states. Presidents have little incentive to handle regional problems if they know those states are unlikely to vote for them in the upcoming election. For example, a Republican president has little incentive to address the concerns of fisherman in the Pacific Northwest, while a Democrat can largely ignore the problems of farmers in the southeast. Presidents are elected to represent all Americans, yet the Electoral College makes them favor some states more than others.

Another problem with the Electoral College is that it potentially subverts the will of the people. Under the rules of the Electoral College, presidential elections can result in a candidate winning the popular vote, but losing the presidency. In fact, the candidate receiving the most votes lost the Electoral College on five separate occasions including: 1824, 1876, 1888, 2000, and 2016. In the most recent example, Hillary Clinton lost the presidential election to Donald Trump despite receiving over 3 million more votes nationwide. Opponents of the Electoral College argue it is an anachronistic system that undermines the will of the majority. After all, the president is elected to represent all of the people. States already have representation in the Senate, so why pervert the presidential election as well. If the president is elected nationwide, it makes more sense to weight everyone's vote equally. Although the Electoral College worked as a compromise at the convention, it is outdated and lacks support by most of the American people (Saad 2013).

Opponents of the popular vote argue that while the Electoral College focuses attention on rural states and swing states, the popular vote would favor large cities. Presidential candidates would focus on large population centers because they offer more bang for the buck in campaign stops and political advertising. Conversely, a popular vote may allow candidates to largely ignore the unique problems of rural areas throughout the country. Supporters of the Electoral College argue that it forces candidates to pay attention to urban, suburban, and rural voters, rather than focusing exclusively on large cities (Gregg 2012). Indeed, the Electoral College requires candidates to form large coalitions of voters from geographically diverse states, which will help them govern once in office. Under a popular vote, Congressmen would see little incentive in compromising with the president that lost their home state or district, making it very difficult for the newly elected president to accomplish his agenda.

Partisanship over Principles

Despite all of the logical arguments for and against the Electoral College, the main reason a popular vote is unlikely comes down to partisanship. Voters with strong attachments to one of the two political parties will likely support or oppose Electoral College reforms depending entirely on its electoral benefits for their preferred party. Aldrich and colleagues (2014) found that prior to the 2004 presidential election, people supported Electoral College reforms that helped their preferred candidate win, but opposed changes that helped the opposing candidate. At any one time, one of the two political parties will benefit from the Electoral College. In recent elections, it is Republicans that have benefited as both George W. Bush and Donald Trump won their elections, despite losing the popular vote. Since the winning party benefits from the Electoral College rules, congressmen and the president have little incentive to push for change.

Unfortunately, too many debates about governmental and electoral reforms are ultimately decided on the basis of which political party happens to benefit at the moment. Given that Electoral College reform would require a constitutional amendment, it is very unlikely that there will ever be two-thirds of each house of Congress, and three-fourths of state legislatures that are willing to change to a popular vote. As long as one of the two Parties benefits, there will be sufficient political will to *block* any change to the Electoral College. Unfortunately, partisans will typically accept *any argument*, no matter how weak, as long as it helps their team win the next election and maintain political power. The same is true of the debate over partisan gerrymandering, the filibuster, and voter suppression tactics. Support for political rules is too often based on political self-interest, rather than principled reasoning about what is fair and just in a representative democracy.

Review Questions

1. How does the Electoral College give greater weight to the voters in less populous states?
2. What are the main arguments against the Electoral College?
3. Is the Electoral College consistent with other features of the United States government?
4. What are the main arguments against establishing a popular vote for president?

Discussion Questions

1. Is the Electoral College an undemocratic institution?
2. Should the U.S. Senate be apportioned based on population?
3. Why should people in rural areas have more political power than people in urban areas?
4. Is it possible that your opinion about the Electoral College is biased by the outcomes of recent presidential elections?

Sources for Further Inquiry

Books

Best, Judith. 1996. *The Choice of the People?: Debating the Electoral College*. Lanham, MD: Rowman & Littlefield.

Bugh, Gary, ed. 2016. *Electoral College Reform: Challenges and Possibilities*. New York, NY: Routledge Press.

Burin, Eric, ed. 2017. *Picking the President: Understanding the Electoral College*. Grand Forks, ND: University of North Dakota Press.

Colomer, Josep, ed. 2016. *The Handbook of Electoral System Choice*. London: Palgrave Macmillan.

Edwards, George C., Wilson H. Kimnach, and Kenneth P. Minkema. (2004). *Why the Electoral College is Bad for America*. New Haven, CT: Yale University Press.

Shaw, Daron R. (2008). *The Race to 270: The Electoral College and the Campaign Strategies of 2000 and 2004*. Chicago, IL: University of Chicago Press.

Journal and Newspaper Articles

Edwards, George C. 2012, November 2. "Five myths about the Electoral College." *Washington Post*. Retrieved from https://www.washingtonpost.com/opinions/five-m yths-about-the-electoral-college/2012/11/02/2d45c526-1f85-11e2-afca-58c2f5789c5d _story.html?utm_term=.28908049a651

Pattie, Charles, and Ron Johnston. 2014. "'The Electors Shall Meet in their Respective States': Bias and the US Presidential Electoral College, 1960–2012." *Political Geography* 40: 35–45.

Peterson, Josiah. 2018, May 4. "Keep the Electoral College, Because States Matter." *National Review*. Retrieved from: https://www.nationalreview.com/2018/05/electora l-college-important-states-have-unique-political-interests/

Posner, Richard. 2012, November 12. "In Defense of the Electoral College." Slate.com. Retrieved from http://www.slate.com/articles/news_and_politics/view_from_chicago/ 2012/11/defending_the_electoral_college.html

Rakove, Jack N. 2004. "Presidential Selection: Electoral Fallacies." *Political Science Quarterly* 119(1): 21–37.

Ross, Robert E. 2016. "Federalism and the Electoral College: The Development of the General Ticket Method for Selecting Presidential Electors." *Publius: The Journal of Federalism* 46(2): 147–169.

Shaw, Daron R. 1999. "The Methods behind the Madness: Presidential Electoral College Strategies, 1988–1996." *The Journal of Politics* 61(4): 893–913.

Villegas, Christina. 2017. "Electing the People's President: The Popular Origins of the Electoral College." *Perspectives on Political Science*, 1–9. DOI: doi:10.1080/10457097.2016.1254492

References

Aldrich, John, Jason Reifler, and Michael C. Munger. 2014. "Sophisticated and Myopic? Citizen Preferences for Electoral College Reform." *Public Choice* 158: 541–558.

Colomer, Josep M. 2016, December 11. "The Electoral College is a Medieval Relic: Only the U.S. Still Has One." *Washington Post*. Retrieved from https://www.washingtonpost.com/news/monkey-cage/wp/2016/12/11/the-electoral-college-is-a-medieval-relic-only-the-u-s-still-has-one/?utm_term=.987537286be7

Gregg, Gary. 2012. "Electoral College Keeps Elections Fair." Politico. Retrieved from http://www.politico.com/story/2012/12/keep-electoral-college-for-fair-presidential-votes-084651

Reynolds v. Sims, 377 U. S. *533(1964)*.

Rudalevige, Andrew. 2016, November 8. "Why on Earth do we Even Have an Electoral College Anyway?" *Washington Post*. Retrieved from https://www.washingtonpost.com/news/monkey-cage/wp/2016/11/08/wait-why-do-we-even-have-an-electoral-college/?utm_term=.dc0ebea360fd

Saad, Lydia. 2013. "Americans Call for Term Limits, End to Electoral College." Gallup. Retrieved from http://www.gallup.com/poll/159881/americans-call-term-limits-end-electoral-college.aspx

U.S. Census. 2010. "Interactive Population Search." U.S. Census Bureau. Retrieved from https://www.census.gov/2010census/popmap/ipmtext.php

INDEX

accountability: democratic 132; public
    139–140
activism, judicial 136
ad hominem attack 47
ads, negative 23, 131
affirmative action, policies 94–102
Affordable Care Act (2010) 60
Afghanistan War (2001–present)
    75–77
African-American sounding names 98
Ahler, Douglas J. 3
Alaska 86
alcohol abuse 89
Aldrich, John, *et al.* 156
Alford, John R., Funk, Carolyn L. and
    Hibbing, John R. 12
American Association of Retired People
    (AARP) 129
American dream 68
American Revolution (1765–1783) 127
Americans, native-born 108–110
ancient Greece 43
animosity, political 2, 28
attacks: *ad hominem* 47; elite 36
attitudes, political 12–14
Australia 119, 144–145

baby-boomer generation 109
Bartels, Larry M. 23
Basic Educational Opportunity Grant
    (Congress) 66
Bastardi, Anthony, *et al.* 26

Belgium 144
bias: cognitive 21; media 35–37; political
    35–36, 39
bias blind spot 25–26, 28
biased interpretation 23
bill of rights 57, 146
Bin Laden, Osama 34
Binning, Kevin R., *et al.* 26
birth characteristics 13
black market 90
Blagov, Pavel S., *et al.* 34
Bracero Program 104
Braman, Donald, *et al.* 23
Brown v. Board of Education (1954) 94
bureaucracy, federal 76–78
Bush, George W. 2–3, 14, 46, 104–106,
    154–156

California 155
campuses, college 115–123
Cantril, Hadley, and Hastorf, Albert H. 23
Carey, John M., *et al.* 132
Cato Institute 109
Center for Strategic and International
    Studies report (2014) 80
Cheney, Richard (Dick) 14
Children's Health Insurance Program 60
China 75
citizens 144, 145, 153
citizenship 108, 144
civil discussions about politics 43–53
civil liberties 16

Claassen, Ryan L., and Ensley, Michael J. 23
Clawson, Richard A., Oxley, Zoe and Nelson, Thomas E. 16
Clinton, Hillary 67, 155
Clinton, William (Bill) 2, 46, 106
Cochran, Thad 80
cognitive biases 21
cognitive dissonance 34–35, 39, 45
Cohen, Geoffrey L., et al. 26
Cold War (1947–1991) 75
college: admissions 5; free 5, 68–72; tuition 66–74
college campuses, students carrying guns 115–123
Colorado 86, 89–90
Columbia 152
communism 57, 77
Comprehensive Crime Control Act (1984) 85
compulsory voting 144
Congress 58, 66, 75–82, 90, 103, 127–135, 137–138, 151–152;
Congressional elections (2014) 143, 147
Conover, Pamela Johnston, and Miller, Patrick R. 46
conservative bias 36
conservative leaning 67
conservative media 37
Conservative talk radio 22
conservatives 2, 33, 44, 136, 140
Constitution 94, 127–128, 136, 145, 151; second amendment 115–116, 121; fourteenth amendment 115, 153; seventeenth amendment 136–138, 151; twenty-third amendment 152
Constitutional Convention (1787) 151
Controlled Substance Act (1970) 90
credibility 47; media 36
crimes, gun-related 119
culture, American 68, 109–110

Daily Kos 33
Davisson, Erin K., et al. 27
Declaration of Independence (1776) 94
decriminalization of marijuana 89
Deffler, Samantha A., et al. 27
democracy 6, 39, 137, 144–145, 154; direct 138; industrialized 143; representative 5, 28, 130, 139, 145, 156
democratic accountability 132
democratic governance 139
Democratic Party 1, 16
Democrats 1–2, 15–16, 22–23, 34–37, 44–46, 76–78, 128–130, 153–155

Department of Defense (DoD) 80
Department of Homeland Security (DHS) 106
Diebels, Kate J., et al. 27
Dilliplane, Susanna 22
direct democracy 138
disagreements, political 1–2, 11, 21
discrimination 94, 98, 103
discussion: civil 43–53; political 43, 47–51
discussion groups: heterogenous 44; homogeneous 43–44
dissonance, cognitive 34–35, 39, 45
District of Columbia v. Heller (2008) 115, 120–121
diversity 95
Doherty, David, et al. 13
Dowling, Conor M., et al. 13
dream, American 68
Druckman, James N. 16
Drudge Report 33
drugs, mind-altering 85–87
Dunning-Kruger effect 48

Eastern Europe 103
education: higher 66–72; public 59, 66, 69–70
Eisenhower, Dwight 75, 79–80
elections: Congressional 143, 147; judicial 138–140; national 143–150; non-partisan 137; partisan 137; presidential 1, 143
Electoral College 6, 137, 151–158
electorate, uninformed 137–138
eleventh century 151
elite attacks 36
elites, political 25
employer-sponsored health insurance 57
Ensley, Michael J., and Claassen, Ryan L. 23
equality 95–97, 98
ethnicity 97
Evans, Danieli, et al. 23
exposure, partisan selective 37–38
extreme partisans 147

families, low-income 70–71, 96
federal bureaucracy 76–78
federal government 66, 72, 85–93, 115, 147
federal spending 76
federalism 90–91
Federalist Papers 127, 138
firearms 115
Florida 154–155
foreign policy 76–77, 80

formal equality 95–97
Fourteenth amendment 115, 153
Fox News 22, 33–34, 38
framing 15–17
Frank, Barney 78
Franklin, Benjamin 109
fraternal twins 12–13
free college 5, 68–72
free press 32, 43
free speech 43, 116
free-market health care 59
Frimer, Jeremy A., Skitka, Linda J. and
    Motyl, Matt 34
Funk, Carolyn L., Hibbing, John R. and
    Alford, John R. 12

Gallup poll 2, 67, 76, 85, 128
Garst, Jennifer, et al. 24
gay marriage 14
GDP (gross domestic product) 62
genetic inheritance 13
genetics 12–14
Georgia 67–68, 155
Gerber, Alan S., et al. 13
Gore, Al 154
governance, democratic 139
government: effectiveness 146–147; federal
    66, 72, 85–93, 115, 147
grants, Pell 67–68
Gratz v. Bollinger (2003) 95
Greece, ancient 43
Green, Donald, Palmquist, Bradley and
    Schickler, Eric 46
Griswell, Michael L., et al. 3
groups: opposing 38, 43, 46; social 94
Grutter v. Bollinger (2003) 95
gun control 5, 22, 116–121; debate 120;
    supporters 117
gun-related crimes 119
gun-related homicides 117–119
gun-related violence 117
gun(s): ban 117; laws 118–119, 120;
    owners 118–120; restrictions 117–119;
    rights advocates 120; students' 115–123;
    violence 120–121
Guttman, Amy, and Thompson, Dennis F. 43

Ha, Shang E., et al. 13
Hamilton, Alexander 103
Harenski, Keith, et al. 34
Harmann, Stephan, et al. 34
Hastorf, Albert H., and Cantril, Hadley 23
health care 5, 57–60, 63; free-market 59

health insurance 59–60; employer-
    sponsored 57; private 60–61
Heitland, Kirsten, et al. 26
heterogenous discussion groups 44
Hibbing, John R., Alford, John R. and
    Funk, Carolyn L. 12
high-skilled jobs 107
higher education 66–72
Hispanics 110
Hoffman, David A., et al. 23
homicides, gun-related 117–119
homogeneous discussion groups 43–44
homosexuality 14
hostile media effect 35
hostility 37–38; partisan 38–39; political
    1–7, 32–42, 107
House of Representatives 127, 130, 133,
    136–137, 152
Howard University 94
Hoyle, Rick H., et al. 27
Hsu, Lillian, et al. 26
Huber, Gregory A., et al. 13
human rights 77
humility 21–22, 27–28, 48

identical twins 12–13
identity: national 103; personal 45
ideological polarization 146
ideology 11–13, 26, 35, 47, 138, 139, 140
illegal immigrants 5, 103–114
illegal immigration 103–104, 109–111
illegal workers 109
immigrant workers 107
immigrants 108–109; illegal 5, 103–114;
    legal 108; unauthorized 104–106;
    undocumented 105
immigration: debate 5, 103–105, 109–111;
    legal 105, 109; opponents 106
Immigration Act (1924) 103
Immigration and Naturalization Act (1965)
    103, 111
Immigration Reform and Control Act
    (1986) 103–105
incumbency advantages 130–131
individualism 103
industrialized democracies 143
inequality, social 96
insurance, health 57, 59–60, 60–61
intellectual humility 21–22, 27–28
internal inconsistency 33
international trade 78
internationalism 76–80
interpretation, biased 23

introspection illusion 25
Iraq 3
Iraq War (2003–2011) 75–77
Isherwood, Jennifer C., *et al.* 27
isolationism 76–80

jobs, high-skilled 107
Johnson, Lyndon 94
Joiner, Amber J., *et al.* 24
Jongman-Sereno, Katrina P., *et al.* 27
judge's ideology 138
judicial activism 136
judicial elections 138–140
judicial ideology 140
judicial independence 138–139
judiciary, legitimacy of 13

Kahan, Dan M., *et al.* 23
Kahn, Kim F., and Kenney, Patrick J. 131
Kansas 90
Kennedy, John F. 94
Kennedy, Kathleen A., and Pronin, Emily 26
Kenney, Patrick J., and Kahn, Kim F. 131
Khama, Kabir, *et al.* 27
Kilts, Clint, *et al.* 34
Korean War (1950–1953) 57
Ku Klux Klan (KKK) 16

laborers, low-skilled 107
laws, gun 118–119, 120
leaning: conservative 67; liberal 67
Leary, Mark R., *et al.* 27
legal immigrants 108
legal immigration 105, 109
legalization of marijuana 5, 14–15, 85–93
legislative behavior 131–132
legitimacy of the judiciary 13
Lewinsky, Monica 46
liberal bias 36
liberal leaning 67
liberal media 37
liberals 2, 15, 33, 44, 110, 136, 140
like-minded media 33–36
like-minded partisan media 37–38
Limbaugh, Rush 34
Liu, Thomas J., and Steele, Claude M. 45
Lott, John 117
low-income Americans 146
low-income families 70–71, 96
low-skilled laborers 107

McCain, John 80
McClurg, Scott D. 44

McDonald v. Chicago (2010) 115, 121
McGoey, Michelle, *et al.* 26
Madison, James 43, 127, 138; market place of ideas 43
Maine 152
mainstream media 4, 33–37, 38–39
mandatory voting 143–150
Marbury v. Madison (1803) 136
Marihuana Tax Act (1937) 85
marijuana 85–89; decriminalization 89; legalization 5, 14–15, 85–93; prohibition 88
market place of ideas 43
marriage, gay 14
mass media 32
mass shootings 117–119
media: bias 35–37; conservative 37; credibility 36; hostile 35; liberal 37; like-minded 33–36; mainstream 4, 33–37, 38–39; news 1, 2, 4, 32–42; partisan 4, 33–39; social 1
Medicaid 58–60, 68
Medicare 5, 57–65, 109–111
Meffert, Michael F., *et al.* 24
merit system 137
middle class 6
military spending 76–81
military-industrial complex (MIC) 79
Mill, John Stuart 43, 50
Miller, Patrick R., and Conover, Pamela Johnston 46
mind-altering drugs 85–87
motivated reasoning 24–25, 28, 34
Motyl, Matt, Frimer, Jeremy A. and Skitka, Linda J. 34
MSNBC 15, 22, 33, 36–38
Munger, Michael C., *et al.* 156

naïve realism 11, 17
national elections 143–150
national identity 103
national popular vote 151–158
National Rifle Association (NRA) 22, 129
native-born Americans 108–110
Naturalization Act (1790) 103
Nebraska 90, 152
negative ads 23, 131
negative stereotypes 3, 99
Nelson, Thomas E.: and Braman, Eileen 25; Clawson, Richard A. and Oxley, Zoe 16
Netherlands 144
Nevada 86, 90

new immigrants 107, 110
New York 67, 155
news, partisan 22
news media 1, 2, 4, 32–42
Niemi, Richard G., *et al.* 132
non-partisan elections 137
non-voters 143, 146
Northern Illinois University 117

Obama, Barack 2, 23, 34, 75, 106, 120, 154
objective era 32, 39
On Liberty (Mill) 43, 50
opinions, political 45
opponents, political 26, 44
opposing groups 38, 43, 46
opposing party 39
Oregon 67, 143
out-groups, social 2
Oxley, Zoe 13; Nelson, Thomas E. and
    Clawson, Richard A. 16

Palmquist, Bradley, Schickler, Eric and
    Green, Donald 46
partisan elections 137; non- 137
partisan hostility 38–39
partisan media 4, 33–39; like-minded 37–38
partisan news 22
partisan polarization 146
partisan selective exposure 37–38
partisans 2, 16, 23, 33–35, 147; extreme 147
partisanship 23, 26, 47, 156
party: identification 13; opposing 39
party affiliation, absent 138
Paul, Ron 77–78
Pearl Harbor (1941) 77
Pell Grants 67–68
Pennsylvania 155
personal identity 45
personality 12–14
Pew Research Center 1, 14, 76, 146–147
Philadelphia 151
polarization: ideological 146; partisan 146
policy: affirmative action 94–102; foreign
    76–77, 80
political animosity 2, 28
political attitudes 12–14
political bias 35–36, 39
political disagreements 1–2, 11, 21
political discussion 43, 47–51
political elites 25
political hostility 1–7, 32–42, 107
political ideology 140
political opinions 45

political opponents 26, 44
political power 25
politics, civil discussions about 43–53
popular vote, national 151–158
populous states 155
pork barrel spending 132
Portman, Rob 14
Powell, Lynda W., *et al.* 132
power, political 25
pragmatism 105–106
prejudice 97–99, 103; racial 98, 110
presidency 155
presidential campaign (2016) 1
presidential election 143
press, free 32, 43
principles 105–106
Prior, Markus 129; *et al.* 27
private health insurance industry 60–61
Pronin, Emily, and Kennedy,
    Kathleen A. 26
Pryor, John B., *et al.* 3
psychosis 88
public accountability 139–140
public education 59, 66, 69–70
public policy 139
public safety 16, 116
public schools 68, 96, 116

race 97, 110
race-based affirmative action in college
    admissions 5
Rachlinski, Jeffrey J., *et al.* 23
racial prejudice 98, 110
racial segregation 94
racism 109–111
radio 22
Raimi, Kaitlin T., *et al.* 27
Reagan, Ronald 2, 75, 85; administration 23
realism, naïve 11, 17
reasoning, motivated 24–25, 28, 34
Reeder, Glenn D., *et al.* 3
Regents of the University of California v. Bakke
    (1978) 95
Reifler, Jason, *et al.* 156
representative democracy 5, 28, 130, 139,
    145, 156
Republican Party 1, 16
Republicans 1–2, 14–16, 34–37, 44–46,
    75–78, 128–130, 153–155
Reynolds v. Sims (1964) 151
Romney, Mitt 154
Roosevelt, Franklin 57
Roosevelt, Theodore 77

Ross, Lee, *et al.* 26
Rush Limbaugh Show 33

safety, public 16, 116
Sanders, Bernie 58–62, 67
Sanders, Richard, and Taylor, Stuart 99
Schickler, Eric, Green, Donald and Palmquist, Bradley 46
schizophrenia 88
schools, public 68, 96, 116
second amendment 115–116, 121
segregation, racial 94
self-esteem 45–46, 99
Senate 136, 155; seats 152
Senators 131, 138, 151
Serviceman's Readjustment Act (1944) 66
seventeenth amendment 136–138, 151
Sherman, David K., *et al.* 26
shootings, mass 117–119
Skitka, Linda J., Motyl, Matt and Frimer, Jeremy A. 34
slaves 94
social groups 94
social inequality 96
social media 1
social out-groups 2
Social Security 109–111, 129
social upbringing 13
sociotropic evaluations 32
Socrates 43
Sood, Gaurav, *et al.* 27
sounding names, traditional white/African-American 98
Soviet Union 75
speech, free 43, 116
spending: federal 76; military 76–81; pork barrel 132; wasteful 78–80
Starr, Paul 62
Steele, Claude M., and Liu, Thomas J. 45
stereotypes 2–3, 39, 97–100; negative 3, 99
Stevens, John Paul 128
students carrying guns, on college campuses 115–123
substantive equality 95–97
Sungeun Chung, *et al.* 24
Supreme Court 5, 95, 100, 115–116, 120, 128, 131–133, 136–142

Taylor, Stuart, and Sanders, Richard 99
Tennessee 67

Texas 108, 118, 155
Thompson, Dennis F., and Guttman, Amy 43
trade, international 78
Truman, Harry 57
Trump, Donald 2, 57, 75–77, 155–156
twentieth century 32, 85, 107, 127
twenty-first century 1, 14, 129
twenty-third amendment 152
twins 12–13
tyranny 139

unauthorized immigrants 104–106
undocumented immigrants 105
uninformed electorate 137–138
United States of America (USA) 6, 26, 66–70, 75–78, 94, 103–104, 107–108
University of Houston 118
upbringing, social 13
Urban Institute 62
U.S. Term Limits, Inc. v. Thornton (1995) 128

value salience 15–17
violence: gun 120–121; gun-related 117
Virginia 85, 151, 155
Virginia Tech campus 117
vote, national popular 151–158
voters 129–130, 146; non- 143, 146
voting: compulsory 144; mandatory 143–150

Washington 86, 115, 143
Washington, George 76
wasteful spending 78–80
welfare 68
well-being 66
West, Darrell M. 32
Westin, Drew, *et al.* 34
white-sounding names 98
Wkas, Leah, *et al.* 24
Wohl, Michael J. A., *et al.* 3
workers: American 107; illegal 109; immigrant 107
World War II (1939–1945) 57, 66, 75–81, 104; Pearl Harbor (1941) 77
Wyoming 90–91, 155